Your Love Horoscope 2006

Your Essential Astrological Guide to Romance and Relationships

Sarah Bartlett

HarperElement
An Imprint of HarperCollins*Publishers*
77–85 Fulham Palace Road,
Hammersmith, London W6 8JB

The website address is:
www.thorsonselement.com

and *HarperElement* are trademarks of
HarperCollins*Publishers* Ltd

First published by HarperElement 2005

1 3 5 7 9 10 8 6 4 2

© Sarah Bartlett 2005

Sarah Bartlett asserts the moral right to
be identified as the author of this work

A catalogue record of this book
is available from the British Library

ISBN 0 00 720 086 2

Printed and bound in Great Britain by
Clays Ltd, St Ives plc

Contents

To P.

Introduction

Astrology is about how we are, not why we are.

Your Sun sign offers you the chance to understand more about love relationships that occur in your life, and how you deal with them. Through becoming more aware of who you are, you can begin to understand what kind of patterns and experiences you are likely to encounter in the future, and also discover how to deal with your own rhythms and cycles of feelings, emotions and moods. Knowing what to expect from yourself and your relationships prepares you for the wonderful highs and the inevitable lows of romance, emotion and sexual desire.

This book guides you astrologically through 2006 with your personal month-by-month love forecast. It also reveals the secrets of how to seduce any man of the zodiac, how to manage him every month, with whom you are compatible and who might pose a few problems – both in bed and out of it. Enjoy.

Astrology Key Words

What is Sun-sign Astrology?

Popular astrology describes the effects that the other planets have in relation to your Sun sign, and subsequently their influence on your destiny, as they move through the zodiac during the year.

The Movement of the Planets

The planets appear to move through the sky against the backdrop of the zodiac. And, similarly, they seem to move through your horoscope, which is a snapshot of the sky at the time when you were born. As they move, they sometimes appear to accelerate or they slow down and almost seem to stop altogether. Planets like Mars and Mercury often seem to 'surge' forward into the next sign and slower ones, like

Saturn, almost lumber. All planets except the Sun can also appear to move backwards – this is called retrograde motion. I use terms like 'backtracking' or 'doing a U-turn' or 'turning turtle' to describe this motion. The effects are usually to slow down events and give you time to reflect on issues. But Mercury retrograde, for example, also signifies delays, hiccups, machinery breaking down or plans being delayed.

The Planets Are ...

The Sun The Sun takes approximately one month to move through each sign of the zodiac. It influences your personal destiny, love goals and aims.

The Moon Taking only a few days to move through one sign of the zodiac, the Moon's cycle affects your emotional reactions, needs and feelings on a daily basis.

Mercury Fast moving but erratic, Mercury affects your communication throughout the year and the way you interact with lovers and friends.

Venus Venus influences your eye for beauty, pleasure and sexual happiness, and the kind of people who are drawn to you. Throughout the year it energizes your attraction factor and your charisma.

Mars Mars affects your sexual desire, how you go after what you want and how you get it, but it also makes you angry and reveals how you confront experiences and relationship issues.

Saturn　Saturn influences structure and boundaries in relationships. But it also brings you back down to earth with a bump if you've overshot the mark.

Jupiter　Often called the planet of 'luck', Jupiter brings adventure, risks, high romance and excitement to your love life.

Uranus　Unpredictable and radical, Uranus brings sudden events and surprise meetings, and is often the catalyst for that electrifying chemistry between strangers.

Neptune　Dreamy Neptune casts a romantic glow over everything, but also glamorizes people and events, and sometimes confuses you about your true feelings.

Pluto　Transformative Pluto influences your deepest emotions, your sexual passion and triggers off the greatest changes in your relationships, for good and bad.

Ruling Planets

The planet which rules your Sun sign is very important because it adds another flavour to your Solar journey. Every sign of the zodiac has a 'ruler' or a planet which is the henchman for your Sun:

Aries is ruled by Mars
Taurus is ruled by Venus
Gemini is ruled by Mercury
Cancer is ruled by the Moon
Leo is ruled by the Sun
Virgo is ruled by Mercury
Libra is ruled by Venus
Scorpio is ruled by Pluto
Sagittarius is ruled by Jupiter
Capricorn is ruled by Saturn
Aquarius is ruled by Uranus
Pisces is ruled by Neptune

Aspects

Aspects occur when there is a resonant dynamic played out between two planets in the sky and in your horoscope. It appears as if they form an angle and the most important ones are called trines (120 degrees apart), squares (90 degrees apart), conjunctions (when they appear to be in the same degree), sextiles (60 degrees apart) and oppositions (180 degrees apart). Aspects to your Sun add a very powerful combination of the energy or characteristics of the planets involved in the aspect.

Zones

These are areas of the Sun-sign chart which are divided up into twelve 30-degree segments to make up the complete horoscope of 360 degrees. As the planets move through the zodiac, they emphasize these different areas of your love life.

The Phases of the Moon

The cycle of the Moon lasts approximately 30 days, as it appears to move round the zodiac. We usually notice the Full Moon because this is when the Sun is directly opposite the Moon and casts its light upon the Moon's surface. The Moon only stays in one sign for about two to three days and will influence your personal Sun sign for a few days every month. The other phases of the Moon which affect your Sun sign are the New Moon, the First Quarter Moon and the Last Quarter Moon. For example, a New Moon on June 29 in Cancer will be followed by a First Quarter Moon a week later, then a Full Moon about one week later, a Last Quarter Moon a week after that, and another New Moon on July 29 in Leo. The New Moon is a time to start out on a new quest, adventure or love affair. Make plans for the month ahead, make that phone call, go on a first date. The First Quarter Moon is for seduction and persuasion. The Full Moon is a critical turning point in the Moon's cycle when it's time to make decisions, face your true feelings or complete what you set out to do under the New Moon. The Last Quarter Moon is for being realistic about your relationship.

Lunar/Solar Eclipses

These happen a few times a year and used to be considered bad omens by the ancients. Actually, they just bring into focus personal issues you might be avoiding or are not aware need attention in your relationships. A Lunar eclipse is when the Earth gets in the way of the Sun's light shining on a Full Moon and there appears to be a dark shadow moving across the Moon. The easiest way to remember what a Lunar eclipse means is to say 'the present blots out the past'. (The Moon is usually associated with past in astrology.) For example, whatever issues you need to clarify in your current relationship, think about them; don't dwell on the past. A Solar eclipse is when the Moon gets in the way of the Sun, so we lose its light temporarily at various places on Earth. The easiest way to interpret a Solar eclipse is to say 'the past blots out the future'. (The Sun is usually associated with the future.) For example, there are things which you have bottled up, denied or avoided from your past patterns of behaviour which now need attention before you can get on with the future of your current relationship.

The Elements

Each Sun sign is also one of the four elements. It's useful to know them because signs that are of the same element are often highly compatible.

The element of Fire: Aries, Leo, Sagittarius. The Fire signs are highly motivated, passionate visionaries.

The element of Earth: Taurus, Virgo, Capricorn. The Earth signs are sensualists who build solid relationships.

The element of Air: Gemini, Libra, Aquarius. The Air signs are romantic geniuses.

The element of Water: Cancer, Scorpio, Pisces. The Water signs are sultry, sexual lovers.

Your Love
Horoscope
2006

Your Love
Horoscope
2006

Aries

The Ram

March 21 – April 20

Love Check

Why you're fabulous

- There's no one who can rival you when it comes to hunting or chasing the lover of your dreams.
- You're bold and dynamic and always the first to take the initiative.

Why you're impossible

- Sometimes you're impatient for sex and want it all NOW.
- Relationships with no challenges and no fun don't last long.

Your love secrets

- Romantic but feisty, you don't want the thrill of the chase to ever end.

- You're not easily led astray, except by your imagination.
- You don't want to be hunted yourself.

Your sexual style
- Direct, passionate, volatile and competitive.

Who falls for you
- Romantic idealists or dynamic career types who know you are as fiery and motivated as they are.

Who you fall for
- Someone who picks up the pieces when you've stormed around the place creating chaos. Earthy sensualists and dark horses.

You identify with
- Celebrities, crusaders, heroes and heroines.
- Anyone who has a 'mission impossible' and succeeds.

Your greatest temptation
- Falling in love with someone already involved.

Your greatest strength
- Determination to win at any cost.

Passion Profile for 2006

With taskmaster Saturn backtracking through your romantic zone until April, you really don't know whether to commit yourself to a long-term love affair, or stay single. Even if you are attached, early on this year you feel like breaking free or finding more space to do your own thing. And that, of course, brings a load of guilt into the equation. But if you are not tramping around the social circuit, down your professional corridors or stalking new deals, you wouldn't be true to your fiery self. So this year, aim to please you first, resist those doubts and fears and prove that you are the sexually enlightened and loyal woman that you really are. (More space doesn't mean you're cheating on him, remember!) By midsummer, the emotional heat is off and the physical one is on. With your ruler Mars surging into your romantic corner on the 3rd June, it all becomes tangled sheets and passionate encounters. By the autumn, you are promised mystery admirers, love triangles (if you can handle the heat), and glamour and excitement beckon. The planets are giving you the chance to show off, strut your stuff, or just sizzle in someone's eyes.

Just remember to check your feelings sometimes. They are there to remind you that beneath all that war paint and feisty image you have a gentle, vulnerable side. Don't neglect it and love will be the magical gift you want most of all by the end of the year.

Best bets for Mr Right this year: Libra for eternal romance, Gemini for hilarious romps, Aquarius for a free-spirited friendship.

2006 Month by Month

January

Independence and freedom are two things you value most in life. And more often than not you like to keep them sacred. Even in intimate or personal relationships, commitment is a word rarely used, and love is not necessarily about being tied to one person. The New Year begins with an unusual amount of high profile romance and light flirtation. And you have a real optimistic feeling about your love life, whether single or attached. With your ruler Mars in sensual Taurus, you enjoy the company of one like-minded adventurer in the art of sexual indulgence. The Full Moon in home-loving Cancer on the 14th enables you to have a riotous time with friends. Even though you'd rather be exploring new social circles, the ones closer to home count for a lot. But the rest of the month is set for clowning around, infuriating friends with your speedy change of heart as you go on a string of unpredictable dates, and the attraction of new romantics into your life. Of course, you are always one to flirt, but you do so with a genuine innocence. Respect the fact that you want to be friends and lighten up people's lives rather than be motivated by any deep sexual power struggle.

One intimate relationship is put to the test on the 18th, when Mars squares up to Neptune and you find you have got in deeper than you wanted to. Always ready to communicate, and often more garrulous than you intended, you say something totally tactless on the 21st. You realize that your partner or lover adores your small talk, but is thoroughly irritated by your blunt and sometimes tactless comments and observations. Take care you don't get yourself into scalding hot water. After all, there is a rival out there, and if you are single, you could lose the very dateable interest you had eating out of your hands a few weeks earlier. The end of the month gives you valuable breathing space. The opportunity to see where your plans and commitments are leading you, and whether you can let them continue without sacrificing your freedom.

Best days for romance: 3rd, 30th
Best days to seduce: 14th, 21st
Best stay at home day: 11th

February

This month you may be faced with a new challenge and, as you know, any challenge is better than none. Yet it is always the essence of the challenge itself rather than the solution or the answer to it that fascinates you. If the challenge involves yourself in relation to a lover or partner, then it becomes more than that; it becomes an adventure and may be even a new role you can try out for yourself. Exploring any relationship is fun, as long as you don't get too involved in the emotional waters that run deep beneath the surface. With a sexy New Moon on the 13th in Leo, followed by a link between cheeky Mercury and madcap Uranus on Valentine's Day, you can be assured of surprise cards, roses or simply a new face on your doorstep. Go on, admit it, you are actually a secret romantic who wants roses round the door, a Lear jet or helicopter pad, and a man who brings you the kind of wild and exciting lifestyle 24/7.

But the old iron fist of the zodiac, Saturn, is also putting a restrictive influence on your self-expression, while it's backtracking through fellow fire sign, Leo. You have no choice but to be realistic about relationships. Sometimes there is all the washing up, dirty floors and his headache to contend with. It's when your man is down, got the grumps or a cold and acts like a four-year old that you want out. That big grudge-bearer, responsibility isn't your favourite, and that's why the challenge this month is to accept there will be times when life isn't romantic, liberating or adventurous. But with your ruler, Mars, plummeting on into Gemini on the 17th, any brief romantic attachment that may have evolved into friendship from last month will now add a touch of sexual enticement to your e-mail inbox. Whether a brief flirtation or a closer but liberated relationship, this one might just be the necessary challenge you've been looking for.

You enjoyed a mild flirtation, and why not? And then there are all those letters you haven't posted, the CDs you haven't put back in the boxes, and suddenly you smile. The planets at the end of the month give you reason to laugh too. For once the man of your dreams is living up to your high ideals again. Throw yourself into bed, or throw him out, but one thing's for sure, you've got the energy now to prove that if life isn't exciting, you'll make it so all by yourself.

Best days for romance: 1st, 28th
Best days to seduce: 3rd, 19th
Best stay at home day: 5th

March

You are feeling a pulsating rhythm within everything you encounter this month. The deep throb of the city, or the rush of the ocean, sends an electrical current through your body reminding you that vibrant spring is taking over from the cool frostiness of winter. On the 1st, the Sun's collusion with Uranus encourages you to honour your sensuality, but Jupiter's U-turn in your chart on the 4th blinds you with over-optimism. This double whammy brings great passion and increased intimacy, but while flames of passion burn hot, no one should expect soppy, romantic gestures. Joint affairs are heightened around the 14th, when the New Moon encourages you to put the object of your desires before all else. Intimate thoughts in the office see you too busy sending seductive texts and e-mails to get much work done. Things start to get messy on the 17th, when everything you say lands you deeper in the mire; in fact, it's one of those days when you wish you'd stayed under the duvet – alone.

Spending time reflecting on the dynamics of your relationships and accepting your role in the confusion, rather than eschewing blame confrontationally, will prevent you from saying the wrong thing and give your lover time to appreciate you. By the time the Sun enters your own sign on the 20th, if he is not suggesting an exotic jaunt, someone else is. So, however difficult it feels, it is worth sitting back and letting time make decisions for you. The passionate solar eclipse in your own sign on the 29th makes you idealistic about your desires; you are more in the mood to dream about your perfect sexual relationship than to actually make it happen. Reflection breeds excellence, so give yourself all the time you need this month, and you'll get it spot on.

Best days for romance: 10th, 25th
Best days to seduce: 3rd, 18th
Best stay at home day: 1st

April

Exciting feelings are one thing, but when you are jolted into having to make a decision between spreading your wings or staying put, that's not so easy. Stagnation is the last thing you want right now, but a gallant rogue seems to be working on the assumption that you'll get up and go without question because normally it is you who's craving excitement. Wisely take your time to think things through. Later on this month the potent effects of Mercury's leap into your own sign will at least give you the chance to discuss things honestly, even if a tad flamboyantly.

Right from the 4th, you are fishing for compliments where one new liaison is concerned. Whether single or attached, your flirtatious character is certainly causing a stir. Jupiter and Mercury are also triggering off that special weakness you have for a face in the crowd, or a red-hot male challenge. And around the 12th, an envious friend or colleague tries to steal the show. Maddeningly precocious though you are, you worry for a few moments that perhaps you are going too far. Secretly, you just want to have fun, but if you take things to the limit you're going to be in trouble, either with a current amour, or because you make all kind of crazy promises which you realize are impossible to keep.

To cap it all, the Full Moon on the 13th in your relationship corner adds fuel to the fire. And you wonder if you're ever going to make yourself understood. And also whether you really understand yourself. Confusion reigns for a few days, and torn between loyalty to what you know is a fine romance, and the temptation of a very outrageous one on the 17th, you begin to play a few mind games. Just don't get yourself into deeper waters when you could be swimming in the crystal clear waves of sheer sexual spontaneity. There is nothing worse than a guilt-ridden Aries, except of course a trapped one. Sort out your true needs from those you think you should have. With Mars causing outbursts and pillow fights from the 21st, there is going to be some sexy fireworks. But then, where would you be without that explosive drama in your life?

Best days for romance: 17th, 19th
Best days to seduce: 5th, 21st
Best stay at home day: 30th

May

Venus moving into your own sign on the 3rd gives you the chance to communicate clearly, focus on your relationships and sort out your true needs and desires. Don't waste time this month, get down to the nitty-gritty. What you want is to know who you can really rely on and trust. And the loyalty you are about to receive will give you the confidence to move on to better things.

Nine times out of ten, you are willing to adapt to your lover's change of plan. But around the challenging Full Moon in Scorpio on the 13th, you are convinced you know best, and he thinks he knows better. Of course, being flexible does have its benefits, and undoubtedly there are times when it is worth agreeing just for the sake of peace and harmony. But just this once consider if his suggestions for domestic reshuffling are really what you want for yourself. Real love depends on voicing your true feelings too.

If you are single, even though you sense things are beginning to improve where a particular liaison is concerned, it does seem to remain a bit of a struggle and test. Yet what you are discovering is that sticking to your own values and beliefs is what unconditional love is all about. If this admirer won't respect your need for individual goals, perhaps it is time that he found a few of his own.

With Venus surging quickly through your sign until the 29th, you feel high-spirited and enthusiastic about love again. And Venus's romantic cosmic link on the 19th sparks off a string of exciting encounters, dates and decisions. Is one glamorous rogue really too good to be true, or is he truthfully good for you? By the 22nd, you take a leap in the dark. After all, life is for enjoying, and this is a chance to defy those friends who see everything as an uphill struggle. Flirt, laugh and make eye contact. It's the look in his eyes that says it all.

If you are attached, and your man's being awkward around the 26th, or playing hard to get, don't assume it's your fault. Sometimes you have to let go of the feeling that you are responsible for every mood he is in or gesture he makes. All this getting nowhere fast will at least give you time to think clearly about your own needs. Rather than jumping to conclusions, take it as a learning curve for you both.

Best days for romance: 2nd, 5th
Best days to seduce: 3rd, 7th
Best stay at home day: 20th

June

Possessions are not exactly something you cling to. And you carry little baggage through life, whether emotional or physical. It is always easier to move on to the next experience, the next love, or romance. Keeping romance alive is something you have a natural talent for, simply because there is never time to get involved or emotionally intense. You must always get on with something else, meet up with new friends, get back to work, or go on a trip before you have time to sit down and become trapped by circumstance and relationship. The less conflict, the fewer emotional demands you experience, and the more likely you are to stay around and even agree to some kind of 'open' commitment.

Aries is a sign, like the other fire signs, who often fall blindly into marriage because at the time it seemed like a good thing. (Roses round the corner are very similar to rose-coloured spectacles, remember.) But once tied to anything which resembles a doorpost (apart from the fun of being tied gently to the bedpost now and then), you usually want to get away as quickly as you can. Having your fun this month means love is in the air again. The Full Moon in adventurous Sagittarius on the 11th puts you in party mood. And with Venus in light-hearted Gemini from the 24th, even your friends will enjoy your light-hearted and mischievous attempts at flirting with all and sundry (and that includes their boyfriends). The rough and tumble outdoor life keeps you busy after the 25th, while the ubiquitous barbecues are leaving smoke rings all over town, and al fresco sex is on offer from one rogue you can't get out of your system.

But your social life is full to brimming, and whether single or attached, you're simply in the mood to play. You don't want heavy dramas, but you do want theatrical romance. And if one very special person can keep up with your penchant for being the leader of the social pack, then you'll take him along for any ride. Dance, exercise, chase a few rainbows, and enjoy yourself. It is time to get ready for the hot summer of sex and fun you're about to be rewarded with.

Best days for romance: 3rd, 10th
Best days to seduce: 21st, 28th
Best stay at home day: 16th

July

'To boldly go where no woman has gone before' is probably a notion you have an affinity with. Outer space is like 'out of mind', and out of mind is when we fall headlong into an infatuation with someone for no apparent reason other than they have the right eyes, look, body, smell – you know the stuff. Infatuation puts you on a high, and if the object of your desire is equally infatuated then fireworks result. This month you move through social circles which include mostly men. And whatever has recently begun as a mere seed of attraction or a mild and harmless flirtation sizzles into full-scale fiery passion. Thanks to the Sun's move into your romantic corner on the 22nd, you have all the charisma, energy and cheek to move closer to someone and get your way.

If you are attached, make sure you are sure of your motives for romantic flirting, and perhaps re-direct your passion towards your partner. With your ruler Mars moving into focused Virgo on the 22nd, it is time to communicate your real needs to your partner. There could be a conflict of opinion on the 23rd about where you are heading romantically. Is it round the world together on an exotic trip of a lifetime, or to sit watching the TV every night? You know which is for you, and not only are you restless for adventure, you know that if you play the game – sparkle, flirt and tease him into at least looking at those travel brochures – you'll win the head-to-head clash. A contest of wills is something you always rise to, and the end of the month should be no exception. Time to plot your grand schemes and plans, and move forward. With or without him.

Best days for romance: 5th, 23rd
Best days to seduce: 1st, 30th
Best stay at home day: 8th

August

An exciting lover equates to an exciting life. And although you may be advised by friends or family to take care, your blind faith in love and your impulsive way of exaggerating the truth will see you through any embarrassing moments this month. With a stunning array of planets in your romantic corner, you are on the hunt for summer love if single, and more of anything as long as it's wild, spontaneous and energetic if you're attached. With a powerful link between your ruler Mars and unpredictable Uranus on the 13th, any sexual uncertainty is finally rewarded, and a relationship becomes more involved than perhaps you would care to admit. The testing strength of any relationship is when the whirl of romance has faded, but with your usual verve for the light and risky side of life, you just want to have fun. Yet your lover or partner wants to be settled, consistent, mutually working at your goals. A long-term partnership might be in jeopardy if you are considering any sudden changes, but if you are happy within a solid and lasting bond, then this month just might teach you that faithfulness and reliability are just as visionary as opportunist love.

Romantic contacts after the 21st prove inspirational one minute, impossibly complex the next. Expressing yourself without causing a row is, of course, a bonus. But you might put your foot in it if you assume that others have the same views as you. The planets are certainly giving you the chance to distribute a few messages. Just make sure you deliver them to the right doors.

Impeccable though a friend's reputation is, you would be wise to check out what is actually motivating his interest in you on the 26th. It might just be that he genuinely believes in what you are doing. But he could also have a rather cunning plan up his sleeve to use your amazing ideas for his own ends. Of course, you are not easily deceived, but it pays to think in the shadows rather than spill all your secrets in the light of day.

Best days for romance: 13th, 27th
Best days to seduce: 18th, 21st
Best stay at home day: 23rd

September

Purring around someone's ankles is usually what cats do, but there is someone out there who has a very feline approach to love, and they are looking your way. On the 1st, take it as a compliment – after all it might be an irresistibly sensuous experience that you just can't afford to miss. By the 15th, it seems as if one lover is talking absolute nonsense, and due to Mercury's deceptive link with Neptune you just can't trust anything anyone says. That includes yourself, so take care you don't get too enthusiastic about making joint plans which you won't be able to fulfil at a later date.

A spot of brainstorming at a social bash inspires you with noble ideas on the 14th. But a flashing smile from someone-to-die-for gives you a few wicked thoughts too. You'll know what to do next, but just make sure it's legal and utterly delightful. Around the 19th you wake up to that kind of 'wow' feeling. All you want and need from love is well within your grasp. Catch your breath, choose your moment and be courageous. Venus is giving you the panache and powers of persuasion to get away with anything. Being a little bit of a sucker for fame, glamour and the glitzy life, you're realizing right now that if your whims are not being indulged, then you'll look elsewhere for that sense of being special. If you are attached, of course, this could present a problem. And this month, Venus and Mars bring charming but high-powered business associates, colleagues and frankly gorgeous rogues popping up in your life when least expected. Flirting isn't just about a grand seduction act that leads to infidelity, however. If friends or family assume that your flamboyant fun-loving persona negates loyalty to your lover, then maybe that says more about their faithfulness than your own.

Flirt with life and people, because it feels good to be you. And being the sunshine person you are, there is no one to stop you. Transmit your joy all around, and love grows for yourself and for others too. So, if you are tempted to smile, be amused, and shine brightly in various admirer's eyes, it might just be the kick you need to realize that the grass is just as green in your own patch. If you are single, this is your chance to reel in a string of dateable men or just one desirable match.

Best days for romance: 3rd, 19th
Best days to seduce: 8th, 30th
Best stay at home day: 1st

October

The ups and downs which reflect the essential polarity of love are simply swings and roundabouts you handle with either great energy or without vindication or regret. Capable of jealousy and a passion that blazes ever on through your love life, you also manage to come to terms with rejection and shrug your shoulders and move nobly on. Being an optimist invariably moves you on round the next romantic corner, and you bear few grudges, preferring to remain friends with past lovers than to become enemies. Love often takes this route, and although you need a passionate and highly spiced sex life, you also want a partner who is as much a pal or friend as a bed companion. Sex isn't the whole meaning of life to you, only a part of it.

The heady romantic blaze of the summer is still in your mind, and with a Full Moon in your own sign on the 7th, don't waste time making it clear what you will and won't put up with in one relationship. And with Mars firing its way on through the most intimate and sexual area of your chart after the 23rd, expressing your sexual desires becomes an ego contest. Although talking about sex gives you a libido boost, it also is putting your current relationship under strain. And this is simply because you or your partner are not being totally honest about your feelings, wants and wishes.

Mars makes a series of important aspects at the end of the month. The first with the Sun on the 23rd inspires you to express to your lover that emotional sob stories have little purpose in your life. The second when Venus sidles up to Mars on the 25th, will break any fragile bonds, or the power of your feelings get the better of you. If single, you fall into a sexual relationship too quickly and too deeply, or it's time to unhook yourself from someone who could be in a position to use manipulative tactics against you in the future.

Best days for romance: 16th, 22nd
Best days to seduce: 20th, 25th
Best stay at home day: 19th

November

Romance quickens around the 17th, when Venus moves into adventurous Sagittarius to give you a host of imaginative ways to keep the momentum fast and furious and deliciously on edge. Yet a friend keeps reminding you that love isn't just about romantic adventure, it is about settling down to an ordinary life. Ordinary? How could you ever be ordinary? Take care, because if you are not living your life to the full, passionate about your man, or on a personal or mutual quest, then you are not living out the true potential that is your right. Frankly, if anyone tries to pin you down this month, you will be even more determined to go your own way. Around the 22nd, trust in your intuition rather than that well-meaning lobby who think they know what's best for you.

This month you could be swept off your feet by new love if you're single; if attached, take care that one handsome rogue doesn't have you dreaming of him as you gaze out of the train or bus window. Your impulsive nature could set you off on a trip around town, or a weekend jaunt away on the 24th, when Jupiter moves into your travel corner, and all you want to do is fly away from anything towards something new and enticing. You may not have even time to rationalize why you are going, or who with, but your extraordinary buoyancy gets you the attention you crave, and men are dazzled by your energy and charisma. When you meet up with someone new on the 25th, the electrifying chemistry between you reminds you that love is a mystery that you will never work out. And if this rogue is someone who can match your passion and your intellect, as well as able to accept your need for freedom, you might just have met the perfect match. But, remember, you can also imagine you've met Mr Right, when he's simply a Mr Right Now, so take it one step at a time rather than leaping and bounding madly into the festive season.

Best days for romance: 1st, 29th
Best days to seduce: 11th, 24th
Best stay at home day: 5th

December

Mars, your ruler, surges into Sagittarius on the 6th to bring you energy, dynamic feelings and, of course, new romance if you are single. But feelings this month are also about loyalty and trust. Being true to yourself is second nature to you, but you could feel a few moments of self-doubt creeping over you when someone special forces you to consider what is really going on in your heart. It is not exactly a test of will or of you having to make compromises, only a real sense of what matters to you. Ask yourself whether your need for mutual respect and honesty is being discussed openly enough. With Mars and Mercury's liberating influence, it is time to set the record straight so that you are set for a wonderful festive season.

Sexually your intimate relationships are on a high after the 11th, and you're in the mood to indulge in the party spirit. This is a time to reconnect to your real romantic spirit. Your inspiration and ability to enjoy yourself will bring much happiness to someone who may not have the same self-awareness as you. The end of the month is about chasing up on those real emotional dreams rather than endless rainbows. Courage and motivation are the two words to remember as you slide into the New Year with fresh self-esteem. At last you know that the excitement and desire you have for one special person is now a reality, not just a vague unfulfilled longing. Listen to your inner voice, it is from deep within, and in those moments of utter tranquillity you will know the truth of whether this relationship is worth a big commitment. If you are single, that admirer you met early in the month returns with the kind of New Year present that smacks of romantic adventure. So be your dynamic, impulsive self and take a weekend jaunt over the festive break or into the New Year and enjoy the liberated, confident new you.

Best days for romance: 6th, 27th
Best days to seduce: 1st, 20th
Best stay at home day: 25th

Your Love
Horoscope
2OO6

Taurus
The Bull

April 21 – May 20

Love Check

Why you're fabulous

 Serene and sensual, you live for every moment of love without worrying about the past.

 You adore the seduction game – the longer it goes on, the better.

 Earthy and smoochy, you have a stabilizing effect on your partner.

Why you're impossible

 When you see someone beautiful to the eye, you just have to own them.

 Your attitude to finances can cause more ups and downs in your relationships than anything else.

Your love secrets

 A connoisseur of the good things in life, your hedonist desires are often underrated.

 You often accuse your partner of being the jealous possessive one, when really it's you.

Passive seduction is your innate art – you don't
have to cultivate it.

Your sexual style
Feral, primeval and slowly arousing.

Who falls for you
Sexually dominating powerful partners, who want
to possess you.

Earthy pragmatists, who realize you're as shrewd
in the bedroom as out of it.

Who you fall for
Hypnotic, intense partners who are also sensually
beautiful and very mysterious.

Fiery visionaries, who don't know how to sit down
and relax.

You identify with
Financial wizardry, beauty, nature.

Connoisseurs of the luxuries and pleasures of life.

Your greatest temptation
Men who are impossibly vain, and refuse to catch
your eye.

Your greatest strength
The patience to wait for him to realize you're worth
every moment of your time spent doing so.

Passion Profile for 2006

No one can doubt you have the sensual charm, the feminine wiles and the calm, good-natured and sweetest way of seducing any man to your side. This year your loyalty is beyond question, your sexual desires fulfilled, and your constant search for mutual respect and happiness understood. Throughout Jupiter's reign in your opposite sign of Scorpio until November, you can expect larger than life characters, wild adventurous lovers or simply the chance to strut your stuff. Wherever you go, men find you sizzling company, and in the spring you prove that you are one of the most creative and determined lovers around. The summer brings exciting encounters if you are single, and a deeper bond if attached. Your sexual needs are rewarded by the autumn, and you begin to realize that you are being true to your own inner voice. Steamy nights and scintillating sexual encounters mark the end of the year and you are blessed with the kind of lover who knows you inside out and back to front.

Best bets for Mr Right this year: Capricorn for ambitious relating, Virgo for sensual togetherness, Scorpio for utter passion.

2006 Month by Month

January

With Jupiter's challenging influence, the year kicks off with a realization that it's time to commit yourself to one long-standing relationship if you're attached, or give it up altogether. Confusion reigns for the first week of the year, and your lover's unreliability will give you cause for serious thought. But Mars in your own sign brings out the flirt in you, and no one can resist your charm. Then the next day you feel guilty about your behaviour. But why? Is it because someone in your past once said that to be taken seriously you have to always be placid and polite? It's time to enrol into the university of love's more fun-loving ways. Enjoy the spirit of romantic adventure for once, because no one else can enjoy being you more than yourself. And if you feel you can't have a laugh without your man's approval, perhaps he needs a few lessons in love himself. This is the month to restore your faith in love too. You are feeling vibrant and alive thanks to Mars and Venus's stunning link on the 22nd. So don't listen to anyone who moans about how pointless relationships are – you know you're on to something exceedingly tantalizing.

If you're single, thanks to Venus's incisive link with the Sun, by the 13th you can take a long hard look at what you really want from an on-and-off romance. If it is worth pursuing, you won't have much trouble in making it permanent. If you feel it is time to call it a day, you'll be ready to cut loose with no regrets. And then, of course, you meet a new professional contact, your hands touch by accident, there are electrifying moments as you both smile, and you wonder, just wonder, if this could be the start of something big. While your ruler Venus is back-pedalling through your adventurous zone it would be worth holding back. Don't leap in the flames too fast. The beginning of February isn't far away, and then you will know if it's for real or not.

Best days for romance: 3rd, 16th
Best days to seduce: 11th, 30th
Best stay at home day: 7th

February

If you are attached, you're still wondering if it's worth all the effort you're putting into one relationship. And even though you've tried hard to make it work, there still seems to be something missing. But remember, if your man isn't giving as much as you are, then maybe it's time to express your worries. With your ruler Venus's change of direction after the 3rd, he might just be in need of some extra TLC. Rather than expecting him to cultivate those ambitious joint plans, go out and play, romance, feast and take him out of himself.

Someone you thought would never get in touch with you again does around the 8th. But it's all hit and miss. He's vague, complicated and can't make up his mind, and you know deep down inside that you want straight answers, honesty and the kind of man who respects your serious outlook on life. But an honest discussion over dinner wouldn't do any harm to put the record straight.

If you're single, the fated attraction at the end of last month looks set to fade in the wash. Luckily you held back, and realized that it was never really meant to be anything other than a brief encounter. Ah well, by the 14th you're attracting a younger admirer in your professional camp. Without a doubt this one is too good to miss, so prepare yourself for a major seduction scene after office hours around the 17th, as Mars crosses the cusp of your sign and moves on into fun-loving Gemini.

If you're attached, you just can't resist acting like a couple of kids in the winter landscape as the pressures, both emotional and professional ease off, and you both realize that maybe you are trying too hard to act like the perfect couple. It is time to lighten up and look forward to a year of self-esteem and acceptance of what you can achieve. And with your lover by your side, you'll be the power behind his own throne too.

Best days for romance: 6th, 10th
Best days to seduce: 1st, 26th
Best stay at home day: 19th

March

Jupiter's stalling effects from the 4th are making you a little over-confident, simply because you are bored with having to be nice all the time. A loved one is certainly fascinated by your every word, and they are happy to play second fiddle to your exquisite performance. But they also have rules and boundaries like anyone else. Respect their contribution, otherwise you could find you are playing to an empty auditorium.

Realistically, you know what you can and can't do, especially where a particular intimate relationship is concerned. But, on the 10th, thanks to Saturn's serious link with Venus, you become convinced that you've perfected the art of courtship, and acquired the voice of authority. Next you begin to imagine that if you change certain conventions in your life, and act a little more radically, maybe you can have your cake and eat it. The celestial line-up is certainly provoking you to take a very unprecedented move. But check what you might lose if you do.

Unsure as you are about changing developments in a current love affair, you are also beginning to realize that maybe the unknown isn't such a scary place. And with the total eclipse of the sun on the 29th, you widen your perception and take a more objective view of love's mysterious ways. Of course, you want to maintain a sense of continuity with a partner. But unlike an oak tree, you don't have to leave your roots behind to branch out into unmapped territory. This is one very important month as you discover that free will and committed love aren't mutually exclusive, and you and your partner have the right to both. It may not seem as if anyone else has noticed, and you might feel a tad invisible in his eyes as the month draws to a close, but you have little choice but to respect his very different viewpoint. The Taurean gripe is that most other people are wrong. This month maybe you have to concede that he is probably as right from his own perspective as you are from yours.

Best days for romance: 4th, 19th
Best days to seduce: 10th, 22nd
Best stay at home day: 8th

April

'Beautiful eyes, shame about the trainers' might be a diary note around the 5th, when if single, you're looking and feeling more than a trillion dollars and Venus in sultry Pisces gives you the seductive charms of a femme fatale. Your attraction to beautiful things, whether works of art or a face in the crowd comes in very handy. You spot bargains, fall in love with the kind of charmers who make all your friends wish they were you. But this time, you just can't forget those ghastly things on his feet. Could it be a clue that there's something equally blowsy behind the boxers? By the 10th, you realize that this one really isn't worth the chase, and resigning yourself to working on your own fitness you're jogging through the park or getting down the gym. It's there you're most likely to bump into the kind of man you'd wash his trainers by hand for.

On the 15th, if you're single, your emotional energy is on a high, but you're in the mood to squander it when a passing comment from your partner or male colleague makes you secretly seethe. Just take care you don't play too many games – even though you're controlled about your feelings, there are moments when you have to express yourself and it could all come out the wrong way. If you're attached, you may be in for a night of silent anger, if single, you feel that no one understands you. So curb that stubborn streak and, by the 18th, you'll be feeling ready to share your true thoughts and smile at the world again.

With the Sun moving into your own sign on the 20th, followed by a sensual New Moon on the 27th, you are blessed with the seductive drive and motivation to attract the man who makes you melt. You have no choice but to reveal your intentions, otherwise how will you ever know what he really thinks about you? And it's all good news.

If attached, you are feeling more aware of your body image than ever before. His body may need a little pulling and tucking here and there, so together you agree to give up your favourite (but awfully bad for you) addictions, and take a rain check on window shopping. Dive into the bedroom, it is the best exercise you can get, and you'll remember how good sex can be when you're both dazzling, positive and body-polished.

Best days for romance: 2nd, 27th
Best days to seduce: 6th, 25th
Best stay at home day: 9th

May

With Mercury moving into your sign on the 5th to join the Sun, you're positively steaming sexiness this month. If you're single, your allure is compelling and admirers are tripping over each other, but your vulnerable side still urges to be cautious. What you don't need is to fall head over heels for someone who doesn't know the difference between a G-spot and a G-string. With a delightful link between Jupiter and Uranus in effect all month, it seems you're up for sexual bliss with your current lover. Whatever problems you have recently had with your man, you are beginning to communicate on a deeper level. Then a lively social event around the 18th confuses your feelings and you are uncertain whether to retreat quickly from your boyfriend's suspicious gaze or show him that actually you do care. A brief flirtation can sometimes stir you both into realizing how much you depend on each other for a sense of confidence and esteem. With a Full Moon in your opposite sign on the 13th, you'll be feeling sensual, erotic and dizzy with desire for your man again. Your emotional and physical charisma is at a peak, and you feel utterly confident about yourself and your future. Arousal levels reach an all-time high on the 20th, and you recognize that it's time to gently assert your sexual needs, no matter how difficult it is for you. If you do so when Venus moves into your sign on the 29th, you can sink into his arms knowing that the pleasure will be mutual from then on.

If you're single, seize the opportunity for a fling after the 25th. You've known someone has been interested for some time, and although at first he didn't seem like the prefect dream-boat, on second thoughts he might have the kind of wicked charm to keep you amused for a few dates. Here comes seductive Venus on the 29th to trigger off an exciting romantic adventure. You're so irresistible at the end of the month, men just can't stop being fascinated by you, so make sure you choose the one who respects your true needs. (And by the way, he's got wicked green eyes). Sexually, you can't go wrong, hormones are racing, libidos are rising and there's a sparkle in your step as you walk into a tantalizing June.

Best days for romance: 10th, 13th
Best days to seduce: 5th, 29th
Best stay at home day: 17th

June

A stunning day for sensual pleasures on the 3rd, followed up by a seductive gesture from an infiltrator on the work scene a few days later, and one which could put you into touch with someone extra special. Get to know him in your own time and on your own terms. That way you can be sure he has got the patience and integrity to deal with your professional discretion and also respect your need for honesty in relationships.

If you're attached, you are now at your most sensuous and loving, so if you are spending all your free weekends with a boyfriend or lover, break the habit around the 19th and suggest doing something you've never done together before. It doesn't have to be exotic – mind you, if you fancy going to Prague, Budapest or Venice, then why not? But it could just be that you roam around your own town or have a wicked weekend in the country.

If single, make sure you get invited to all those midsummer parties around the 21st, whether business or pleasure. Luck is on your side after the 20th, so go out and meet up with some dream catches. It may even be that gorgeous, quietly determined Capricorn you know at work.

Whether single or attached, you now have a renewed faith and belief in yourself, and what a lover or partner really stands for in your life. This is an important time of year when you begin to feel the power of your own credibility and sense of achievement, both with regard to your professional as well as personal life. This makes for an excellent time to begin any project or finalize plans. With your partner, you both feel emotionally well-balanced; shimmering and vivacious, you can flirt a little and enjoy the company of male colleagues too. Don't feel guilty that you're smiling at the world. The kind of charm you radiate is the key to meeting a VIP contact around the 28th, who can help with your professional progress.

Best days for romance: 11th, 27th
Best days to seduce: 15th, 20th
Best stay at home day: 4th

July

You're probably wondering, why should it always be you who makes the effort, sacrifices and allowances for the demands of others? Well, until the 22nd, Mars is urging you to create the domestic set-up you need, whether you want to or not. Luckily, the Sun in the creative area of your chart converts this task from a chore to a pleasure, and you are blessed with the charm and good humour to laugh and romance your lover into the bedroom. Enjoy the experience and, whether you're single or attached, as Jupiter changes direction on the 6th you will satisfy your heart and win the eternal battle for true love.

It is one thing making love happen and another keeping it alive, but Venus gives you the determination to create time alone together, away from family responsibilities before the 17th. Share sensual evenings with your partner and as the Sun moves into fiery Leo on the 22nd, he'll be responding with more suggestions for days, nights and months of projects and plans 'a deux'. Jupiter's move forward this month triggers off mutual aspirations, while a lovely lunar aspect on the 24th brings comfort in each other's beliefs. You are soulmates, providing the stability and security you desire in your closest relationships. It is time to reach out, open up and share your deepest thoughts. As Mars moves into fellow earth sign, Virgo on the 22nd, you'll discover powerful levels of commitment, removing any fear of loss or insecurity. To have the courage to be honest with a partner and realize you won't be shunned or rejected creates the most meaningful future imaginable. A relationship based on trust is a veritable Nirvana.

Best days for romance: 3rd, 21st
Best days to seduce: 17th, 31st
Best stay at home day: 11th

August

If you are single, Jupiter's change of direction last month has also brought you new insight into your passionate nature, and you decide it's time to put happiness on the top of your agenda. You are in dazzling form at the beginning of the month, and you are lusting after that gorgeous male friend's sexy voice on the 5th. By the 10th, with a stroke of luck, you'll be hearing it down the phone. Take a chance and tell him you are fascinated by his body as well as his mind, especially if you get past the first date.

Watch out that you don't get into a seriously complicated liaison with the wrong man on the 11th. You are in the mood to take a risk, but falling into the arms of someone who's already attached isn't going to make life or love very easy. With the summer heat rising, by the 20th the planets also start to give you hot thoughts. And a rival's less than flattering remarks won't stop you from going on a minor manhunt on the 23rd, when the New Moon in your romantic zone has you vivacious and witty. This one could be long-term, so take your time, and don't feel you have to push for instant results.

If you're attached, August is a month of changeable sexual thoughts. After the 12th, you feel trapped one day, and the next thoroughly happy and committed. You want to maintain your personal space, but you also want to be loved. On the 27th your lover tells you about his special feelings for you. And it becomes obvious he wants a deeper commitment. Then, on the 29th, you're convinced you can maintain your independence and still be coupled up. Facing the reality of your mutual needs becomes a major issue, so make sure you tell yourself and your man the whole truth and nothing but the truth.

Best days for romance: 9th, 22nd
Best days to seduce: 6th, 19th
Best stay at home day: 10th

September

The truth drug is a problematic one, and for a few days early on in September you turn a little cynical about romance. You know, you start to think, 'Well, what's so special about it anyway? In the end, doesn't it always turn to routine, chores and who's right and who's wrong? Look at what's happened to so many marriages.' And if the truth be known, how many of your friends are having affairs or telling white lies about how perfect their man is. But beneath all that hard edginess, you know that your judgements on love are simply a defence against your own craving for eternal romance. You want that never-never land to exist, and yet good old reality always brings you back down to earth with a bump.

Funnily enough, the lunar eclipse on the 7th makes you

extra dreamy, and if you are attached, the magic returns and your sensual desires are fulfilled. You are now at your most sultry and, around the 15th, you break with tradition and suggest to your lover doing something you have never done before. It doesn't have to be radical – it could just be a weekend break in a cultural city, or a mad romp in the countryside – but it will bring back that old sparkle.

If you are single, plan your seduction campaign with big business in mind. Get on the party list, be cool, sophisticated and glamorous, and luck will be on your side after the 12th. It is time to meet up with that dreamboat you fell for last month. With the Sun moving into Libra on the 20th, you have a new sense of belief in the kind of lover you really want, and what he must stand for in your life. He would give you a sense of the independent, confident part of yourself, as well as knowing how to run your bath and where to meet you after a hard day's work. He would understand your ambitions and that you need a goal or a materialistic challenge to bring out the best in you. And if he doesn't exist? Well, now is the time to meet up with him if you're single, and if attached, don't feel guilty that you're still smiling at the world and not him every day. The kind of charisma you're radiating will bring you success, with or without him. If he can fulfil your wish list qualities, then hang on to him tenaciously.

Best days for romance: 6th, 25th
Best days to seduce: 1st, 22nd
Best stay at home day: 12th

October

Recent discoveries have given you magical powers of self-belief and greater understanding of how other people value you. In fact, you are so deep in thought that you might not notice that a sultry rogue has his eyes on you. Be sure to keep yourself free for a sizzling date around the 2nd, when Mercury's cheeky influence in your love corner brings a younger, dashing hero into your working life. A spot of retail therapy will give your ego a boost, so go on a spree for an outfit that accentuates your best assets, and that sexy rogue won't be able to take his eyes off you. Remember though that you deserve simply the best – and don't take anything less. Your high ideals might be hard to live up to though, and by the 15th one love interest starts to feel a little trapped. Remember, your down-to-earth acceptance of love's tangled ways is far more important than any vague or wild promises or fantasies about long-term commitment, especially as right now you just need some fun.

After the 22nd, the Sun, Mars and Venus all surge into your relationship corner, bringing enthusiastic, exciting encounters, and inspiring you with ideas and seductive offers. Enjoy the spirit of romance, and revel in being the centre of attention while you are Miss Popularity herself. Dazzle friends with your charm and exploit your natural gift of pleasing everyone. If you are single, this is your chance to be exploited yourself in the most delicious way.

If you are attached, you are now both a force to be reckoned with, and this is your chance to make a successful twosome.

So make the end of the month one where emotionally, physically and materially you both agree that you can work together to create something special. With Venus and Mars's superb link in Scorpio on the 25th, it is time to open up about your true needs and true love will be all yours.

Best days for romance: 19th, 26th
Best days to seduce: 9th, 24th
Best stay at home day: 15th

November

Once an intimacy is formed, you are reliably faithful, but can be possessive without even realizing it! You don't get led astray (except by a beautiful face in the crowd), and your discretion and tact are exceptional qualities. Yet you are feeling inevitably drawn to the same conclusion about love – that there is something always missing! A feeling that however committed someone is to you, or you to they, there is a piece of the jigsaw puzzle that simply doesn't fit. With a wealth of planets in your relationship zone for the first two weeks of this month, it's worth seeing whether you are trying too hard to make this the perfect romance you've seen in films or read in books. Remember, you are ruled by Venus, and the planet of love is about an ideal of love too. And it is one that no one can really live up to, including yourself. And it's probably your own sense of being 'only too human' that makes you disillusioned at times like this. With Mercury's liberating change of direction on the 18th, you at last give up trying to control every minute of your love life. You see your man as a separate entity, and you understand that the puzzle of love is never complete. In fact, the pieces are endless and that in itself is a joy to discover. With a powerful link between Jupiter and the Sun on the 21st in your love corner, a commitment can be made or the chains that bind you can be broken. It's all or nothing, yes or no, and time to come clean.

If you are single, a rogue you've desired for some time begins to take more interest in you too. His larger-than-life attitude is dangerously attractive, and he's up for adventure and sexy pleasures. Take your time, seduce him passively, and watch the flames grow between you as the month draws to a close.

Best days for romance: 5th, 27th
Best days to seduce: 6th, 20th
Best stay at home day: 3rd

December

You aren't quite convinced that someone close shares the same enthusiasm or belief in you. And the more you ponder, the less you feel secure about their loyalty. With Mars, Jupiter and the Sun all in your most intimate part of your chart, you are being seriously tested on all counts of love. There are moments you feel it's not worth the effort, you'd rather live life alone, seeking towards greater independence. There will be other moments when all you want is someone who understands you and is there for you.

By the 20th, you're beginning to see that you can win, and will do so. Determination and integrity are your allies, so spend more time on self-dedication and less on worrying about what your partner thinks about you. With the Sun finally moving into your adventurous zone on the 22nd, you glow with charisma, and radiate good feelings all round. Make the festive season one where you lighten up a stranger's face if you're single, and lighten up your lover's world if attached. Indulge in a sensual, worldly sort of day on the 28th, and don't feel guilty about your hedonistic streak. You can be simultaneously mythical and down-to-earth, and all it takes is the right companion. But with such potent planetary activity, come the 30th a friend issues an ultimatum. Don't feel guilty if you believe your work must come first. Just recognize that perhaps they are pushy out of a fear of rejection. So stir the ingredients of love carefully. You might have to make another compromise, but just this once, it's worth keeping everyone happy, including yourself.

With the end of the year comes a feeling that you've come through some difficult times, and yet have always been true to yourself. With a lover deeply committed to you, don't give up on your long-term plans. Things will work themselves out, and the more love you give out to the world right now, the more will come back to you tenfold in the months to come.

Best days for romance: 1st, 17th
Best days to seduce: 24th, 31st
Best stay at home day: 16th

Your Love
Horoscope
2006

Gemini
The Twins

May 21 – June 20

Your Love
Horoscope
2006

Love Check

Why you're fabulous

 You always put a smile on other people's faces.

 Men find your witty, light-hearted approach to life magical.

 Pals love hearing you gossip on the phone.

Why you're impossible

 You can't keep a secret.

 Making up your mind where to eat out drives him crazy.

Your love secrets

 You flirt with your best friend's man.

 All that superficial fun disguises a very sensitive soul.

 When you're trying to catch a man, you never let on you are.

Your sexual style

Unpredictable, cheeky, but utterly romantic.

Who falls for you

Down-to-earth rugged hunks who admire your brain or want to control your scattered approach to life.

Light-hearted gamblers who just want to have fun.

Who you fall for

Independent freedom-lovers, travellers and gurus, or men who can tell you stories in bed all night. Or you go to the other extreme and hook into dreamy, elusive types.

You identify with

Communicators, mobile phone fanatics and anyone who's up for the latest gossip.

Your greatest temptation

Having two boyfriends, in case one rejects you.

Your greatest strength

You'd rather know the truth than live in a fantasy world.

Passion Profile for 2006

Whether deeply in love, or daring to dive into the waters of a transformative relationship, this year is one for some big changes in your love life. The year starts on a sexual boost to your libido, as Venus continues to bring you some hot rewards during a cold winter. You are hungry for more of anything – as long as there is more. By the spring, if you are single the seductive influence of Venus in your adventurous corner triggers off a delight of new blood in town, and a delirious period of romance if you are attached. Yet you are still wondering if one ex could still hold all the trump cards, and by your birthday you realize that even though there is still a magic spark between you, it is time to let go. The summer sun brings a fresh outlook on what relating really means to you, and it encourages flirtatious fun and sexual highs throughout August. But are you ready for that sudden whirlwind affair that takes you by storm in September? Dare to commit yourself and you'll be in sexual heaven for the rest of the year, resist and you might regret missing out on the love of a lifetime. Your destiny will be everything you want it to be now that you are learning to love yourself. If you can, so will someone else.

Best bets for Mr Right this year: Sagittarius for letting you be a free bird, Leo for passion personified, Libra for intellectual stimulation, Gemini for a hoot.

2006 Month by Month

January

Get ready for a scintillating social month. Reward yourself with a leg wax and facial on the 9th, indulge in aromatherapy or lash out on some earthy hues for your dazzling eyes on the 10th so that you are prepared for the onslaught of sexy attention. A sudden flurry of work around the 14th involves extra demands on your time, yet it is through those contacts and encounters in your professional world that you will meet the kind of partner or lover who will keep you spellbound – well, until the end of the month at least. Around the 22nd, Mars and Venus line up to provide you with all kinds of dishy dates if you are single, or romantic jaunts if you are attached. Snap out of feeling guilty about going to that party around the 24th, after all you've got the vitality for any event and any eventuality, so go for it. If you're not delighting everyone with your presence then you wouldn't catch the eye of one dark horse who's been secretly fancying you for the past few weeks, would you?

By the 25th, you wonder whether love is more complicated than a differential equation. Yes, you want to see X, but Y keeps calling, and Z just hasn't realized that you want your freedom. Start working out down the gym and stretch those beautiful limbs. You'll be eye-catching first, men-catching second. If you have a lover, then saying what you truly feel on the 26th makes for sexual bliss. Let him know what you love best in bed and don't be shy about revealing your deepest needs. However, a lack of communication with a lover at the end of the month makes you feel distinctly uncomfortable. Usually you avoid scenes, you walk away, turn to the phone, hunt out your friends and pretend nothing bothers you. But just this once it's worth sticking out the irritation and asking yourself what it is that you can't agree on. Talk things over with him on the 30th, and at the end of the month you'll know if your heart, and his, is truly in the right place. Funnily enough, this is the time of year when the sun is emphasizing your excitement corner and you can't resist seducing anyone just for the fun of it. But take care, if you are attached you could end up causing more problems than you bargained for; if single, the list of admirers just gets longer and longer.

Best days for romance: 6th, 28th
Best days to seduce: 10th, 31st
Best stay at home day: 1st

February

Romantic game playing is something Geminis do best. And even if you refuse to admit that you adore those kind of challenges, this month you have little choice but to join in. Flirtation makes people happy, it brings smiles to faces, it allows us to penetrate the barriers and boundaries we all put up in the world. With Mars, the planet of rampant mischief, surging into your sign on the 17th, just go with the flow. Whether single or attached, you can't help but laugh in the rain, jump when the phone rings, and wait eagerly for those secret text messages.

But what about Valentine's Day, you cleverly remember. With whom, what, where and how am I going to spend it? Domestic urges take hold around the 12th, but a gourmet dinner could be heavy on the expenses, so arrange a sexy picnic to get his juices flowing. Novelty is everything as you know, and you feel fabulously inventive thanks to Mercury's link with Uranus on the 14th. Invite your lover or admirer to dine out by a deserted riverbank or in some tranquil field. The weather could be raw and chilly or the sun may shine, but enjoy the fun. With the planets giving you fantastic ideas for sexy pleasure, anywhere that is different, daring or spontaneous will give you both a brilliant sexual rapport.

Any romantic complications get sorted out around the 20th, and you'll start sensing a positive new direction in a sizzling relationship. Passion runs to perspiration point on the 25th, so remain committed to your feelings, and know you are number one in your man's life. If you are single, surf the net, or simply surf the new employees in your professional world; a new dateline or dating strategy will give you oodles of choices. Around the 28th, listen carefully to your answerphone – there is someone out there who needs your good heart. They may not be the most glamorous, to-die-for person around, but they do understand what love is truly about. And for you this is the chance to play, to shine, to have time to chat to your friends and to have some space. They could give you all that and more.

Best days for romance: 17th, 27th
Best days to seduce: 4th, 19th
Best stay at home day: 7th

March

Mars is still ruling the roost in your own sign, and you're vibrant, scintillating and know that you are wanted. Being headhunted by professionals is one thing, but being romantically hunted for your charisma and unbelievable charm is another. Luckily, you are up for both this month. With Venus moving into airy Aquarius on the 5th, you are en route for a vibrant month – but watch out for some unpredictable moments on the way.

A know-it-all friend has your best interests at heart, but keep your intimate secrets to yourself on the 6th. Be wise, follow your nose and trust your judgement, not theirs. Otherwise, she could become a rival for your current lover or a match for any male competition. Take an out-of-town break with your amour and get close to nature in his arms. If you are single, a weekend jaunt between the 12th and 20th proves that men just can't resist your glamorous aura. Dump the friend if you have to; after all, if she is scheming and two-faced you won't be able to trust her when you leave her with Mr Right Now for even five minutes.

Meanwhile, Venus is drawing you towards all the gorgeous things life has to offer, apart from romantic Romeos, what about a new pair of shoes, or maybe that new make-over that's on offer? But are you truly content with the superficial things in life? Even though the material world is tempting, what you need right now is a deeper sense of belonging, a knowledge there is someone who understands your unpredictable way of living life, and who gives you enough space to do so. With another stunning link between Mars and Venus on the 25th, accompanied this time by seductive Neptune, you suddenly feel more inventive sexually, and want to express your physical desires. If you are attached, your partner begins to click on a different level and bedroom fun turns to a more intimate togetherness. Now you are both sharing long-term goals rather than just the wine, and you are plotting and planning how to make your life more fulfilling. If you are single, a hilarious rogue takes you out of yourself, he might just be a one-date wonder, but it's enough to give your ego a boost.

Best days for romance: 10th, 13th
Best days to seduce: 3rd, 18th
Best stay at home day: 28th

April

With Venus moving into your career corner on the 6th, take the chance to explore new ideas, goals, and even that sneaky little word 'commitment' with a boyfriend. Think about how dedicated you are to your own success, and whether he is devoting himself to his own, or helping with yours as well. Rarely do you admit to your own deeper emotions simply because it is easier to be rational and reasonable. But you could experience a moment of anxiety about appearing desperate and needy on the 9th, simply because sometimes you have to admit to having feelings. Go on, admit that you would love to be part of a long-term double-act, but the problem is that you also want your freedom. Likewise, you want to create a lifestyle which gives you time to play as well as work. If your boyfriend is a fellow air sign, Libra or Aquarius, he may understand because his own vocation and lifestyle will be run pretty much along the same lines. But if he is Taurus, Cancer, Scorpio, Capricorn or Leo, he will simply want you to dedicate yourself to the double-act, and nothing but. Do you cut ties or do you commit? These are big questions this month, as the airy Full Moon in Libra on the 13th brings it all out in the open. You may not shout in his ear, you may not even whisper across the pillow, but the crux of the matter is how do you maintain your individuality when committed to coupledom?

Ideas flow thick and fast around the 18th, as Venus and Uranus bring surprise professional opportunities your way. And freedom that these may bring to be yourself seem to be staring you in the face. If your lover or partner doesn't respect your independence, then maybe it is time to start thinking if he really is the right man for you. I know you hate to give up on others, and anything for an easy life, but don't give up on your own ambitions and aims on behalf of someone else. For what is love if it is not to adore someone for who they are, warts, freedom, quirks and all, rather than trying to change them?

If you are single, look out around the Full Moon on the 13th for a dreamy type who lingers longer than most at the office, or in your social circle. He could be younger than you, so enjoy the attention, and if you are ready for more than a one-off date, keep your eyes firmly fixed on him.

Best days for romance: 5th, 23rd
Best days to seduce: 16th, 19th
Best stay at home day: 3rd

May

This is the time of year when you are approaching your birthday. A solar cycle is nearly complete, and with it comes a feeling that all the things you've achieved in the past year have been worth the worry, heartache and effort. But what are your true romantic goals? If you are a true Gemini, then you know you need to keep the happy, sparkling side of your relationships intact. It's when the routines, the same old arguments, the same old bedroom scenarios begin to fill your weeks that you become bored, and subsequently long for what you had in the beginning. With Mercury, your ruler, moving into Gemini on the 19th, followed by the Sun on the 21st, you want to play. Your ideals are on a high, and even if you have to move the furniture around in your bedroom, at least something has to change. We all suffer that same human gripe about 'why is life so dull', 'why can't I do something different', 'why isn't my love life perfect'. The answer this month is to make those changes yourself. No compromises, just pure self-confidence about what you want from your partner and how much you are prepared to give of yourself. Don't be afraid to air your thoughts on the 25th, and show how utterly magical and warm-hearted you are, but also that you're an idealist. Illusions are great when we are dreaming them or even living them, but don't forget they can turn to disillusionment when others can't live up to your image of how you want them to be.

This month you are growing in awareness. Perfect romance and ideal love is a hard act for anyone to follow, so brew your own love potions based on knowing who you are rather than what you think others expect from you. Know your limitations as well as how to charm or seduce anyone into your life, and you'll discover that love isn't an illusion unless you choose to let it be so.

With a stunning New Moon on the 27th in Gemini, promise yourself this is the start of your solar year for romantic highs, success in love and, most of all, to simultaneously honour your individual needs and desires. Don't give up on the very part of yourself that is your destiny – in other words, your character, your sense of purpose and fulfilment in life through relationships. As much as your partner or a lover can bridge the gap, it is you who have to cross the bridge to knowing who you actually are – he can't do it for you.

Best days for romance: 9th, 21st
Best days to seduce: 19th, 27th
Best stay at home day: 10th

June

Hey, after all that serious stuff, aren't you just ready to party? And if you've just had a birthday or are about to, now is your chance to prove how irrepressible, stunning and magical you are. Single or attached, you are creating attention wherever you go. Mercury's swift move into Cancer on the 3rd, followed by a seductive link between the Sun and Neptune on the 10th, are making fun your top priority. Venus's provocative influence has you writing poetry and spinning tales. And your hilarious social antics entice an especially sexy lover into your arms. Use Mercury's sensual but cheeky influence in Cancer to take the seduction one stage further.

But tangling yourself up in a complicated web of intrigue is all too easy around the 19th when Mars squares up to Jupiter and temporarily blocks lines of communication. If your lover or boyfriend hasn't called or e-mailed don't leap to silly conclusions. Consider all the possible options before charging round to his office or home to check out if there is someone else, or if he's decided to cool off. You have such a vivid imagination that it is easy to think the worst. And being a Gemini, you want answers, facts, the truth and honesty, painful as it can sometimes be, rather than wallowing in doubt. And you want it now. So try to be patient for a few days, hang out with friends, and enjoy the sun because, with Venus finally arriving in your own sign on the 24th, you realize you were just panicking for no reason. You are charismatic, on top of the world and in control of the romantic stakes. Just don't give up your time too freely or seem too keen, and you'll recognize your chance for real happiness and how to obtain it. Dazzling self-belief and certainty of where you are heading is irresistible and it sees you rising phoenix-like from the ashes of self-doubt with one very sexy amour clinging to your feathers.

Best days for romance: 11th, 21st
Best days to seduce: 18th, 29th
Best stay at home day: 6th

July

Make the most of Venus's ongoing influence in your own sign until the 19th. Romantic dreams will fill your days, and the summer heralds that feel-good factor with a run of exciting days of fascinating encounters at home or on holiday. Things have been a little up in the air concerning your home or family ties, but now you can come to terms with making the necessary changes. At last you can feel confident about your own personal objectives and trust in your own judgement without fear of disapproval. However, Mercury's U-turn in your chart until the 29th continues to trigger confusion about your inner security and sense of stability. Early on in the month you are moody and impatient one day, vibrant and ready to take on the world and its mother the next. With Mars moving into Virgo on the 22nd, a part of your chart concerning home, relaxation and a sense of inner well-being, you will probably be happy to take a break from the summer fray to enjoy cosy nights at home, or share a cocktail with that lover under a parasol.

Brilliant days around the New Moon of the 25th give the opportunity to exchange information with friends about your personal happiness and your need to develop certain aspects of life, both materially and emotionally. There is a grand opportunity to make yourself heard by a lover or partner on the 29th, when Mercury moves forward again, and anything can be sorted out – from money and possessions to personal values. So listen to what he has to say too, but only make changes according to your true needs. For once, don't compromise just to prevent an argument. You need to stick to your principles, not sacrifice them to win approval. Approval is not love after all, so never forget the difference. We all seek approval in some form or another, because it makes us feel we are wanted, and it takes away our insecurities and fears. But people have a nasty habit of manipulating us (albeit unconsciously) to get their own way and gain power over us. It is often the one who plays the victim in a relationship, you know, 'All I do is work my socks off while you just go out partying', who is actually controlling the relationship. And then the approval seeker will act contrary to their own desires, and reply, 'Ok, I won't go and meet my friends, I'll make your supper every evening and stay by your side.' Take care. The planets right now are suggesting a shift in your relationship pattern; it won't be an overnight change, but there is something distinctly fragile in the air at the end of July.

Best days for romance: 5th, 16th
Best days to seduce: 11th, 21st
Best stay at home day: 29th

August

Commitment always sounds a very necessary prize. Yet, with a curious twist of your mind, you see that perhaps it is not all it is cracked up to be. Somehow there must be a way of loving one person, but still honouring your freedom. With a radical Full Moon in Aquarius on the 9th, and Mercury moving into fiery Leo on the 11th, followed by Venus on the 12th, you might force a lover to make an all or nothing decision. But do you want to end up lonely? The big paradox for Gemini is that you want company, friendship and a good social network, but you don't want to be doing what's expected of you consistently – routine sex, set mealtimes, social niceties. These you often rebel against, just to be contradictory. This month, you will be tested in your loyalty if you are attached, but if single, you'll know where your true loyalty lies and that is to yourself. Yet with the calming effects of Mercury's rapid move into sensible Virgo on the 27th, you begin to accept that reflection and adjustment are necessary rather than making rash decisions.

However insecure you feel about your relationships, there is a purpose behind the impasse. Mid-month, he seems to be holding back on his feelings, and at the end of August he doesn't even seem to want to talk about the weather. Is it you? Have you done something wrong? Or is it merely that you have reached a turning point. Either way, you have an uncanny feeling that change is in the wind, and you have known this since last month. Single or attached, there is anticipation in the air, a sense of someone better, sexier, round the corner who can bring the romance you long for back into your life. Or that, maybe, at long last you can make a relationship work and still honour your own freedom.

This is a month when the most important thing to remember is that understanding and acknowledging your feelings reveals more about your greatest desires. More than any other time of the year, now is your chance to really focus on your love goals and to remember that whatever direction you take, it will always be the right one. No to regrets, yes to refreshed values.

Best days for romance: 17th, 27th
Best days to seduce: 1st, 6th
Best stay at home day: 10th

September

So, if you are single, are you ready to embark on a new relationship; and, if you are attached, are you prepared to leave a lover, or start afresh? This month a new affair beckons, thanks to a host of planets in the romantic corner of your chart. It all kicks off on the 8th, when feisty Mars pushes on into Libra, followed by your ruler Mercury on the 12th. Whoever you bump into in your social circle, whatever the scenario, you'll realize this person could be Mr Right Now, or even Mr Right. Charismatic and enchanting, the partial eclipse of the Moon on the 7th provides the seductive aura that will attract any man. But take care if this is a clandestine affair, as the electrifying link between Venus and Uranus on the 16th could bring it all out into the open via someone who does not have your best interests at heart. But with the seductive powers of Cleopatra, you are also the life and soul of every social whirl. A nagging thought crosses your mind on the 25th that perhaps there is a rival in your circle who is after the same man. But, don't worry, it is your personal charm and self-confident approach to love and life that gets you noticed and hunted by that gorgeous enigmatic stranger.

If you are still involved in a relationship, then the end of September marks an emotional turning point. You start to open up about your sexual needs, and how you need passion and romance from morning through to night. Remember your own need for space and freedom too? Well, the planets are giving you the chance to prove that your career and personal ambitions are just as important as loving your partner. Tell your boyfriend honestly how you feel on the 30th, when Venus alights in your romance zone and your every word is peppered with magical stardust. It is time to create the kind of relationship that really works for you. Either that, or you might have to accept that it just won't work on his terms. It is make your mind up time – do you honour your personal goals, or give up on them for the sake of that old foe, approval?

Best days for romance: 8th, 12th
Best days to seduce: 23rd, 30th
Best stay at home day: 15th

October

By now you will have made a choice, or met your match. And the bonus is that this is a super month for pleasures of the flesh as well as the mind. The Full Moon on the 7th gives you free rein to be passionate and assertive. Make sure you ask for what you truly want from a sexual rendezvous of the most intimate kind. If you are single, a dark horse will be ready for some erotic phone conversations, so switch on that mobile phone. Accept an unusual invite for a wicked invitation on the 14th – he is raring to keep up with your libido now it's on a high. Again, if you're single, a fascinating romantic encounter occurs on the 22nd, enhanced by the scintillating New Moon in Libra. Within the next few days you'll be at your most stunning, and sexually buzzing, and with the Sun surging on into intense Scorpio from the 23rd, the adrenaline will be racing and a mutual craving develops between you and a male colleague. Don't give up on those long-term dreams and desires now that you're about to discover a new and deeply moving experience of love – in more ways than one.

This is an excellent month to communicate your sexual needs without getting into a flap. And if you're breathlessly waiting for that phone call on the 25th, don't worry; your vibrant personality won't let him forget you. But your boyfriend could get a mite possessive on the 28th, when you'd rather be dreaming of an escape route. By the end of the month, you realize why sometimes that twosome thing you dream of is still important in your life as well as your sense of freedom. It is time to set the record straight with a partner who knows how to give you the space to be yourself. Remember, sexual passion, romance, travel and fun are the key points on your wish list. So make it clear that is what you're about. Commitment to the washing up bowl or laundry? Never!

Best days for romance: 7th, 18th
Best days to seduce: 1st, 9th
Best stay at home day: 11th

November

If you thought October was passionate, then this month you are going to be fired into sensual bliss, romantic intrigue and maybe even some double-dating. With a host of planets moving into your opposite sign of Sagittarius, let the fun commence. Just take care you don't hurt anyone. Remember, sometimes even the truth needs to be tweaked a little, as long as it's done with the intention of not harming someone. This is simply because you are still being pulled in two directions either by a choice of prime candidates or by your own twin soul. You want it all ways, and somehow you are determined to have your cake and eat it. Your imagination, perception and eye for a likely candidate is on a high around the 5th, and again on the 10th. With Venus moving into Sagittarius on the 17th, don't be surprised if the fiery rogues out there are soon firing their arrows in your direction. Even if you are attached and loving it, there will be temptations this month. Particularly when Jupiter moves into Sagittarius on the 24th, and larger than life characters just seem to pop out of the woodwork. Take care, though, that you don't play too many games yourself, and try not to tell all your friends what you are up to.

But any romantic panics will soon calm down to a slightly less frantic pace. So take a few sensible moments around the 26th to put an end to a secret flirtation that's going nowhere or an affair that's run its course. Jupiter will be in your relationship corner for nearly a year, so it is the beginning of a period of liberated love, free and wide open choices, and the realization that there are men out there who aren't just dream material, they're dreamboats sailing your way. Around the 29th you might be tempted to take up a sexy away-day offer with a new admirer who has integrity, belief in you and the ability to treat you as an equal. This could be one of those romantic adventures that boosts your ego, arouses your libido and, most of all, makes you realize how good it is to be you.

Best days for romance: 17th, 24th
Best days to seduce: 25th, 26th
Best stay at home day: 2nd

December

And so it continues! With Mars surging on into your relationship corner on the 6th, followed by cheeky Mercury on the 8th, there is no stopping you from flirting your way into the festive spirit. However, watch out when a few doubts about your own desirability rating arise on the 5th. A Full Moon in your own sign brings a myriad of emotions, memories and thoughts reeling through your head. You remember an ex who always scolded you for being so contrary, you remember how another wanted serious conversations about politics while you were only interested in who was getting off with your best friend. Why did none of those men understand you? Perhaps, after all, regrets aside, you have made the right choices over the past few months and now it's time to unclutter your heart and spring into romantic life again.

The next day, creative thoughts and sexy urges are bubbling over, and you know you have got to do something to make a relationship move forward, but you are not sure what. But by the New Moon of the 20th in sassy Sagittarius, your eyes are suddenly opened wide and you have a clear vision of what you have to do to make a love affair work out. Mars and Venus propel you to throw out long-held ideals for a wonderfully fresh approach. And on the 21st, you know what you want for Christmas and it's not that snazzy bag you saw on the 15th and could not afford. A brilliant surge of communication channels open, and you ask the very questions you've been so far avoiding. Does the man of the moment really want some kind of commitment, or is it just lust? And, more importantly, could you envisage spending a lot of time alone with him? If the answer to both questions is yes, then make it clear how you really feel and enjoy a festive season in the most tantalizing and sexy way. By the New Year, you will be raising your glass to toast each other, no strings, no commitments, just live for the moment and enjoy the sparkle of each other's company.

If you are single, you'll either be the star of the Christmas show, or surrounded by delicious hunks on a mission to snag a hot date thanks to your glamorous image. One man out there understands that you don't need mistletoe to prove you're adorable, just the joy of being true to yourself. What happens next? It's a secret. But just to give you a clue, any wishes made on New Year's Eve are likely to come true.

Best days for romance: 6th, 8th
Best days to seduce: 17th, 21st
Best stay at home day: 26th

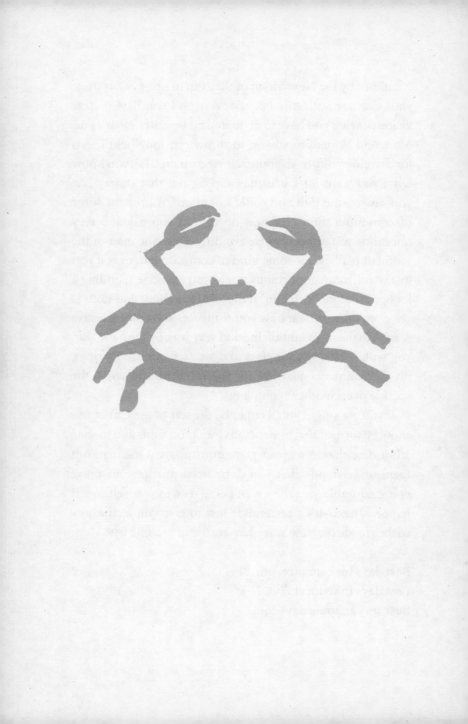

Your Love
Horoscope
2006

Cancer
The Crab

June 21 – July 20

Your Love
Horoscope
2006

Love Check

Why you're fabulous

 Men just can't resist your sensual aura.

 Once you include someone in your sacred personal space, you'll do so for life.

 You are totally loyal to your tribe of family, colleagues and friends.

Why you're impossible

 Your moods swing like a pendulum.

 You take things very personally and then react defensively.

Your love secrets

 You're restless, unpredictable and sexually wild.

 You're a match for any man who tries to seduce you.

 Sexually, you're very aware of what does and doesn't turn you on.

Your sexual style
Sensual, sultry and magnetic.

Who falls for you
Macho men who want to control you, or mummy's boys who hunger for your warmth.

Who you fall for
Ambitious whizz kids, successful down-to-earth business magnates, airy intellectual types and cool operators.

You identify with
Men who have a sense of family and history, dynasty or tribal law, but also emotional honesty.

Your greatest temptation
Playing the victim–saviour game to win a man.

Your greatest strength
Being able to cope with all his moods as well as your own.

Passion Profile for 2006

With the passion of Jupiter behind you this year, you are a force to be reckoned with. Your eyes are wide open to the romantic games people are playing, but how can you make those dynamics work for you too? Throughout the spring, you are in demand, full of vivacity and a bit of a party animal. Yet you wonder if any man can ever understand you. By May, it is time to put on your dancing shoes and play the seduction game. Shimmering and sensual, you spend the summer in two minds. One says commit, the other says stay free and easy. The chances of a long-term affair or relationship are high as you go into the autumn. But big changes are in the air – do you move forward with the one you love, or alone? By the end of the year, you become more realistic about your long-term love goals. You know that the one person to care about is yourself, and whether single or attached you have learnt that love is as unpredictable and as changeable as the wind. It's time to show that you have the passion, instinct and ability to adapt to circumstances and love's tangled ways.

Best bets for Mr Right this year: Taurus for soul-mating, Virgo for security, Scorpio for sexual fantasy, Pisces for a laugh a minute

2006 Month by Month

January

They say that January brings the snow, but for you it also brings necessary warmth from friends, lovers and the knowledge that the cycles of nature are turning towards the summer. Being born in the summer makes the winter harder to bear, yet with the Sun in your relationship corner until the 20th, you are in demand – and loving it. So be at your most passionate and live by your principles and intuition. Sometimes the romantic light does go a little fuzzy, and we have all experienced the worry whether we'll have that bright magical spell cast over us again. But rarely will it be clouded by self-doubt for long this month. Your optimistic side and renewed joy for living will give you more reasons to listen to yourself than anyone else.

With a Full Moon in your own sign on the 14th, this is a month to remind yourself that transformation and the quality of love you seek comes from within, as well as from without. And because you've been very secretive about your feelings, get ready for a probing attempt from a lover or partner on the 17th to find out what you're thinking, when Venus and Mercury's inquisitive link forces you to open up and reveal your thoughts. Now is the chance to reveal your own motives and how radical you can be when it comes to expressing what it is you want for your own future. Of course, there are times when you say more than you should do, and your lover doesn't know where he stands; but, equally, there are other times when you're feeling moody or insecure, that you say nothing, and yet your man knows exactly what's going on behind the quiet smile. With Venus backtracking through your relationship zone until next month, this will be an ongoing test to prove that you are not holding anything back, nor projecting your fears onto your partner. It is time to take mutual responsibility for your aims and ambitions. Speak with conviction and you will be amazed how logic and reason can turn the tables exactly the way you like them. In your direction!

Best days for romance: 3rd, 14th
Best days to seduce: 10th, 22nd
Best stay at home day: 5th

February

Romantic attachments are becoming more curious by the day, and you are finding yourself involved in something particularly clandestine. Then some friend or other keeps asking you, 'Well, explain it all, what's it about, give me a reason'. Yet, as you well know, not everything is a mathematical equation or about justifying feelings. We are creatures of instinct first, with rational judge and jury tagging along behind. But this February love story fits only the former. You can't expect to tell anyone why you feel this way, and you can't expect to find a mental solution to something which requires a gut reaction.

A New Year's encounter returns to haunt you in the nicest possible way. Just make sure you are not being led down the kind of path that means you get so thoroughly involved right up to your neck in complex arrangements, that you can't get out when the going gets intense. Valentine's Day starts off icy over breakfast, but hot and steamy by the evening, and the deep feelings you have for your man make you realize that it is when you feel out of control of your love life that you start to get jealous, moody or suspicious. But you also have a secret inner force which compels you to take risks, when another part of you would rather play it safe, or you push your man to extremes, when you'd rather he was predictable. Understand this much about yourself this month, and you can and will have the kind of happiness you crave.

If you are single, thanks to the Sun's influence after the 19th, someone is wondering whether you have an ulterior motive for being so charming. And, of course, you wouldn't be you if you didn't live without taking a few risks in love. With an expressive New Moon in enigmatic Pisces on the 20th, you have exactly the allure to do so. By the 27th, you have proved that where there's a will there's a way. And any new relationship that begins, or an old one that ends, confirms your need to live close to the edge. And with Uranus's radical influence in your romantic zone, it's time to define clearly what you want from your love life and go for it.

Best days for romance: 7th, 27th
Best days to seduce: 1st, 20th
Best stay at home day: 12th

March

This month you feel in a cul-de-sac about where your personal journey is going. With Mercury's tell-tale influence in your relationship zone, you are aware of the issues, the doubts, the differences and the swirl of polarities between what you want, what he wants, what you value and what is politically correct. You have no other choice but to take the plunge into your deeper feelings and sort it all out.

After all, it has been difficult to know how far to go with one relationship. There are days when you feel 'this is it', and nights when dark thoughts fill your head and you can't be sure of anything. Spring is in the air, friends believe they have all the answers to your love life (not even knowing how to sort out their own). And yet you haven't told them quite everything about how you really feel. The guarded, secret, private part of yourself is on red alert around the 13th, when either nosy neighbours, curious Geminis in the workplace or well-meaning but probing friends frustrate you into turning the tables on them. Frankly, a spot of espionage reveals you are right, their romances are unreliable, confusing, and these perfect couples aren't so perfect after all. But your own secrets are best kept that way up until the 30th. Whether you are deeply in love and don't know how far down the relationship road you are going, or caught up in a clandestine affair, the celestial influence is urging you to understand what you truly want, and transform your love life into pure magic.

Best days for romance: 9th, 16th
Best days to seduce: 11th, 25th
Best stay at home day: 28th

April

This is a month for putting the S back into spice and sex. And although it might seem a safer bet to sit patiently waiting for your lover to call, the intelligent thing to do is to get on with your social life and keep him guessing. Once he realizes you have a life of your own, you can begin to assert your sexual needs. Be careful on the 3rd – if you become too possessive he might put the brakes on any future plans you have. By the 11th, you will be dazzling him and quickly forget your differences. With Venus in dreamy Pisces from the 6th, making an electrifying link to Uranus on the 18th, adventurous sexual techniques are on your mind, so make sure you give him a guiding hand before you attempt the unimaginable!

If single, you'll be looking your most sensual and luscious thanks to Venus, and if you are feeling left out in the cold then don't worry, there's someone out there who's taken notice.

Watch out on the 18th for an eccentric charmer with a twinkle in his eye. This could be the beginning of a short-term relationship, but one which could transform the way you look at life. Then with Mars moving into your own sign on the 14th, you suddenly have the courage to take control of the relationship reins. Whether single or attached, you are proving how conscientious you can be towards a lover, and how caring and sensitive you are towards his needs. But just remember, yours have to be attended to as well. The end of the month you swap your serious side for the pursuit of fun. Your new-found air of liberation will be so arousing that you'll be pursued by new admirers wherever you go.

Best days for romance: 15th, 21st
Best days to seduce: 3rd, 9th
Best stay at home day: 13th

May

So many of your relationships are dependent on a sort of 'all or nothing' means test. If your lover isn't giving you every minute of the day his full attention or time, you worry that you are not g_____old Cancerian complaint of 'no one re_____' starts to create bubbles_____charm, sw_____into the by throwing the guilt on your partner, or by reproaching yourself. With Jupiter's inspiring link to Mars in your sign on the 7th, you begin to wonder if a current love affair or new admirer will truly fulfil all your sexual and passionate desires. Around the 13th, thanks to a stunning link between Mars and Uranus, you take a deep breath and admit to your feelings. Yes, you are deeply insecure, find it difficult to maintain any boundaries, and are emotionally malleable, but you do have an inner strength and an extraordinary love to give out to the world. With an equally passionate Full Moon in Scorpio on the same day, it seems as if either all your dreams are going to come true, that you'll merge into each other for ever after, or that too much of a good thing is giving you the feeling that you need some space away from him for a while.

I am afraid that another Cancerian pattern of behaviour that you fall into so frequently appears at the end of the month. Sometimes you want to be so close you are like butter melted into roux; the next day you are distant, cool and want your space. The problem here is that you actually loathe being separate from the one you love. Yet you crave autonomy at the same time. Your mood swings are an expression of this, and like your ruling Moon, you are governed by the rhythms and cycles of the cosmos. Go with the flow this month. It may be hard to see a way through the jungle of emotions, it may be difficult to honour your values but you are gradually coming home to a deeper connection with yourself.

Best days for romance: 19th, 24th
Best days to seduce: 2nd, 23rd
Best stay at home day: 11th

June

You are realizing that it is time to take positive action where your personal wishes are concerned. The fruits of your labour are beginning to show, and it seems crazy not to take advantage of those who understand you have something very valuable to say and do. So don't waste time, start making tracks. For some time you've been worrying about what a lover really wants from you. Use the enlightening effects of Mercury moving into your own sign on the 3rd, and Mars moving out of it into your realistic zone, to clarify exactly what are their objectives and limitations. Of course, there is always some envious friend or family member who will want to throw a spanner in the works, but that in itself could be a fascinating challenge. Prove that where love is concerned, it is you who make the choices.

With the Sun moving into your own sign on the 21st to mark the summer solstice, your joy for sexy, steamy love is on a roller-coaster ride. This is the beginning of your solar year, and a time for change. Even though there is a restlessness you can't quite put your finger on, a few special dreams are hatching. And whether you are attached or single, an unexpected encounter on the New Moon of the 25th triggers off a sexier rapport and you can't resist playing a game of cat and mouse. At last, you are developing an ability to have things your own way, and on your own terms too. Don't back down now because you are on a wave of independent action. After all, compromising will only make you feel that you have taken one step back. Be clear about what you truly desire, and start working towards crossing the bridge to personal paradise. Never one to take things lying down, (even in bed you like to be on top – admit it!), you are certainly showing you have the energy and the willpower to aim for some very satisfying romantic goals.

Best days for romance: 3rd, 21st
Best days to seduce: 25th, 29th
Best stay at home day: 9th

July

This month, be aware of your present needs, current feelings, and the chance to let go of hurts, resentments, hates and fears and embrace yourself as you are now. With the Sun in your sign until the 22nd, and Venus taking up residence on the 19th, it is also a time when you can accept that transformation comes from within as well as without. Because you have been very secretive about your feelings, around the 4th be prepared for an outburst from a current lover or an ex who wants to know why you have been so mysterious. This is one of those months to reveal your own motives and what you truly want for the future. With Mercury backtracking through Cancer after the 10th until the 29th, facing difficult, emotional interactions will be an art that you will naturally handle well. Don't turn back, but look at the truth of who you are, and what you truly want. So, when you feel that your relationship is dull, shapeless and going nowhere, then around the 11th, thanks to a Full Moon in your opposite sign, Capricorn, you have a chance to shake or wake things up in the boudoir.

Venus demands you take a closer look at your own image and romantic behaviour during the second half of the month. Are you ready to take responsibility for your own needs and desires? Or are you still floundering with the fear of upsetting someone else if you make your own choices? Family or clan expectations do matter to you, but it is worth remembering that you must live out your own wants and wishes too. Otherwise, unresolved issues could arise through any intimate relationships you have in the future. Whether single or attached, once Mercury shifts gear on the 29th, and with a bounteous Jupiter surging forward in your romantic corner again, the high summer looks set to be one where the magical moments you long for are generated by the enigmatic revamped you. And you are beginning to prove that you are worth every minute of waiting for.

Best days for romance: 6th, 29th
Best days to seduce: 3rd, 27th
Best stay at home day: 31st

August

Emotional passion is an exhausting process, whether it comes from your natural sensitivity, or if it has been forced on you by other people's ups and downs. Like anyone else, you need time to recharge your batteries and your passion for life. By the middle of August, your sensual needs have been met, thanks to Mercury and Venus's move into the physical pleasure zone of your chart. But with the Sun moving into Virgo on the 23rd, followed by a New Moon on the same day, your social life is now highlighted. Begin to enjoy the company of family and friends, put on hold the questions, fears and doubts about your lover's motivations, or your lack of motivation to find new love. Rather than just letting other people's ideas wash over and through you, you return to your more inspirational and empowering self. The harmonious energy around the 25th, favours all social and intimate activities. You are on top form again, and your light-hearted input will outweigh any emotional discord. The cosmos is reminding you that it is time to restore your closeness with friends as well as partners. Remember, they have faith in your determination to make a success out of your love life. With Mercury's light-footed entry into Virgo on the 27th, you now have the voice, wit and charm to get your sexy way.

If you are single, you are unsure about getting involved with someone who could put you into a position of power. Talk things through with a confidential and impartial friend, and don't commit yourself until you're 100 per cent convinced it's the right thing to do. Other than your mother and your-self, no one has your real best interests at heart.

Best days for romance: 12th, 23rd
Best days to seduce: 8th, 16th
Best stay at home day: 1st

September

This is a month when you rediscover a lost piece of treasure from memory lane, or nostalgic thoughts that are enough to make you blush when you mentally replay a sexual scenario with an ex-lover on the 1st. With a partial eclipse of the Moon in Pisces on the 7th, you are considering doing something about hotting up your sex life. Either establish contact with that ex if you are single, or re-create the sexual fantasies with your current lover, and September will be hotter than August. Show him what you want, and find sensations or words that stimulate you both. With Jupiter still pushing on through Scorpio, surprise your man – or a new one – by revealing the power of your seduction and your personal beauty. You know that you must stay on top of your feelings, but just for once you cannot resist being more carefree and wilful than you have been for a long time. Have it all your way, both in and out of the bedroom, and by the 25th you are in the mood to con-sider a return match, but this time you let him take control.

When you are at your most profound, you are usually trying to resolve a problem in your own or someone else's life.

Around the 27th, you need to analyze your own feelings when the cosmos forces you to confront a growing sense of restlessness. Uranus triggers off a desire for some kind of domestic reorganization, and with other professional changes in the wind, and a sense of a better lifestyle ahead, it feels as if you just have to move on. A lover may be ultra-suspicious of your motives, and you just can't seem to say the right thing. Every time you try to explain that you are tired of your work or domestic situation, he becomes less and less responsive. Don't forget he might just be feeling insecure and imagining that you are thinking of splitting up; and because your self-esteem is growing, he may be feeling left out in the cold. By the end of the month, you finally reach an agreement of what you both want for the future. Be prepared for a change of direction, together or apart. You know there's no other way than forward.

Best days for romance: 7th, 16th
Best days to seduce: 10th, 24th
Best stay at home day: 19th

October

You are at your most smouldering and hypnotic this month, thanks to a host of planets moving into your romantic corner. Sassy, charismatic and vibrant, use your incredible talent for getting to the heart of any matter and clarify your lover's true intentions on the 2nd. The likelihood is that he is confused about his role in your relationship, or can't see where he fits into your long-term career plans. Ask yourself whether you do have space for him in your life, and if you are ready to share more of it with him. Is there something missing or inhibited about your personal life together, or do you fear that if you get closer, you will become too dependent on him? With Mercury crashing headlong into probing Scorpio on the 2nd, followed by the Sun, Venus and Mars on the 23rd and 24th, you won't have time to sit and think about your emotions and you'll be feeling ready to air your views. So be passionate and as emotionally honest as you dare.

Just take care on the 24th and 25th, when Venus and Mars produce some fireworks. If you are single, a spell-binding encounter raises your adrenaline levels, and if you stay poised and zen-like you know you'll hypnotize him with your magnetic aura. Intimate pleasure is guaranteed and you radiate a feminine charm that no one can resist. If you are attached, you may still be thinking that eternal bliss is on the cards, but dare you go for it? Will he be more confrontational than you expect? It's not that you're doing anything wrong, just that any unspoken feelings or fears between you are making him a tad uncomfortable. So try to understand that he might also fear your ability to pull away, get too close, or control the moods and sexual tensions between you. Remember, you need to express openly why you are torn between happy ever after and a more free and easy relationship. It doesn't hurt to discuss, it might to deny.

Best days for romance: 2nd, 23rd
Best days to seduce: 24th, 25th
Best stay at home day: 30th

November

The sensual happiness you seek is not long away. With Jupiter still lingering in your most romantic corner until the 24th, and Venus until the 17th, you still have chances where new love is concerned, and to create stability and long-term commitment in any attachment. Yet someone you thought was just a friend of the opposite sex becomes more than a wall to bounce ideas off around the 8th. And, of course, showing any signs of vulnerability can be very attractive to someone who wants to be a protective hunk for ladies in distress. If you are single, around the New Moon in Scorpio on the 20th, this may develop into a physical relationship, and you just can't keep your hands off each other. He's a bit of a hero, so let him take the lead, but don't put him on a pedestal. He may be your personal bodyguard, but the transition from friend to lover is tough and by the end of the month you may wonder if you've made a big mistake.

If you're attached, Jupiter is still giving you very idealistic thoughts about love. You see it all as a 'happy ever after' romantic novel – you the heroine, being swept off your feet or walking together into the sunset along some deserted beach. But deep down you know that it is not exactly like that. There are feelings, and pain and hurts from the past, and you find it hard to express your doubts and fears, and you can't sometimes separate your feelings from his. So what is to be done? Wait until Jupiter moves out of dark horse Scorpio on the 24th. Although it has been an exciting inflated romance of the century, you will begin to come back down to earth with a gentle bump at the end of the month. Seeing it for what it really is comes as no surprise – a very human relationship, where you both have to learn to make compromises. A sudden surge of affection between you on the 29th confirms that there is something very deeply binding between you. Friends may tell you to break up – 'come on, you've been on and off for months, just bite the bullet' they wail. Family may think you are wasting your time and there's no hope for this relationship, it's going nowhere. But what ever the sourpuss attitude of those who really don't know what's best for you, let alone themselves, it's time to make your own decisions based on your own very acute instincts.

Best days for romance: 18th, 20th
Best days to seduce: 1st, 15th
Best stay at home day: 7th

December

It is hard not to drift from relationship to relationship if you're single, as the deceptive Full Moon in Gemini on the 5th keeps you wondering what is real and what is an illusion. But there's always a light at the end of the tunnel (even if it's just the next train pulling into the station), and you are blessed with the mental agility to put yourself into the arms of someone who responds to your way of loving. With Venus moving into your love zone on the 11th, followed by the wonderful winter solstice on the 22nd, your sexual desires are fired into action and you feel confident that his sexual appetite is as passionate as yours. Suddenly, the present completely overshadows the past in every imaginable way, but more than ever in the bedroom.

If you are attached, the run up to the festive season is full of social events and friends and colleagues can't get enough of your party princess antics. With Venus giving you panache, charisma and raunchy sexual energy, you just won't be told what to do. You are in command and loving every minute of the seductive dance that takes you ever forward into the New Year. Yet you have little choice but to air your feelings and generate a few home truths. And those are ones that mean you now begin to see how to love someone without trying to control every move they make. What do you fear so much? Is it perhaps that deep down inside you feel really vulnerable in the face of love, because instinctively you know it can flip to hate? Whatever you feel, whatever seems wrong or right about someone's behaviour or attitude, remember to observe, respect and honour their differences. And if they can't do the same towards you, then maybe it's time to be honest about what love really means to you. Dishonest feelings only instigate betrayal of self in the end. Don't sell-out on yourself at the end of a transformative, but revealing year.

Best days for romance: 3rd, 17th
Best days to seduce: 22nd, 31st
Best stay at home day: 4th

Your Love
Horoscope
2006

Leo
The Lion

July 21 – August 21

Love Check

Why you're fabulous

- Glamorous, fun-loving and sizzling with energy, you are every man's best friend.
- Men adore your flamboyant sexual style.
- You are totally loyal and committed when you know your man is too.

Why you're impossible

- If you can't have your way, you'll throw yourself on the floor in a tantrum.
- You loathe being ignored and have to be the centre of attention.

Your love secrets

- You'd love to be attached to someone famous.
- Sexually, you are inexhaustible and love to dominate.
- If your man doesn't tell you he loves you every day, you sulk.

Your sexual style

- Dramatic, showy and direct.

Who you fall for

- Men who make you feel number one, and are equally numb with admiration.
- Eccentrics, intellectuals and mavericks, or men who run up impressive expense account lunches without batting an eyelid.

Who falls for you

- Pleasure-loving rogues who want someone glamorous hanging on their arm.
- Down-to-earth rugged types who are spellbound by your show-stopping performance.

You identify with

- Luxury, stylish clothes, glamorous men, celebrities and champagne breakfasts. Being the queen bee at your own party, or the social lioness about town.

Your greatest temptation

- Exhibitionist sex!

Your greatest strength

- Loyalty to your man – whatever he has to put up with, so will you.

Your Love
Horoscope
2006

Passion Profile for 2006

Make this a year to be committed to yourself and your own needs. With serious Saturn fixed in your sign all year, there will be tests, barriers and boundaries to overcome, but your flow of sexual energy and your passion for love will be respected by everyone you meet. With a flirtatious spring, and a romantic summer, you are getting the right kind of reaction. Dynamic and challenging, new relationships are adventurous if you are single, and current flames bring you inspiration and a sense of security. Take the road towards a new challenging way to love this autumn and what you truly desire will follow. Hunt hard, passionately and with self-belief, and you will be amazed at the choices and opportunities open to you. There will be friends who squirm in envy as you prove you are irrepressible when it comes to love throughout the year. And by the end of December, your secret fantasies are coming true. If you look after number one you will be sure to have the kind of year which can only make you stand out from the crowd as the most loved and adorable woman around.

Best bets for Mr Right this year: Aries for mutual ambition, Sagittarius for adventurous sex, Libra for romance and social fun, Aquarius to give you space.

2006 Month by Month

January

This is a time of year when you feel uplifted by the knowledge that the sun is beginning to shine in your favour. And with the solar focus on your relationships from the 20th, you feel revitalized, and ready for hedonistic delights of the sexiest kind. Close partners may breathe a sigh of relief, preferring your show-stopping performances to your fiery temperamental ones. (And don't deny you enjoy the latter, because it makes your life so much more interesting if there's challenge and excitement). This month relax, enjoy the company of friends, both male and female, and you won't be ignored. You are in the mood for every party or event, and if you are not invited, you will probably just turn up anyway!

Fun and romantic games are on the cards if you are single, and with Mercury's mischievous influence after the 22nd, a much younger admirer seems to be following you round the office from dawn until dusk. If lust is on your mind and in his eyes on the 29th, take care; this one is hot property, but do you want the accompanying demands that he might make on you? With the New Moon on the 29th comes a revelation about yourself. Free and easy, yes, passionate about being centre stage, yes, but are you actually a cradle snatcher? No, just having fun.

If you are attached, Mercury gives you permission to communicate to a lover, say exactly what you want, and get away with it. But he may not be all ears with Venus still backtracking through Capricorn all month, and you might find the emotional equilibrium is not quite as easy going as you'd like. Simply, you are both out of balance right now. You are generous, warm and sexually insatiable, he is unsure of himself, feeling miserly and doesn't have the desire for a sex marathon every night. By the end of the month, you make up, kiss and whisper lovely things to each other. It is time to balance the sexual books, with heartfelt understanding.

Best days for romance: 20th, 25th
Best days to seduce: 7th, 16th
Best stay at home day: 1st

February

With the sun still highlighting your love corner, and Venus changing direction on the 3rd, you enhance your image and are attracting all kinds of delicious attention from the right people. The romantic excitement of attracting new moths to your very special and magnanimous flame brings a release of fiery energy, and you feel mentally on top of the world and sexually delighted. The sun beetles its way on through your chart, and the Full Moon in your own sign on the 13th triggers off a brand new commitment. By the 15th, you begin to feel how the depth of sexual and physical attraction from one relationship is enriching your personal world. Your cheerful and optimistic approach has brought a great deal of sunshine into many friends' lives over the past dull winter months, but it has also required extremes of energy and boundless warmth to keep everyone happy. Now you must take time out to relax and steady the flow of energy for yourself.

Over the last few days of February, don't be so kind and extravagant with your time, and keep your energy for your own sexual and romantic interests. There are some fair-weather friends out there, who will stop at nothing to make demands on you. Could it be that they are envious of your style, charisma and ability to smile at life and love? Envy, however, is a dangerous thing unless one is conscious of being either the object of envy, or feeling it oneself. But it is also valuable to acknowledge it, simply because we are usually envious of the very quality or talent that we believe we are lacking in ourselves, but is actually hidden away un-lived. Are you envious of someone? Of the way they run their life, love their partner, are adored by the madding crowd? If you feel such twinges this month, ask yourself whether you aren't really being the true Leo, the one who shines in everyone's eyes, who seeks fame, fortune or simply the best lover in the world. If you haven't got him, then this year is your chance to find that perfect catch.

Best days for romance: 11th, 17th
Best days to seduce: 13th, 26th
Best stay at home day: 4th

March

With Venus finally moving into your love corner on the 5th, things are hotting up. But Saturn's backwards lumbering through your own sign may still be giving you cold feet about any serious long-term commitment. Exerting your power in a relationship is crucial to your sense of well-being, and you know that only you have the ability to create spectacular and exciting relationships. This month could be the starting post for new love, or the change of one very close to your heart, and your whole inner self and approach to life is carefree and yet determined. But being a bit of a control freak won't pay off when Venus's tension with Saturn on the 10th produces a conflict of interests. If attached, you might feel as if you're driving with the brakes on for a few days; if single, you wonder if you've tried too hard to seduce, spoken too hastily or not given enough of yourself.

Around the 25th wonderful things begin to happen. With a sexy link between Venus and Mars, along with a seductive collusion between Venus and Neptune, you simply can't go wrong. Words flow, candles are lit, dinner is magical, lovers give each other presents or wicked whispers are spoken across the pillow. Make the most of this chance to show that deep down inside you are passion personified and also a serious romantic when love is at stake. After the cool days of early March, suddenly it feels like summer and the temperature is rising with your libido to match.

With the total eclipse of the Sun on the 29th in your expressive zone, you suddenly feel more confident about your long-term relationship goal and the direction you want it to take. One chapter in your love life is over and it is time to put yourself first. You'll be ready to listen to seriously important advice about one admirer's interest in you if you are single. But make sure you trust your instincts and avoid trying to find an ulterior motive behind what is being said. You are motivated and in the mood for change, so check out all your options before you make any spontaneous decisions.

Best days for romance: 5th, 17th
Best days to seduce: 19th, 24th
Best stay at home day: 11th

April

Whether it is the result of too much fizz, or too many hours spent with the clan, your enthusiasm for their demands wears thin on the 1st and your energy levels seem to ebb and flow with every moment. You have played the Domestic Goddess, cooked their meals and laughed at their jokes and, frankly, now you'd like a bit of pampering and quality time alone with your lover. With Saturn finally moving forward again in your own sign on the 5th, you begin to feel less emotionally blocked. The determination to make your love life as exciting as you can brings new admirers into your midst if you are single, and you are fired up for a month of passion. Mercury's cheeky influence in fiery Aries on the 16th helps you throw off your apron, put on your heels and be appreciated for the sensual creature you truly are.

If you are attached, flighty Mercury inspires you with the words to tell your lover what turns you on and he can barely function at work for wanting to be back in your arms. But is he the one you are fantasizing about, or is it someone else you visualize in your bed? An ex-lover or secret admirer is in the wings and the thrill of his undivided attention has you flirting shamelessly. But think carefully before going on a mission to seduce. Weigh up the pros and cons of the potential damage you could cause to your relationship, partner or yourself. It is difficult not to give in to the physical and psychological demands of your body and soul around the 20th when Mars makes your desire stronger than your will. But as well as being a creature of passion, you have a strong instinct for preservation. And as the Sun moves into Taurus on the 20th, the idealistic tigress that you are demands total attention, and only someone willing to give you that is worthy of your love. Make sure you know who this may be.

Best days for romance: 1st, 3rd
Best days to seduce: 16th, 29th
Best stay at home day: 22nd

May

Fate is something that seems to draw us into relationships or events over which we have no control. But destiny is different. It is about making choices and accepting responsibility for them. And this month, the more fated you feel, the more you'll be buffeted by that familiar opt-out clause, 'I just couldn't do anything about it'. Romance is a mystery, but being drawn into a brief flirtation and denying that it's your choice isn't going to get you out of an equally tricky decision. With Venus's move into pushy Aries on the 3rd you can expect all kinds of exciting moments. If you are single, this may mean double-dating, and if attached, an amusing romantic encounter. So if it's truly raining men, make sure you know where you stand – hopefully, face to face with someone who won't claim it was 'fate' that threw you together. Rather that it was your mutual destiny and personal choice.

By the 13th, you have recovered your senses a tad, but you still want to take a trip down an adventurous romantic lane. With a potent Full Moon in power-mongering Scorpio, you won't want no for an answer, nor 'another day when I'm not so busy'. You'll want the sexiest response you can get. With your usual ability to turn emotional stalemate into fun-loving progress, take a chance and ask for whatever you truly want. Your lover or partner just won't be able resist.

There have been great highs and obligatory lows in your relationship curve over the past few months, and a 'it's a new life' feeling develops into a serious desire for some kind of togetherness by the end of the month. Yes, you like your independence, but you also want to be wanted and included in someone's life. And thanks to the enlightening Gemini New Moon on the 27th, you realize that there is a chance to have the kind of relationship where freedom and closeness are not mutually exclusive.

Best days for romance: 5th, 9th
Best days to seduce: 24th, 27th
Best stay at home day: 10th

June

This is the month you've been waiting for, as Mars surges into your own sign on the 3rd, and with it your sex drive leaps into action, helping you to discover what and maybe who really turns you on. In the first two weeks of the month, you will also discover a lot about yourself and your own sexual needs. With a powerful link between Mars and Saturn on the 18th, it is time to discuss those needs with your current lover to bring greater mutual understanding. Share your secret dreams, and if he is willing to act out yours, indulge his too. Your open mind and uninhibited sexuality mean you can create the right kind of loving bond. Just take care around the New Moon in your secret corner on the 25th that you don't let slip something you might regret. It might be that you mention an ex or compare him to your lover – or simply you feel that commitment might actually equal confinement.

You don't want to undo all the hard work you have put in so far, do you? But the plus side of Mars in your own sign is enough to let you get away with more than most. And, similarly, you have the energy to juggle with work, partying and, of course, that passionate fun that you enjoy so much.

If you are single, you are inspired by sizzling strangers, or just inspired to experiment and enjoy the delights of taking a trip somewhere just to stand out from the crowd. One dark horse wants to take things further than a drink at the bar on the 26th, but are you willing to give up what you already have? Saturn and Mars push and pull you all month between extremes of feeling. One feeling is that you can have your cake and eat it, but the other is that you have enough self-control to remain virtuous or independent. And you are torn between the desire to be footloose and fancy free or committed for life. What is it about you right now? Probably just that you haven't discovered that real romance, that complete and utter fairytale lifestyle where you are the princess of one man's dreams while still having your own space to be you. Don't let other people's expectations of what a 'real' relationship is about hold you back for one second on your quest to find true love and a real soulmate.

Best days for romance: 15th, 20th
Best days to seduce: 3rd, 28th
Best stay at home day: 16th

July

The summer always brings a smile to your face. You are a Sun child, ruled by the solar light and you need to shine just as brightly. With Mars in your own sign until the 22nd, and the Sun taking over the limelight in Leo on the same day, you feel blessed with charisma. Your sexual energy is on a high and you are beginning to sort out your feelings. Even though Saturn will remain in your sign for the rest of the year, at least it is giving you fresh insight into how to structure your love life into something workable. And, similarly your relationships are now on a more even keel. With romantic liaisons and affairs of the heart playing such a high profile for the first two weeks, you unleash your flamboyant image and realize that a serious double act could be more invigorating than a string of hopeless or hapless dates.

Mars opposes Neptune on the 5th, reinforcing your need to seduce a very provocative rogue if you are single. If attached, your lover seems set on glamorizing your relationship, and you. But is the image your lover has of you a realistic one? We all have an imagined ideal of how we want our lover to be. We unconsciously project it on to them, and if they appear to carry the image, we assume what we see is what we get. But often it is hard to carry such an image for too long, and we return to our true selves, with our faults, weaknesses, hopes or fears slowly revealed as time moves on. It is often then that we 'fall out of love' with our partner, because they don't seem to hold the image for us any longer. Take care this month that you know why you are loved, and more importantly what kind of angel you are supposed to be. As you know, even angels can fall from grace.

By the 22nd, you are firmly in control of yourself and the physical aspects of your life are stunning. All you need to do now is relax, and not let the emotional side of love become a bone of contention. You are on a summer buzz and a sexual high, and if you are single, the creative force of the Sun in your own sign helps you catch that gorgeous dreamboat you've been fancying. Around the 25th you are full of energy, oozing sensuality and whether single or attached, you can now have your wicked way.

Best days for romance: 10th, 25th
Best days to seduce: 21st, 27th
Best stay at home day: 11th

August

A vibrant month, thanks to a host of planets cruising through your own sign. But it is also one where any love affair that's in need of change or adjustment will be strongly emphasized. You may need all your powers of courage and enterprise to develop a close relationship or transform it completely. You are now in a position to organize and put an end to doubts and fears, and to energize and motivate others at will. A dramatic few days between the 9th and 12th signify that what you may have believed to be the truth about your relationships is now about to change. With a quirky Full

Moon in Aquarius on the 9th, followed by Mercury and Venus's transit into your own sign, your love ideals are challenged and your self-esteem and ego boundaries are put to the test. Yet you have the charm, the charisma and, most of all, the seductive tactics to win any man round. He may think differently, he may want a different lifestyle or is less committed than you thought, but your determination to get things out in the open brings you welcome answers rather than unwelcome questions.

By the 17th, you feel that your desire to exert your opinions has paid off, and you can redirect your energy to your own image. New hairstyle, make-up or simply a summer wardrobe, and a spot of retail therapy purges you of all the worries and you're back on track. With Venus and Saturn's cool alliance on the 27th, you back off and resort to being the self-sufficient and independent 'I don't need anyone' vamp that you are. The star of the love show is you, so never ever forget that. And if your partner can't accept that you need to show off, be the life and soul of the party, or just control your own life, then perhaps it is time to take a deep breath and put your cards on the table. This could be the beginning of a new way to love, and the end of emotional conflict. Whether you break up or make up, it is inevitable that your relationship has to click into another gear. No love affair is static. But if it was, wouldn't you just want to stir things up to revel in the passion and fireworks which you truly need in life to sparkle so brightly?

Best days for romance: 12th, 22nd
Best days to seduce: 3rd, 15th
Best stay at home day: 18th

September

But you wonder if it is worth all the effort as Venus moves out of your sign on the 6th. Of course, you have feelings, but there is a side of you that craves excitement, danger and the unknown factors in romance. However, this month the celestial line-up is urging you to think things through. It is one of those restless months with desires all scrambling for attention, and a host of fascinating encounters gives you a chance to sort out if there really is anyone out there who understands you. After the 8th, Mars triggers off a passion for social adventure. You'll be at your most vivacious and extrovert and ready for smooth operators and fun-loving friends.

Feelings of nostalgia are rare for you, but the last week of the month is a time when the challenges of the last few months can now be reflected upon with understanding, and most of all renewed self-awareness. Saturn is a hard task master, but the planet teaches us that if we face our greatest fears we can succeed in overcoming them. Also, Saturn reminds us that the qualities we hate in others are very often the ones we disclaim for ourselves. And that boundaries are there for a purpose, that our defence mechanisms are often pushed too easily by those we love, simply because we are unconsciously signalling our own defensiveness. You may be in demand, loved and desired, but is that enough? Freedom and independence are just two things that cannot be sacrificed, and you know it. Somehow, love still has to fit into your lifestyle, and this is your chance to discover how.

Best days for romance: 17th, 25th
Best days to seduce: 6th, 19th
Best stay at home day: 27th

October

This is the time of the year when your inner child, your outer appearance and your deepest feelings are all under focus. So spend the month clearing up any emotional or romantic loose ends rather than scattering around new ones. Focus on how you relate to others, and to yourself. Are you defensive? What do you do to protect yourself from a seeming threat? For example, if your lover complains you are too demanding or self-confident, or too much of a show-off, how do you react? This will depend very much on where the Moon and Saturn were in your birthchart. But it's worth reflecting on the intricacies of relating, so don't let your long-term plans become confused by any lack of self-belief. The more we know about ourselves, good and not so good bits, the more we can improve our relationships. Now is the time to light a candle for your romantic dreams and watch the adventures begin to come true.

Watch out for an unpredictable or provocative encounter with an exotic stranger around the Full Moon of the 7th. It's not that you are in need of any more drama in your life than you already have, but this could be the chance to show any rivals what you're made of. The perfect seductress!

With a Venus and Mars collusion on the 25th in suspicious Scorpio, trust your instincts about one new admirer and make sure that he's really as squeaky clean as you imagine him to be. If attached, check all the facts before you accuse your partner of deceit or betrayal. Confrontations may be inevitable, but at least you'll know where you stand.

Best days for romance: 4th, 29th
Best days to seduce: 7th, 20th
Best stay at home day: 5th

November

This promises to be another major turning point in the year for you, when a series of surprising aspects not only put energy and verve into a new romance, but also ensure that the expression of love that you thought wasn't forthcoming finally heads your way.

Venus moves into your romantic corner on the 17th, followed by the Sun on the 22nd and Jupiter on the 24th. This could herald a major upheaval in your love life. So expand your energies into new ventures, and become the centre of attention in someone else's life. Your energy and dynamic sexual style attracts all the right attention, and also brings real love and honesty into any existing relationship. The tremendous power of Jupiter in your love corner gives you the belief that you can win above all the odds, whether you cut the strings from the past and move on into a new and more committed relationship, or become involved in a wild, but exciting love affair. This is an excellent time to travel, and with romance in the air you feel wanted and loved. To realize that someone understands you and can accept that even you have a vulnerable side behind that glittery persona can only enhance your image and ensure that the end of the month brings you all the answers you've been hoping for.

If you are not already steaming up the windows with your love for each other, you'll discover a handsome hunk is determined to make you his. Whether you're in a long-term relationship which is rediscovering its heart, or a resurgence of an old one, you just love to be wooed. So encourage him to chase you a little. Just make sure you are running slowly enough that he'll be able to catch you up without wearing himself out. Reliving the chase triggers wonderful memories of youthful romantic interludes and sensual gestures, and that is just what you need to bring back truly dazzling moments into your life and relationship.

Best days for romance: 17th, 24th
Best days to seduce: 1st, 30th
Best stay at home day: 20th

December

Critical or condescending remarks from family or friends are the last thing you need this month. After all, if you want to rush headlong into the flames of new romance, liven up an existing one or get out of a 'don't tie me down' rut, then there's nothing that will stop you now. With cheeky Mercury moving into flamboyant Sagittarius on the 8th to join a rampant Mars, you are up for all kinds of romantic adventures. And there are admirers out there who would wash their own socks for a night out of fun with you. With Venus reminding you that life is about enjoying yourself, not for denying you have one, you are particularly rebellious. And don't freak out when friends comment you're going slightly potty about one love interest around the 12th. They genuinely want to know what's going on. But even if you are rushing between passionate encounters and the hairdressers, do try and find time for a lover who might just be there when you realize you need a helping hand. If you are attached, this isn't an easy month for keeping the more romantic juices flowing. Sexually, you are up for adventure, and if your boyfriend isn't the exploitative type, then think again whether he's really Mr Right or merely Mr Right Now.

With a sudden burst of inspiration about how to kill two birds with one stone, having your freedom and staying in a fun-loving no-strings relationship seems the terrific option for festive fun. And the New Moon in your love zone on the 20th confirms that you are at last being honest with yourself as the sexual sparks fly in one lover's direction. With Saturn making a U-turn in your sign again, you have time to think about your long-term goals. Quite simply, you're in the mood to forget the past and get on with the present. The future? It is looking brighter than ever before, but you will have to work at love to make it work for you. Charm, dazzle and be the belle of the New Year ball, but never forget that while you may be a roaring lion, you are also a little pussy-cat at heart who needs warmth, affection and true respect for your extraordinary talents.

Best days for romance: 15th, 27th
Best days to seduce: 19th, 23rd
Best stay at home day: 4th

Your Love
Horoscope
2006

Virgo
The Virgin

August 22 – September 22

Love Check

Why you're fabulous

 Thriving in the world of words, you can get your message across to any man.

 You care about your body image and always look impeccable.

 That virtuous smile hides a very wicked libido.

Why you're impossible

 You are quick to point out your man's flaws or mistakes.

 Bragging about how knowledgeable you are drives him mad.

Your love secrets

 You are a dreamer when your man's not there, and not as down-to-earth and practical as you make out.

 You won't make love with him if he's got dirty fingernails.

If you have a man you worship, you'd wash his socks for him.

Your sexual style

Earthy, sensual, magical and timed to perfection.

Who falls for you

Lazy men who know how efficient you are around the house.

Dynamic fiery extroverts who adore your down-to-earth sense of humour and love of sensual pleasure.

Who you fall for

Men who know the difference between yoghurt and fromage frais.

Hard-working types, who have stamina and adore routine and ritual. Or romantic dreamers who you can organize.

You identify with

Workaholics, dieticians and men who look after their bodies; keep-fit regimes, organic food and wholesome loving.

Your greatest temptation

Spending all day in bed with him, instead of going to work.

Your greatest strength

Dedication to his sensual needs.

Passion Profile for 2006

This is one of those years where you start off thinking you're happy exactly the way you are, but end up changing dramatically. Your own inner voice is positive and you're listening to what others have to say. Make this a year of self-discovery and around the Full Moon of 14th March the love of someone special allows you to shed your old skin and develop into the individual you've always aspired to be.

Acceptance of each other's differences brings your relationship to greater levels of understanding. And by the summer you're oozing confidence and attracting the sort of reaction from your partner you only ever dreamed of. Throughout the autumn, physical love-making takes on a new dimension. Listen to your body, drop those outdated inhibitions and by the end of December, mutual understanding will also create emotional compatibility into the New Year and beyond.

Best bets for Mr Right: Scorpio for a deeply sensual rapport, Capricorn for a success story, Cancer for emotional closeness, Taurus for long-term friendship.

2006 Month by Month

January

Constructive play is as important to you as constructive work, and that includes constructive relationships. And New Year resolutions aside, someone who has your best interests at heart poses some questions which get you thinking. In some ways, this is just the trigger for you to understand the need to undergo the changes you've been avoiding for so long. Whether you decide that you need more space from a lover, or want to move in with him, you need to clarify your feelings. With Mercury in your romantic corner from the 3rd, you're given the necessary breathing space to think about your long-term relationship goals. After the 5th, the cosmos offers up a new phase of self-indulgence and romantic es-capades. Around the 13th, Venus's influence gives you a strong desire to get away from it all and relax alone, which is beneficial for your state of mind and emotions. Opt either for a walk in the country or indulge in the luxury of spend-ing all day in the bath. But it won't last for long, when Mercury links up with Venus on the 17th, and your energy is redirected towards your man. Sexually, your energy is now at a terrific peak. Try to see that the more you express your true desires and wants to your partner, the more energy you create for yourself.

If single, the offers and dates start to flood in. There may be work to be done, there may be resolutions to be made for the New Year, but somehow your time just flies by with the passing smiles, eyes and particularly the attention of one gorgeous rogue. Don't let him out of your sight. He could be a valuable ally at work, (and an equally good bed companion), but mostly he's giving you a chance to see that you're one of the most sought after women around.

Best days for romance: 4th, 19th
Best days to seduce: 17th, 25th
Best stay at home day: 6th

February

If your man attempts to change the status quo, you can become resentful, and your obsession for routine breaks out into frantic behaviour, like washing up every time a cup is left on the drainer, folding up his knickers or ironing yours! Luckily, this month heralds a possible change in those obsessive ways. And it's one where you might actually enjoy breaking into a different social circle, getting out of a romantic or relationship rut, and generally decide that life can be fun when change is inevitable.

Uranus is still reminding you of the very different attitudes and behaviour of various men – and how right now you are attracted to those who are so radically minded. Your ruler, Mercury, moves into Pisces on the 9th, and although Valentine's day might come and go without an obvious bang, Mercury's link with Uranus brings a new admirer if you're single, and a surprise card from a stranger. If you are attached, it's time to make some plans for the future, and with your quick wit, you will win your man round to your way of thinking.

You'll also feel like mixing business with pleasure this month. A fascinating conversationalist could turn out to be a useful ally in your professional camp. So make a note of his status – both work-wise and love-wise! This is one sexy contact not be missed. But if he's already hitched, don't get involved, it could lead you into dangerous emotional waters.

If you're committed to a relationship then either you'll pour more love into those outstanding feelings of mutual security, or sense that at last you've reached a point where you can both work together to achieve your goals. A superb New Moon on the 28th in your love corner will bring fresh and tantalizing feelings to any existing relationship. If you're single, this dreamy moon will enable you to put your feelers out and get closer to that sexy admirer from last month.

Enjoy the dark days of February as it draws to a close, and indulge in the social and romantic events which are now beginning to thread into your love life. Even more objectivity in the months to come will stand you in good stead, and there's nothing like love in the air to encourage you to dance, sing, seduce and be there for that Mr Right Now.

Best days for romance: 19th, 25th
Best days to seduce: 10th, 14th
Best stay at home day: 15th

March

With the Sun in your relationship corner until the 20th, you're closer to one love interest than ever before. You have renewed faith and belief in him, and also what he stands for in your life. This is an important time of year for you when you begin to feel the power of your own credibility and sense of achievement, both with regard to your personal issues as well as professional ones. The Full Moon in your own sign on the 14th is an excellent time for finalizing any project or formulating your goals. If attached, you both feel emotionally well-balanced and develop a genuinely supportive attitude for each other's success.

The only downside is your ruler Mercury's U-turn in your chart from the beginning of the month until the 25th. You feel the weight of a heavy workload, and ambitions come bubbling to the surface to conflict with your love life. This also means your family life may be in direct conflict with your career, and you feel muddled and confused when normally you have the strength of purpose to get through these glitches. By the 25th, you may resort to the companionship of your closest friends, particularly those who can help take the strain of those odd confrontations you hate to face. It's admirable that you'd do anything for an easy existence, but it's also important to acknowledge that sometimes you have to stand up for yourself. You can't always be the life and soul or the laid-back spirit, and compromising too much puts pressure on your own personal needs. At the end of the month, you feel at least the weight is off your shoulders again. Mercury moves forward on the 25th, and your lover either moves in, or you begin to communicate your deeper doubts and needs.

If single, Mercury's hold-up simply gives you time to reflect on whether an admirer or someone who takes your fancy, is really right for you. There's always a time of the year when we all have to take a step back. Look at what we have, whether it's truly right for us, and then create new openings for ourselves. Whether a change of social location, a new job or travel, these are the arenas in life where you can meet possible new love interests, and throughout March, you can at least start to formulate your plans for change.

Best days for romance: 14th, 23rd
Best days to seduce: 18th, 30th
Best stay at home day: 3rd

April

What a relief. After the uncertainty of last month, Venus moves into your relationship corner, and you begin to set your sails for romantic success. April fool you're not, and as the month brings new growth, fresh spring mornings and lighter skies, your reliable, good-natured side will bring to life any relationship which has been dull or simply floating along going nowhere. Now, remember that you're good at pretending you don't have any feelings. But those rather unpredictable and confusing niggles, doubts, fears, loves or hates are not containable. You can't stick them in boxes and pin labels on them. Some are uncomfortable, others welcome, but sorting them out is a million times more difficult than sorting out the kitchen paraphernalia. But this month, you're up for indulging in sensual delights and *feeling* the pleasure of being wanted and *feeling* the joy of desiring someone too. It won't be just the way you cook up the perfect dinner for two, or the surprise bottle of bubbly you bring to the bedroom one night around the 18th. With Venus's electrifying link with Uranus on that day, this is the beginning of a new phase in a current relationship, or a fascinating encounter with a possible Mr Right if you're single. All of life's little problems will miraculously disappear like the rain. And with an equally stunning link between Venus and Jupiter on the 20th, you'll be adding romance to your weekly shopping-list and champagne to your daily menu.

This is a brilliant turning point. You feel rekindled, alive, animated and have the energy to enjoy the good things in life. Now you're ready to adapt with the minimum of effort to ensure you maintain the harmony and sense of contentment that you value so dearly.

With the fabulous New Moon in earthy Taurus on the 27th, you find the confidence to discuss your personal needs with a new flame. Suggest you go public and test the depth of their commitment to discover just how serious they are. Unless this one can give you what you truly need, cut the cord. And if you're attached, you begin to make plans for that romantic adventure. Whether a wicked weekend away, or simply cultural and gourmet delights in town, you're at last beginning to have your cake and eat it.

Best days for romance: 2nd, 5th
Best days to seduce: 7th, 18th
Best stay at home day: 14th

May

The Sun and Mercury in Taurus for the first few weeks of May give you a feeling that it's time to get out and about. You're restless for romantic adventure, and twitchy about routines. On one hand you like to keep to your rituals, but on the other you want to break free from the structure and duties – whether they are imposed upon you or of your own making. Jupiter's backtracking movement through your chart is still making you feel insecure about doing so. You are not normally bothered by other people's opinions, but a close friend makes some serious criticisms of the way you are handling your love life on the 7th, and you begin to wonder if you can trust anyone. If you're single, you feel a little unsure about throwing yourself passionately into the arms of someone you don't know thoroughly. Knowledge is power to you, it stops you feeling vulnerable if you *know everything* about your man. Like the friends he has, what he has for breakfast, if he wears trainers or polishes his shoes religiously every morning; on the other hand, you don't want to know the more mundane details like whether he leaves his clothes all over the floor, or if he has embarrassing moles or smelly feet. Simply because the latter negate the perfectly ordered kind of romance you aspire to. But this month you have to know everything, and the balance of a current relationship hits a new phase. This time round make sure you really know what it is you want from this love affair because around the 13th hearts could get broken if there is nothing real and tangible between you. It's not that you want this relationship to end, but if it can't stand the test of true love – warts and all – then what is it to you anyway? Stop trying to take control of your partner's every move, the way he combs his hair, the way he squeezes the toothpaste, and you won't be let down by love's mysterious ways. And if you're single, it's fine to want to know every little detail about him before you take the plunge, but if you have a real passion for someone, you'll accept his warts – and all.

Best days for romance: 12th, 19th
Best days to seduce: 6th, 17th
Best stay at home day: 21st

June

A more settled month, where the midsummer sun puts ideas of travel, indulgence and foreign fun into your head. Yet your home life takes first place and you feel good about your work and professional interests. The desire to get out and about is highlighted by the Sun in Gemini until the 21st, and Venus's mercurial influence for the rest of the month. Even if you are away from home more, your usual habits and rituals will still be important to you, and that includes the way you share any new responsibilities with a partner. With no emotional pressure, and a scintillating social life, you're feeling dynamic and raunchy. After the 19th, old flames may make a reappearance, and new ones arrive on the scene if you're single. So stand back and take an objective look at what your real needs are. You'll see more clearly by distancing yourself from the past. Take a week off from emotional demands after the 24th, and sail through all those friends' birthday celebrations with a smile on your face. You're a calming influence on your friends and your lover, and you'll be so adored that you'll reach higher emotional levels than you've ever experienced before. Do you realize how sexually attractive that is?

If you're single, friends will lighten your life with past memories and fun sentiments. Old romance that once seemed faded or worn out could pick up pace again. But the greatest joy is to be found through your professional life. Here, new contacts are fascinated by your cool mystique. With Venus highlighting all romantic contacts in the workplace, you'll be spoilt for choice around the 30th. But what value do you place on commitment? The Uranian influence in your chart is certainly waking you up to a side of yourself you have denied or repressed for some time – those feelings of being unworthy, of not being able to say what you truly feel for fear of rejection. Yet now you're beginning to realize that a little shot of courage, and pride in who you are and what you do, is enough to keep the right kind of dream lover by your side. If you haven't already found him by now, you soon will.

Best days for romance: 13th, 20th
Best days to seduce: 5th, 16th
Best stay at home day: 9th

July

This month sees two important signposts rather than milestones in your life, one of which will be directing you towards personal goals as Mars continues to edge ever closer towards your own sign. The other is your ruler Mercury's backtracking influence from the 4th until the 29th, which will confuse some of your romantic longings and plans, and create disappointment or simply delays and missed dates. Yet, as the month progresses, a genuine holiday atmosphere takes over any disillusionment or worries. A lighthearted and generally sociable time will boost your energy levels which can often be at their lowest this time of year. Sexual temptations abound after the 22nd, when Mars cruises into your own sign, and there is a light, flirty atmosphere wherever you go. The feel-good factor is all yours, and those earlier frustrations seem to disappear with the early morning mist. Enjoy the attention of friends, new lovers (if you're single), and a feeling that the kind of happiness you desire is well within reach. Pass the suntan oil, and indulge in the swimming pool, the beach games or just get out and about with your man while you're feeling so self-assured. Unnecessary niggles regarding work and family are now all in the past, and as the summer sun bathes you in a radiant glow, you feel the load lighten.

The odd feeling of frustration (thanks to Mercury still back-tracking on the 24th) could force you to say things you don't really mean to your lover or partner. Wait until the end of the month, and you'll be true to yourself when you do speak up. Whatever you have felt haunted by, you'll now be able to bring into the light of day. As a true sense of it is now coming out in the wash, make sure it's squeaky clean when it does.

Meanwhile, there is a considerable amount of intrigue going on in your social circle. But take care you express only the truth to a friend who's having problems with a boyfriend; remember everybody hurts sometimes, even you, so don't make any tactless remarks around the 27th. With Mercury moving forward again on the 29th, you'll feel more relaxed, spontaneous and ready to indulge in the sexiest fun with a new amour or current partner.

Best days for romance: 3rd, 21st
Best days to seduce: 24th, 30th
Best stay at home day: 16th

August

A time to refuel your sexual energy, as Mars opposes Uranus in your relationship corner mid-month, which will have a long-lasting effect through the month. This volatile energy could even rekindle the flames of an old romance or regenerate emotional feelings for an ex. Unpredictable events and feelings are something you don't welcome with ease. And yet the powerful effect of a lover or partner will force you to adapt to circumstances that are out of your control. For example, why are you in love with someone you thought had disappeared off the face of the earth and who has now returned with a smile on his face? Or why do you feel so passionately about a new admirer, and can't get him out of your mind when you're in bed with your man? These are radical thoughts and feelings, but you must face the unknown and the bizarre. The planets are now giving you the courage to do so. So seize the opportunity to prove to your lover that you are ready for deeper intimacy and emotional bliss. Expand his awareness of your true sexual needs and show him how easy it is to give and take beneath the sheets.

Then, on the 20th, you suddenly feel less enthusiastic about his feelings, and you are convinced he's playing games. When you are so vulnerable you become possessive or obsessed with every detail of what he says, or you read too much between the lines. Keep yourself occupied so that those niggling worries don't drown you in anxiety. Excessive thinking means you need to channel those thoughts and sexual desires into something tangible and pleasurable. So indulge in your favourite forbidden food for just one day around the 21st as the Sun moves into your sign to herald the beginning of your solar year. Be deliberately provocative or flirtatious with a handsome stranger in a coffee shop, shout at the painting on the wall, not at yourself in the mirror. Bash up your pillows or cushions, not your man. Strong angry feelings don't last long, but projecting them onto your lover will only make him feel claustrophobic, or leave the country! Don't worry, by the New Moon in your own sign on the 23rd you're back in form, and his romantic reaction is equally enticing. With Mercury at last alighting in your sign on the 27th, love is back to normal. Safe, secure, workable and very human.

Best days for romance: 5th, 19th
Best days to seduce: 16th, 23rd
Best stay at home day: 27th

September

This is the pivotal month for romance, sex and commitment. One where you're in charge of the show, where you can direct the events and take responsibility for your own destiny. And if you're not doing so, then why not? Is it because you fear committing yourself to something without knowing all the facts? As you know, where love is involved there are only mysteries, and as I keep telling you absolutes just don't exist. So don't fear the powerful energy that is giving you every right to name your day or have your way. This is the start of your solar year, a time when there is giddy anticipation of what you can achieve – and also a few fears about where you're going next.

Sexually, you're absolutely consumed with lust for someone around the eclipse of the moon on the 7th in wicked Pisces. With Venus also now in your own sign, you radiate the charisma of a sex goddess. Although Mars departs your sign on the 8th, Venus takes the helm and softens every encounter in a magical light. Single? Well, there is still someone out there who won't take no for an answer. Let him come closer, he might be far more squeaky clean (or sinfully wicked) than you imagine. Take advantage of your wonderful aura, and let your lover see the quality of earthy sensuality you possess. With Venus's dramatic link to Uranus on the 16th, you turn on the sexual taps and he just can't have enough of your earthy sensuality. So continue to rustle the sheets with him until the 22nd, when there's another New Moon in your sign (also a solar eclipse). Two New Moons in the same zodiac sign in consecutive months is a rarity, and it's a sign of you being given a double chance to settle with the past and start a fresh. If you're single watch out for more delicious dates down those corridors of power after the 23rd. Someone's spotted you, but have you spotted them? Whether it's body language or pure chemistry in motion, trust in your reactions and your intuition, you'll know when you bump into him that your tingling sensation is for real.

Best days for romance: 6th, 17th
Best days to seduce: 1st, 11th
Best stay at home day: 22nd

October

With the inner planets now moving on into the part of your chart concerned with your values, you become more introspective, inward-looking and self-contained. You realize you have more to offer a partner than just financial co-dependency or being a safe bet on the domestic front. Do you really want to spend the rest of your life tidying up sock drawers and sploshing bleach down the sink wearing your rubber gloves? I think the answer is no, or you wouldn't be reading this book. This kind of inner reflection may only last a few days until the 5th, but it will confirm your sense of knowing that you are the centre of your own private universe, and no one can take that away from you. However hard some-one tries to convince you otherwise, you are beginning to formulate your own values, and know that the only person you are answerable to is yourself.

Around the 20th, you must now make a decision or choice which could affect your whole day-to-day existence. If you feel secure in yourself, this could be a great time to confirm your future with someone. But getting out of a rut is the hard-est thing of all to do. Because the rut is the easy option. You know it and you can deal with it. And by 'it' and 'rut', I mean any relationship you've been putting up with for some years. To ensure your long-term happiness, you need to do some rational thinking, and Mercury's U-turn on the 28th provides you with some much valued time to think things through before committing yourself one way or another. Don't get persuaded by someone to make the wrong decision. Think about what kind of relationship makes you feel good to be you. Take the initiative next month, right now don't forget to listen to your own inner voice. Whatever the external event that triggers your need to sort out your feelings, you gradu-ally know what is right and what is wrong for you.

Best days for romance: 16th, 19th
Best days to seduce: 10th, 31st
Best stay at home day: 24th

November

Around the 5th, you still have feelings of confusion about your relationships. But don't worry, it all begins to wear off by the 10th, and you talk it through with a friend who's been in the same predicament herself. Then it's time to admit to your lover what it is you truly want. The timing couldn't be better on the 18th, when Mercury's change of direction enables you to be objective, and your man to be constructive. And with Uranus's move forward on the 20th, at last there seems to be a bright light at the end of a very short tunnel. You've been through enough show-downs and scenes and worries in your life to come through unscathed. The smile is on your face again, the look in his eyes says it all, and you are back in charismatic form. What you truly value in life and what you truly need is more important than what others expect from you, isn't it?

Venus in your domestic corner from the 17th, followed by spirited Jupiter on the 24th, bring you great pleasure around the home. You can create the perfect love-nest, decorate your place, or simply indulge in wining and dining with the one you love as winter sets in. It's all laid-back, watching films together, working out fascinating plans for the future, setting up a business from home, or simply falling into each other's arms on the sofa. But take care, it's easy to be complacent when you've been through a bad patch, but now is the time to be your most tender and caring self as your partner needs some nurturing and reassurance for his own goals and plans for the future too.

If you're single, your social life will be coloured with loving and affectionate interactions, and the end of the month is all about playing. Look out for a streetwise rogue on the 28th, for a sensual and deeply magical experience, even though it could be short-lived. Enjoy yourself, dump the painful memories, and unwind from the tangles of past doubts and fears. You're on the most exciting and radical romantic route to happiness, just open up to the world a little, and that someone special will find you.

Best days for romance: 5th, 18th
Best days to seduce: 13th, 21st
Best stay at home day: 7th

December

The end of the year brings light and welcome relief. Socially you enjoy the whirl and excitement of the office party or the domestic soirée. Friends will rally round you, and although you still have the odd desire for solitude away from your lover or family, you'd rather be sharing a walk in the hills or a visit to the sea with a lover. With Venus in your romantic zone from the 11th, you see the world through totally different eyes. Now it's rose-coloured, warm, misty, dreamy and escapist. You know that reality isn't like that, but then again whose reality are we talking about? Aren't there other realities out there? Admit that as much as you're a pragmatist, you're also a romance addict. You yearn for secret liaisons, for hidden passion and forbidden love. Yet the good old down-to-earth side of you usually wins. And with the winter solstice on the 22nd, you spend the festive season enjoying the company of one man, and knowing that it might just last forever if you play the right kind of relationship game. You feel that even if you have seen yourself in a new light this year, it has at least encouraged either a partner or a new lover into your life or confirmed your belief that love is a very mysterious and unpredictable force.

The planets are giving you a treat at the end of the year, and as the party season reaches a climax, you arrive at a point where it feels as if there's no going back. Single, or attached, sexual fulfilment is on the cards at last. Make the end of the year one when your physical needs and your emotional make-up are honestly clarified and respected.

Best days for romance: 11th, 21st
Best days to seduce: 14th, 25th
Best stay at home day: 31st

Your Love
Horoscope
2006

Libra
The Scales

September 23 – October 22

Love Check

Why you're fabulous

 Charming the pants off him is your favourite pastime.

 You always look serene, glamorous and alluring.

 Romantic and idealistic, you always make your relationship a harmonious place to be.

Why you're impossible

 You flirt at parties, just to keep him on his toes.

 Being nice all the time means he never knows how you really feel.

Your love secrets

 If you're not in a relationship you'll find your way into someone's heart with the greatest of ease.

 Some men just can't live up to your high expectations and then you feel let down.

 You always look at life in terms of 'we' and assume every man you meet does too.

Your sexual style
🝏 Classy, passive and aesthetically beautiful.

Who falls for you
🝏 All types, because they see in you an image of feminine perfection.

🝏 Streetwise hunks who adore your rational outlook on life, and strong earthy types who want to bring out the wild woman in you.

Who you fall for
🝏 Independent tearaways, whizz kids with time and money to devote to you, fiery men with a dare factor, or intellectual cool customers – as long as they are all beautiful.

You identify with
🝏 Love triangles, perfect manners, beauty and truth. Designers, glamorous celebrities and men who know the difference between Manet and Monet.

Your greatest temptation
🝏 Imagining there's someone better round the next corner.

Your greatest strength
🝏 Knowing that love really does make the world go round.

Passion Profile for 2006

You may have to learn patience, and you may have to rein in a little of that free spirit, but in nurturing one special relationship you'll unearth an undiscovered continent of emotions in your make-up. Wintry nights in each other's arms create that warm glow you've not felt for months and by late February a surprise invitation has you hitting the social scene as a serious item. Work gets in the way of romance in March, but come late April you reconnect with such sparks of passion that you both find that the need for commitment becomes an obsession. The only option is to go for it.

And as Venus moves into your love corner in May, if you're not house-hunting for two, you're at least occupying half his wardrobe. Time spent creating your perfect love nest takes up most of the summer, and by August you're still reeling from the dazzling effects of domestic bliss. If single, Mars's potent energy in your own sign in September brings new rogues piling up in your inbox. But at the same time you begin to panic that it's all too good to be true. Nothing is forever, yet you are in a powerful position to make one relationship work. Take everything a day at a time and you'll soon realize a whole year's gone by and this one is meant to be.

Best bets for Mr Right this year: Pisces for pure romance, Sagittarius for adventure, Aquarius for making sense of everything.

2006 Month by Month

January

Being flirtatious, and also being known as a romantic idealist, sometimes makes it hard for others to understand that you are actually attracted to physical appearances and the luxuries of life. You have great taste in your home and beauty means a lot to you – your own and his. And you know you need to share your world with a partner who is as harmony-loving as you are. Beautiful things include 'love'. But it's often far too easy to fall into a relationship for the sake of companionship or approval, without knowing what your true motives are for doing so. This month the large circle of friends you hang out with may temporarily disappear, or seem moody and introspective while Venus is backtracking through your chart. Your normal social activities, like flashing around at all the best parties, or being the most gorgeous looking thing in the room, seem to stagnate, and even your fun-loving activities aren't up to scratch. But with the Sun moving on into flirtatious Aquarius on the 20th, followed by mischievous Mercury on the 22nd, it won't be long till you're back centre-stage with an admiring audience.

But what about the love bit, I hear you shriek. Ok, it's there, he's out there waiting for you, but the moment of synchronicity, the moment you meet for the first time hasn't quite arrived. Patience is indeed a virtue, and with the New Moon on the 29th in your romantic zone, get out and about, throw a party, or be seen in all the best places. Your chance for meeting him now is high on the percentage stakes. So be on the look out for the one who can't take his eyes off you.

If you are attached, as long as you manage to uplift your social life a little towards the end of the month you'll be back on form. Sexually, you're on a wave of libido peaks and cosy nights together planning your future. But there seems to be something missing. Is this *real* love, or just an illusion? Did you fall into the trap of thinking this was it? And now the first magical moments have begun to wear off, conversations centre around his mates or work, rather than the colour of your eyes? Think carefully what you want from this relationship. Venus's reversal this month is there to give you time to reflect before you make a big commitment which you might regret.

Best days for romance: 11th, 15th
Best days to seduce: 13th, 24th
Best stay at home day: 2nd

February

Remember, self-respect is essential if you're going to find true equality in your relationships. And this month, you begin to take advantage of your light-hearted image as Venus moves forward again from the 3rd. A hunch about how easy it is to make someone close to you happy gives you a new sense of responsibility towards your friends and yourself.

If you're single, internet connections take up a lot of your time, and you feel that being Miss Independent does have its advantages. You have choices, a range of possible dates and a variety of new male and female friends. Just take care you really find out as much about them as you can. One new admirer could be utterly disappointing around the 14th, but with Mars surging into airy Gemini on the 17th, another might seem too good to be true, and you decide impulsively to delete him from your message box. Don't make any commitments this month, because Mars is giving you the chance for a myriad of romantic chances and adventure.

If you're attached, it's hard not to leave him totally out in the cold, but it frustrates you that he can't read your mind. Especially around the 13th when the Full Moon triggers off emotional confusion and you try to avoid saying out loud what you're really thinking. But you might just have to speak out, and if that involves a wrangle or spending some time alone, then at least you'll have been honest. It's important to allow yourself the opportunity to make a success of those aspirations which really matter to you. Around the 15th, disillusionment at the lack of immediately glowing results, combined with a split-second of impulsiveness, make you consider calling it a day with your man. Take a more philosophical approach and, by the 25th, your skills of communication are more lucid than ever and you can't fail to win your lover round to your way of thinking, as long as you stay calm.

Best days for romance: 3rd, 17th
Best days to seduce: 8th, 28th
Best stay at home day: 24th

March

Mars's influence gives you the compelling drive of a professional, and those combined qualities of confidence and wisdom makes it impossible for any man not to succumb to your whims and desires. And isn't that just what you want? Around the 5th, Venus's move into your sexiest expressive zone mean intimate caresses speak louder than any words or text messages.

It didn't seem so long ago that you were unloved, unhappy and downright emotionally bereft. But now that you've got romance back in your life, you're wondering what all the fuss was about. After the 7th, you're seriously considering whisking off to more interesting climes, or at the very least taking up a new course or hobby. You're obsessed with the new or the different, but in all the excitement don't forget the tried and tested. It's all too easy to return to that lonely position you were in last year if you don't keep a rein on your fickleness. Take care until the 25th that you don't deceive yourself while Mercury's backtracking through slippery Pisces has you dreaming of the grass being greener anywhere else but here. The biggest problem you have this month is that you keep gazing into that mirror and hoping to see yourself in a perfect relationship. But right now you really don't know what you want. So let me give you a few clues. I think you want personal freedom, but desire stability; you hate to be bored, but you're scared of walking the tightrope; and most of all you want unconditional, requited love, but you're terrified of being committed to one person. And you're not alone in this. Your partner may well be experiencing the same fears and the way to allay them isn't to run to someone new, but to talk about your dreams and aspirations with the one who loves you most. With the help of the enlightening solar eclipse in your love corner on the 29th, you'll realize that your tried and tested lover can be as enthralled and enthusiastic as any new kid on the block and that actually, his advice is sound, because he has your best interests at heart. By the end of the month, you are tripping the light fantastic together; if you're single, well, men are just tripping up over your feet.

Best days for romance: 5th, 25th
Best days to seduce: 9th, 29th
Best stay at home day: 13th

April

Blissful pleasure comes your way after the 7th, and you feel magical, wicked and ready for any romantic escapades. The Full Moon in your own sign on the 13th reaffirms your belief in yourself. You do have feelings, and you do have doubts and fears like anyone else, but an idealist you are and that's that. Mercury's move into your relationship corner on the 16th puts everything in perspective regarding a boyfriend. On the 17th, expect to seduce him out there in public if you have to prove a point. After the 18th, watch out that you don't cause a conflict of opinion. And stop flirting before your man grits his teeth, raises his eyebrows, or starts chatting up your best friend. The reality of who's going to be cook, or clean the bath are pressing problems, but you know that your sexual needs are just as important – if not more. Your adrenaline level is high, and the spring sunshine is making you feel aroused and attractive. So clear the air with your man, and enjoy some moments of exquisite tenderness after the 20th.

If you're single, the 5th sees you glowing with confidence. You'll also be feeling passionate and feisty on the 19th, so make sure you team up with someone who can match your incredible adrenaline levels. You're romantically afire again on the 26th when a passing wild-boy or gorgeous male colleague notices your charismatic personality. But cool your own passion, I'm afraid to say, he's actually attached.

It is one of those months for close emotional and sexual rapport with either your lover or a newcomer in town, although you could find the possessive side of his nature very scary, especially if he's a Taurus or Scorpio. So don't waste time. Tell him you're ready to share your mind, but he'll have to prove himself worthy of you if he's to share your body.

Best days for romance: 16th, 27th
Best days to seduce: 4th, 16th
Best stay at home day: 11th

May

Rushing into relationships without thinking, or blindly falling in love with love is often how you mistake infatuation for a deeper long-lasting bond. Without a partner, you feel like a lonely ship tossed in an angry sea. And if you're single, you hope that every man you meet will be Mr Right, and if the sexual attraction is there you fall too quickly into the whirlpool of love's deceptive waters. But you're in tigress form this month, and your eyes are hunting from the 3rd onwards as Venus finally arrives in your relationship zone. If you're attached, you're at your most irresistible and feminine. In fact, your boyfriend just can't have enough of you, so use the time to start planning any summer breaks – if you haven't done so already. Choose a very romantic location and watch out for getting led astray by social temptations of the male kind.

Sexual happiness improves after the 19th, when Mercury moves into your adventurous corner and you think up all kinds of new tricks in the bedroom. But feelings of doubt about your deepest desires could surface by the end of the month. On the 31st you have to make some kind of choice, but let your man know you can't be certain of anything right now. Frankly, it's back to one of your less endearing traits, and that's putting off until tomorrow the things that needs to be said today, and then inevitably regretting it later. 'If only I'd said it when I meant it, now I don't know whether I really feel that or not.' Get the picture?

If you're single, there is someone special you've had your eye on for some time. He may be the kind who could charm the birds out of the trees, but you're not making it clear enough to him that you're interested. By the 24th, you're also confused about whether to search for a long-term involvement, or simply enjoy yourself and maintain your sexual and emotional independence. By the 29th, your party mood transforms your outlook on love again. You want to be desired for your charismatic qualities, both physically and emotionally. Perhaps, at last, you can find someone who will give you the freedom to be yourself and love you for who you are, not what you think you should be in his eyes.

Best days for romance: 14th, 19th
Best days to seduce: 21st, 31st
Best stay at home day: 23rd

June

June brings a fresh wave of self-belief, and wonderful temptations abound. With the Sun at the highest point of your chart, your image, look, style and manner are all being noticed, not only by your professional contacts, but also by the kind of dreamboat who could take you further than just a ride down river. Perhaps even as far as the ocean of love's magical depths. But take care. There are several rivals out there who might get in your way around the 16th when the Sun's tense link with Pluto triggers off manipulative behaviour by someone you thought was your pal. But you really have no excuses not to charm the pants off him, or at least make an impression where it counts.

If you're attached, you'd like to move a relationship on to a new level. It's been oscillating between romance one minute, routine the next. But how to ensure your idealistic vision of love is maintained? With Neptune's continuing elusive influence in your romantic corner, it's likely that the dreamy atmosphere you adore about falling in love is top of your list. And yet, like everyone else you know, deep down inside that there comes a time when the illusions fade and good old reality sets in. But how to keep the magic? It is time to weave romance back into your life, to keep it fresh, scintillating and sexy.

Around the 10th, you feel seductive enough to leap in where angels fear to tread, thanks to the Sun's lusty tangle with Neptune. And that devilish mood attracts an array of wannabes to your inbox or voice-mail. If you're single, this presents little problem, but if attached, you may begin to wonder if you're in the right relationship. Again and again you judge yourself too quickly, and that noble voice in your head says, 'I don't deserve any more than anyone else. I'll stick this out and it will all be OK.' If everything really is fabulous, then fine, but don't deceive yourself if it's not. This is one of those months when your ruler Venus is giving you the chance to understand what your true values are all about. Make sure they're yours, not someone else's.

Best days for romance: 3rd, 27th
Best days to seduce: 6th, 17th
Best stay at home day: 12th

July

It's summer, and if you're not dashing off for that romantic holiday, you're surrounded by friends, your social life is whirling like a dervish and frankly you're up every night show-stopping and bopping until you drop. But you're not alone, and sleepy as you are in the mornings, the wonderful intimacy between you and your lover right now inspires you to long, languid days of arousal, rather than docile siestas. Around the 6th, Jupiter's change of direction makes you realize that you'll soon be leaping from under the covers, as life's about to quicken its pace. A sudden trip abroad or an opportunity to be part of a money-making venture quickly turns your mind from thinking about how to please your lover to working out how to negotiate your way through a financially lucrative maze. This speedy *volte-face* might come as a shock, but if your lover knows you well, he'll understand how quickly you flit from hot to cold, or sex siren to chairman of the company. If he doesn't, make it clear that you're not abandoning him, but that you just have to do this one little batch of things and then you'll give him your total attention. Or better still, include him in your plans and ask him what he thinks you should do. Your knight in shining armour will love solving your problems for you and you might just find that what he says makes a lot of sense. Could it be that you've finally met your soulmate in the ideal merger of mind and body? If it feels as good as it should, you have. If he gives you freedom and security all at the same time, hang onto him, enjoy the moment and the prospect that this can continue for as long as you want it to.

With the Sun moving into fiery Leo on the 22nd, followed by an inspiring New Moon on the 25th, you're beginning to put your own needs first. The big Libran 'problem', (as there is for any sign) is that you want to be loved so much that you often opt for approval rather than true love. So if he says, 'let's go to the pub' when you'd rather be going to a fashion show or that smart coffee shop that's just opened, you'll probably say 'yes' just to keep him happy and therefore gain approval for yourself. So perhaps it's timely now to say no for once. Otherwise, the approval seeker in you will unconsciously take over, and you won't really know if your decisions are based on your values or his. It's fine to tip the scales in his favour, but sometimes you need to tip them in your favour too. Now is you chance to liberate yourself into self-love. The more you love yourself, the more someone will love you for being that very special person you are.

Best days for romance: 2nd, 19th
Best days to seduce: 21st, 29th
Best stay at home day: 14th

August

It's a month for adventurous romance if you're single, and fulfilling sexual experiences if you're attached. Your desire for excitement will be fulfilled when a whirl of glamorous events puts you in the spotlight. With Venus, your ruler in feisty Leo from the 12th, you have the chance to write the script and play the leading role in any man's life. If you're single, take centre stage, and make a deep connection to a gorgeous hunk who wants to play your leading man. With Venus creating confusion with Saturn and Neptune on the 27th, the drama intensifies, so don't get jealous if your lover fraternizes with a minor player. It's not serious, but if you get it all out of proportion, you'll be dumped by your romantic lead. So get your Romeo back stage and show him just how desirable you are.

If attached, with the hot August sun comes a series of social occasions, where you can sparkle and be true to your gregarious streak. Around the 19th, you can relax and forget the struggles of emotional confrontation you see around you. Other couples row, stamp their feet, walk out on each other. But you? Calm and serene with your lover, your sexual energy flow is on a high, and you can merge into him without fear, totally uninhibited and sure of yourself. The deep worries about commitment and choices are temporarily shelved, and you can sit back and enjoy the fun-side of life together. But do you take a chance to work at this relationship? Romance is one thing, and you need an awful lot of it in your life, but long-term commitment is still scary, and you innately don't feel comfortable if there is an imbalance in the partnership. Why should you make all the improvements when he's just carrying on assuming everything is hunky dory? At the end of this month, you become aware that your attitudes and ideas must be expressed if this relationship is to continue. It's time to communicate honestly all the emotions that you've been analyzing, and even if you are doing all the work, it's worth it.

Best days for romance: 10th, 14th
Best days to seduce: 9th, 27th
Best stay at home day: 23rd

September

With Mars moving into your own sign on the 8th, there's a feeling that your long-term wishes are not in balance with a loved one's expectations. But if you keep your head while all about you are huffing and puffing, you should make progress without causing all those heavy scenes you loathe so much. Take the opportunity to discuss tactics while a lover or friend is in the mood to listen on the 12th. Your ambitious side may be the reason for aggravation in the love nest, but it is time to act on your right to follow up your desires.

Liberating yourself from one unnecessary romantic pressure is essential this month. A certain admirer may be asking too much, or demanding you make some kind of commitment which goes against your instinct, yet you seem powerless to do anything about it until the 23rd. For the first two weeks you resign yourself to voicing a few borrowed remarks, such as 'It's out of my hands', or 'I can't be bothered'. But don't give up or compromise too readily. With sexy Mars surging through your sign there is a big change in the wind, and you'll have the determination and the resilience to see it through.

If you're single, sensual encounters revive your charm offensive and you're out to seduce a few mind-expanding rogues. Radical though your ideas are for enhancing your sex life around the 28th, don't neglect your lover's needs in the excitement of it all. It may be necessary to play down your enthusiasm until their mood improves. Of course, if the boredom factor seeps into your relationships, you want some way to make it more magical. So shock that gorgeous hunk by your uninhibited sexual response. Challenging though love affairs seem to be, you are never one to complain. Mars is spurring you into taking a new initiative where your deepest desires are concerned. Quite honestly, the options open to you are more than most people could imagine. And the greater your romantic visions, the greater happiness you'll begin to experience.

Although you normally don't tell your friends everything you're up to, (remember, for all your chit chat and gossip, you do have a secret side), at the end of the month you are quite keen to discuss in detail anything from your sex life to your romantic dreams. But others are very wary about your rather obsessive frame of mind. Maybe it would be more appropriate to engross yourself in the things they've overlooked. That way, they won't be able to criticize you later.

Best days for romance: 8th, 12th
Best days to seduce: 7th, 30th
Best stay at home day: 19th

October

With Venus now gracing your own sign, and the Sun and Mars still there until the 23rd, you are truly in your element. This is a wonderful month for self-expression, for communicating your feelings and for feeling close to the one you love. It might also be the month when you make the best and most positive decision you have made for a long time. With harmony almost restored in your love life, you are rewarded with the right kind of feedback on the 7th: sexy, lingering and magical.

The fiery Full Moon in Aries gives you that X-factor. You, and only you, are the one he wants and you can do no wrong. How can you be so perfect? Well, living up to all that idolization is a little harder as you go on through the rest of the month. Because, yes, you do have bad hair days, yes, you do sometimes look a bit red-eyed in the mornings, and yes, you do say things you regret you said a day later. But, hey, who's perfect anyway? And if your lover or boyfriend begins to see signs of a flawed woman in you, maybe he should also think about his own imperfections first. The problem is that you equate love with a perfect ideal. And that's why, much as I'm advocating that this is your month for pure bliss and happiness, I'd also be a fool to give you the impression that life will be a bed of roses from now on. There are thorns, and there will be days when the petals fade and drop off, and the magic between you seems to be temporarily eclipsed by good old reality. But the sensual link between Mars and Venus in sexy Scorpio on the 25th triggers off a deeply erotic connection with your dreamboat, and if you begin to glimpse that love and beauty also include the warts, dirty knickers and snuffling colds, then you're beginning to see also that the imperfect is also loveable. Trying to live up to such a high standard or idealistic expectation is, of course, only natural, because you're born a Libran, and a Libran you will always be. But if you carry too many illusions about love, then inevitably it's dangerous, because one day the illusion will turn to disillusionment, and then you will either become a writer of romantic twaddle or a cynic. And I don't think really you want to be either do you? In other words, see the flaws, paint your beautiful image of love with a touch of humour, and see your lover and yourself as just two more players on the world stage, no more, no less.

Best days for romance: 3rd, 22nd
Best days to seduce: 12th, 27th
Best stay at home day: 20th

November

This month you are more frank and honest, and generally aware of who you are and where you are going. As Venus surges on into fun-loving Sagittarius, you're light-hearted and ready for an upbeat phase in your love life. You find the strength to climb down off your pedestal, thanks to an irrepressible urge to create a sound relationship. The Full Moon in Venus ruled Taurus on the 5th helps you put love before pride, and you learn to meet your lover half way. However comforting it feels to keep your emotions tightly under wraps, a moment's fragility will pierce an admirer's heart a thousand times deeper than a lifetime's control. As Mercury moves forward again on the 18th, his emotional cool will melt at a glimpse of your vulnerable side. But there is more than one man who's dazzled by the softening of your attitudes and as loves arrows fly, temptations are placed in your path. Consider your options carefully and don't gamble a sure, but outdated thing, for potential flash-in-the-pans. Update, rather than up-sticks and avoid someone who seems like the most attractive prospect, as in fact, he's just a jealous cad who'll revert to type once the competition's over.

A serious opportunity for emotional commitment comes on the 14th, but someone inevitably feels rejected. Thankfully, for once it won't be you, and as the Sun moves into Sagittarius on the 22nd, followed by Jupiter on the 24th, a loving exchange of vows and intentions helps you realize that your soulmate is the one who is by your side, as well as in your heart. Around the 27th, Pluto stir up a battle of the sexes.

There is more than one way to win a fight and the best way is not to confront him at all, so use subtle tactics to get what you want. Take comfort in the knowledge that you're both battling for the same thing. And what's that, if not each other?

Best days for romance: 1st, 21st
Best days to seduce: 17th, 30th
Best stay at home day: 11th

December

December begins with you in a positive mood about your ideals and future happiness. A tantalizing Full Moon in Gemini on the 5th might entice you to seek a change of climate, or to go on a jaunt away from the usual festive routines. However, even if you do widen your horizons early on you will still be energetic enough to accept the strains or ties of family expectations. With Mars and Mercury moving on into Sagittarius on the 6th and 8th, the social whirl picks up and whether far away on some exotic shore, or on your home ground, you're dazzling, charismatic and having fun wherever you go.

If you are single, a flirtatious encounter with a charismatic entrepreneur around the 12th gains you the upper hand, or is it just Venus urging you to drive a hard bargain? Either way, your brilliant smile and sex appeal get the deal or the man – or both. Ignore any twinges of negativity around the 14th; with Jupiter on your side you simply can't fail. Even if you are longing for the impossible, the possibilities are endless this month. You want more, and you know you deserve it. Set your aims high and don't ever put yourself down or try to be something you're not.

If you're attached, the festive spirit is hot. Your man's happy to nestle down in front of those log fires or up for exploring a new continent. This is your chance to make choices, ask for what you really want – both sexually and emotionally – and prove that when you make a decision, you'll stick to it. And what about the little approval-seeker inside? Well, happily she's begun to realize that approval doesn't equate with love. The balancing act you are now performing is pure artistry. And with a little help from a New Moon in liberating Sagittarius on the 20th, the last weeks of the year are ones when sexual affinity, and positive belief in yourself are sparks which will set your love-life on fire for a brilliant start to the new year. Go for it!

Best days for romance: 5th, 20th
Best days to seduce: 13th, 25th
Best stay at home day: 26th

Your Love
Horoscope
2006

Scorpio
The Scorpion

October 23 – November 22

Love Check

Why you're fabulous

 Erotic and mysterious, you can sexually inspire
any man you want.

 You are passionate about life and love, so it's all or
nothing when it comes to relationships and work.

 Friends know they can trust you with their secrets.
Rivals know not to cross your path.

Why you're impossible

 You can become totally obsessed with sex.

 When you want someone or something, your
tactics are very manipulative.

Your love secrets

 Controlling sexual relationships is a way of
defending your vulnerability.

 You are intensely probing, but give little away
about yourself.

 Sex must be a transformative experience.

Your sexual style

Hypnotic, intense and totally all-consumingly passionate.

Who falls for you

Serious men who want to transform your life forever, sensual rogues and gypsy types, men with secrets, money or another partner hidden away somewhere.

Who you fall for

Artistic types, style gurus, practical, down-to-earth hunks with money in their wallet, rock stars or men who are already involved with someone else.

You identify with

Mystery, magic and intrigue. Survivors, people who are dark horses, and anyone who can talk about sex, money and death.

Your greatest temptation

Men with money or power.

Your greatest strength

You will never submit to anyone or anything.

Passion Profile for 2006

This year your thoughts turn purely to sexual love, and you're wondering how best to express them and how much you can say before frightening any true love away. The affection you feel is mutual, so there's nothing to fear, except for your own feelings of inadequacy. Learning to love yourself is vital to your relationships – romantic and professional. So learn to accept the idea that actually you are a beautiful fish in a pond of sardines and consequently a pretty desirable catch. With Jupiter bringing larger-than-life characters into your world all year, and a bigger and better sense of what your sexual needs are all about, you can't resist anything, from dangerous liaisons if single, to committing yourself to a secret love if attached. But whatever happens, your extremes of feeling run ever deeper this year, and you'll know in your heart of hearts who you love and, most importantly, why.

Best bets for Mr Right this year: Taurus for sexual equilibrium, Capricorn for mutual empowerment, Cancer for emotional understanding.

2006 Month by Month

January

The sensitive Full Moon in Cancer on the 14th reminds you that it's all very well dreaming about what might have been, but it won't resolve one current emotional issue. No two relationships are ever the same, even though you are still you and haven't changed that much yourself. But the dynamic when two people meet creates an energy all of its own. Yes, looking back at past love affairs, wistfully with regrets, with anger or with pain, has its place if we can acknowledge it as simply that, looking back. But getting on with love now requires acceptance of your needs and values. Don't renege on them. Doing so means you might be dependent on the approval of others to give you a sense of security. The Full Moon is there to tell you it's time to respect your heartfelt desires, and break free from the inner judge and jury.

With Mars surging through your opposite sign, confidence bursts through any self-doubt, and you are armed and ready for emotional clarity. You are on a quest to make your mark, and whether you take up the gauntlet to get one special person to notice you, or just knock them dead with seductive skills, you are about to make the kind of impact which is unforgettable. Whether you like it or not, around the 22nd you make a deep impression on someone. The harmonious link between Mars and Venus brings exciting, unpredictable romance, electrifying sexual energy all around, and you just can't resist. (Well, if you do you might regret it, so no indecisiveness about taking a romantic chance – promise, please!)

If you're single, you could be whispering explicit come-ons around the 26th and if you are attached just think of your favourite (and very legal sexual fantasy), and live it out together. With mischievous Mercury scrambling lines of comm-unication around the 25th, you feel as if you're suddenly driving with the brakes on. You want to get this re-lationship flying high, but there is a time factor involved, a nervousness and a fear of going too far, too soon. A part of you craves belonging, permanence, but another desires space, no strings, emotional self-sufficiency. Which is right, which is wrong? By the 27th, you are more realistic and know that you can combine the two. It's time to reveal to someone what you really want.

Best days for romance: 3rd, 16th
Best days to seduce: 14th, 18th
Best stay at home day: 17th

February

As Mercury soars into your wilful zone on the 9th, it's your personal image which is top of your agenda, rather than your relationships with others. But the two run parallel and the liaisons you're involved in ultimately affect the way you see yourself. Make use of the frivolous Leo Full Moon on the

13th to stop worrying about the negativity of others and rediscover the self-confidence you've been hiding under a bushel for far too long. Dressing to impress boosts your powers of personal positive thinking and attracts ego-boosting flattery and attention. A combination of romances past and present becomes tricky around the 17th, when you're on the receiving end of some seriously flirtatious e-mails and intimate remarks. But you're not the fickle kind, so act on your deepest intuition and if it doesn't feel right, don't get involved.

Jupiter's expansive influence in your chart makes love nothing if not complicated, especially around the 22nd, when your motives are exaggerated and blown out of proportion. Luckily, even if you can't do the right thing, saying the right thing is made easier after the 26th. The determination to build bridges is uppermost in your heart and you are surprised by an offer you can't resist, as the Sun encourages you to stand up and be counted. Your foresight is admired by someone who wants you to help him see into his future – and he's visualizing it with you. Counterbalancing the old and the new is made easier by the dreamy New Moon in Pisces on the 28th and it seems like you can, and will, conquer the world – and best of all, the heart of the man you love.

Best days for romance: 7th, 18th
Best days to seduce: 14th, 25th
Best stay at home day: 20th

March

Jupiter changes direction in your own sign on the 4th, and you remember that every close sexual relationship for you is a mysterious and sometimes tangled web of passion, desire and excitement. You've had the chance to show someone special how you feel, but you've also reassured yourself about how much they care for you as well. You are in the mood for closer intimacy with your lover after the 1st, as the Sun's electrifying link with Uranus makes you crave closeness and sexual bliss. Feelings of doubt might creep into your mind, though, about whether this is really Mr Right, so think clearly and open your heart to your true feelings. You do have extremes of one day wishing him far away, and the next loving every bone in his body or hair on his chest. This month will prove no exception so try to understand that your own love-hate relationship with the world doesn't reflect on those things or people you love or hate, more upon your own ability to experience both emotions.

The Full Moon on the 14th tempts you to do something radical and different, whether it is simply to be more forward about putting your desires across, or actually suggesting an expedition of a lifetime. Whether you take off for a jaunt around the Himalayas or simply a jog round the park or visit your favourite restaurant, mid-month is a great boost to your self-confidence and ability to make a deliberate choice.

Being so acutely aware of other people's moods, you also feel insecure about your own long-term plans around the 20th, when there's a distinct air of frustration about your personal life. But by the 29th you realize that this was only a temporary – if necessary – blip to open you up to a new and creative way of thinking about your relationship. If single, on the 27th you relive some magical moments with an ex, either over the phone or face to face, and a new admirer can't wait to date you. Keep him on his toes – he's going to be chasing after you for weeks to come. And don't you just enjoy keeping one step ahead of the game?

Best days for romance: 3rd, 27th
Best days to seduce: 9th, 21st
Best stay at home day: 4th

April

Of course, it's virtually impossible to be philosophical about our relationships when we're right bang in the middle of them – especially if they're proving painful, wonderfully escapist or intensely involved. And as much as others might goad you on to analyze your feelings, it's not exactly easy or desirable right now. The first few days of April (and, no, you're not a fool for love either) you feel as if you've been short-changed where love is concerned. Whether you are struggling to come to terms with a past rejection, or wanting a new commitment or love in your life, it will still feel uncomfortable and that's that. What is missing, what is that sense of deprivation all about? These are questions I hope you will try to answer – or at least acknowledge that they might need some kind of response.

Yet by the 6th Venus moves into escapist Pisces bringing you an empowering realization that you are no longer emotionally dependent on others for your happiness. Finding that light within, the inner voice of soul and spirit, is both liberating and crystallizing. What is being formed is likened to Jung's definition of free will: 'the ability to do gladly what you have to do'. And this is also about making your own choices in a relationship rather than feel you're being carried along on someone else's tidal wave.

By the New Moon in your opposite sign of Taurus on the 27th you are ready to express your most secret of desires to someone special. It may be you've felt neglected, it may be you wanted to be so close that they couldn't handle that kind of dependency, but now you're realizing that you don't have to cling to someone to be loved. You can be separate, individual and adored for being you in your own right. Make the end of the month one where you can begin to share the secret side of yourself.

Best days for romance: 6th, 20th
Best days to seduce: 10th, 27th
Best stay at home day: 3rd

May

Brief encounters and passing fancies are not something you usually indulge in, but with the influence of Mars and Jupiter on the 7th, and Mars and Uranus on the 13th, you might just surprise yourself. It's not that you are planning to abandon your moral values, but if you are in the mood to try new and exciting liaisons, it's going to be hard to hold yourself back. And frankly, why should you? We all need a little boost to our ego now and then, and whether that involves a holiday romance, or fresh ways of spicing up your love life, don't feel guilty about enjoying being you. With Mercury's influence this month, you begin to realize the importance of self-acceptance. You are a sensitive, sensual woman and need to be treated as such.

Around the 13th, a Full Moon in your own sign encourages feelings of loneliness and it over-exaggerates qualms about a ticking biological clock. Flirting will help dull the sounds and gain you an admirer or two, who gloriously remind you that you have a libido which is worthy of attention. Whether you've been single or just under-sexed for too long, your body is waking up to the fact that it is spring and time for romance. Jupiter's malingering influence is finally forcing you to focus on your personal needs and desires. It's about time you put yourself first and around the 26th say no to family demands. If you are single, a sudden surge of renewed vitality gets you noticed and adored by a hunk who makes your spine tingle when you gaze into his eyes. Don't panic, his spine is tingling too.

Best days for romance: 6th, 15th
Best days to seduce: 11th, 29th
Best stay at home day: 15th

June

Sensual intimacy hots up and you begin to unwind, swap life-stories and old love wounds. And if you're single, a flirtatious encounter with a like-minded male colleague gives you renewed faith that some men are actually more sensitive than given credit for. There is something in the way he moves which draws you to him. He has feelings, not macho feelers. And, of course, that means you feel liberated and not pressured. After all, do you really want to listen to those men who moan about money, their job and the latest political scandal when you could be hearing romantic overtures about your future? But with Jupiter still backtracking through your sign, it's hard to know if you're being taken advantage of or misunderstood by other flash-in-the-pan admirers.

If you're attached, Venus's difficult link with Saturn on the 4th triggers off a few days of frustration. Do you settle for what you have got, or are you still sneakily worried that another Mr Right is out there somewhere? However much your man seems to adore you, something seems to be lacking. Maybe it's time to really ask yourself if your sexual needs are being met. With Mercury in the expressive zone of your chart until the 28th, you can voice your feelings, and be free of inhibitions. If you accept that what you have here and now is far more liberating than being bound to future expectations of what might be, you will spend the rest of the month with a smile on your face.

Around the 27th, you are in two minds about meeting up

with someone from the past who once seemed so perfect. But plans are delayed, or he doesn't live up to your nostalgic thoughts. But, think about it. Maybe that's just love's way of telling you you've moved on, been there, seen it, done it. Now's your chance to really get on with the present and take each day as it comes.

Best days for romance: 19th, 23rd
Best days to seduce: 7th, 18th
Best stay at home day: 4th

July

One special relationship seems to be tearing down the facade of your usually guarded vulnerability and a part of you wants to tell that special someone how much you really feel about them. This will be made easier around the 6th when Jupiter moves forward again in your own sign, to bring a change not only to the way you perceive others, but in the way you perceive yourself. Consequently, a fresh approach to your relationship heralds levels of intimacy you never imagined possible.

The influence of Mars in the career zone of your chart until the 22nd sidetracks you and you are putting all your energies into a work project. But remember, emotional honesty is needed now more than ever before, especially on the 14th when Venus's power-tussle with your ruler Pluto forces your head to rule your heart. Luckily, Venus moves into your excitement zone on the 19th, to make your lover seductively persuasive and whether he woos you with flowers, or wines and dines you at your favourite restaurant, you can't fail to end up in a steamy clinch. Venus brings all sorts of scintillating ideas to liven up your sex life and free up your inhibitions, and this makes you much more relaxed around your lover. For once, you seem to be living out the role of princess, and your knight in shining armour wants to hold you in his arms and make you happy. It doesn't have to just be a fairy tale, you need to believe that romance exists in real life, however much misery has been caused you before. The past is best buried and healed by the belief that wonderful things are possible and if you truly believe in them, they really are.

If you're single, flirtatious gestures from colleagues or friendly rogues makes you more sexually confident than ever. But feelings and emotions run deep for you, and it looks as if you're about to catch the relationship bug. Keep your eyes wide open and, by the 29th, candidates will come running thick and fast. The planets are bringing you not only a new man or romantic encounter, but a new value about your own image in other people's eyes.

Best days for romance: 5th, 19th
Best days to seduce: 8th, 23rd
Best stay at home day: 30th

August

A period of serious navel contemplation and self-analysis provides the catalyst for the next stage of your journey into the labyrinth of love. It's time to discover what it is you really want from your relationships. Put it down to Jupiter's ongoing presence in your sign and the force of the Sun lighting up areas of your life which you need to work on.

Seeing the sacrifices that others are willing to make for you around the 6th, highlights the fundamental truth about how to make one lover happy. You are now at a point where you want an all-or-nothing partnership, and you're willing to work for it. The Full Moon of the 9th brings an end to a secret desire for something or someone who no longer makes you feel good about yourself. Venus, at the highest point of your chart from the 12th onwards, makes you aware of your emphatic beauty and sex appeal, helping you to sweep away self-doubt and gilding you with a gloriously attractive, positive glow. You have a golden opportunity to nurture the sort of relationship which makes you feel on top of the world. Ignore any subtly undermining and, frankly, suspect remarks from someone in a position of authority; their interests are not yours, however much they imply that they are. Turning your back on them on the 23rd will open doors to far-reaching opportunities in your personal life.

Surprisingly sensual moments abound and nights of passion turn to words of love as you resurrect feelings you've been keeping buried for far too long. By the 31st, hurt is a thing of the past and the only thing that's suffering is your sleep pattern, thanks to those long, hot, sexy nights in the arms of the one you love. You've been living in a dreamier world than ever before, but now those feelings of not living out your true potential suddenly change and you begin to have a clearer picture of where you are going in your life again, and more importantly who with.

Best days for romance: 10th, 23rd
Best days to seduce: 6th, 24th
Best stay at home day: 1st

September

The more you look at life with a twinkle in your eye, the more you realize how much affection you can gain. It's not that you particularly want sentimental endearments right now, just to know that you are special and wanted. But express your desires with as much feeling as you can muster on the 8th. It's not easy, of course, to ask for emotional support in any straightforward way, but Mars is giving you the chance to do so. Especially as someone is picking up on the nuances that have been floating around you for so long. Being elusive is one thing, but don't forget you are human too. If you are single, one handsome rogue in the workplace is thinking aloud, and they seem to be divulging some interesting information about how they fancy you. You may have been vaguely suspicious of them in the past but listen with an open mind. It could lead to the kind of liaison you're seeking.

Venus's sexy link with Pluto on the 25th will make your lover take note of your sensual power, sit up and probably kiss you to pieces. Just take care, though, as a blast from your beautiful past could show up when least expected around the 28th. But then, isn't a little wicked wistfulness just what makes you so magical? Current admirers will be flocking like gulls in your wake if you're single, and if you're attached, revel in the attention, rather than those fantasies about 'what might have been'. Then suddenly it's back to domestic issues. Hmmm, in the harsh light of day that means putting 'arse into gear'. In fact, if you whizz around the place like a dustbuster, you'll feel like virtue personified when you go on that surprise date, or simply indulge in your man's loving arms, knowing why he's worth seducing over and over again.

Best days for romance: 7th, 29th
Best days to seduce: 13th, 30th
Best stay at home day: 5th

October

You know it's coming. That feeling of – 'it's *my* time of the year', when the anticipation of your birthday looming over the horizon is enough to make you reach for the internet dating line, or call your favourite rogue for company and sexual indulgences. And it's because you are deep down the most empowering, hypnotic and sometimes demanding diva of love's ways that you know you have to be in relationship rather than out of it. Even if you're not actually living with someone, or dating them. The power of keeping a man spellbound by your presence, or lack of it, is what keeps you buzzing. Remember that hunk a few months back who was on the hunt, and you never let him catch up? Well, he's still lolling around every window-box, behind every closed door and across the coffee machine. Yes, he's followed your every move, knows how you stare into space when you get bored and wonders if you're thinking of him. Don't let him know right now, as delicious flirtations with a very radical colleague become steamy on the 15th.

By the 24th, Venus, Mars and the Sun are all swarming into your own sign to bring you the kind of wicked, sultry, intense and utterly crazy love life for the last week of the month. Whether single or attached, you'll be drawn into a love triangle, or the kind of geometry that defies logic. Somehow, you're double-dating, calling his bluff or meeting in clandestine locations. You are up for steamy sex and power battles, text messages and secret phone calls, or a spot of espionage into why your man's got a lipstick mark on his collar when you don't even wear the stuff. Intrigue, however revealing, however exposing or however unbelievable, is what you're made of right now. In your element, you can take on any romantic crusader, and love passionately and intensely any man who can fulfil your heart's desire. Don't give up on your incredible theatrical love of life, while you have the seduction skills of Cleopatra.

Best days for romance: 2nd, 24th
Best days to seduce: 25th, 30th
Best stay at home day: 15th

November

Mars and Venus continue to plunder your sign and with Jupiter finally crossing over the cusp into Sagittarius on the 24th, make the most of this bountiful energy early on in the month. This is a great time for libido peaks, sexual surrender and passionate encounters. You feel wicked, so plan a night of languorous sensuality around the 5th with the Full Moon in your love zone. Or simply be romantic and spontaneous under the stars, however chilly the weather, you know the heat between you is intense.

If you are single, you have an incredible talent for bewitching any man right now, whether it is a handsome admirer or simply the boss. Wisely impress the latter by sorting out a minor conflict of egos down the corridors of power on the 16th. And, while your knack for problem solving is inspiring those around you, let a friend confide in you about a romantic obsession. Their insights, experiences and perhaps even their rejections could be of great personal use for your own personal quest later on in the year.

Enjoy a flirtatious or clandestine weekend around the 21st with a dark horse. But, however aware you are of his passion for you, he's not Mr Right, although he's worth dating for his charm, looks and humour. You're still sexually at your most stunning, so choose your men carefully and with discretion. You don't need one-night stands in your life right now, however much you want male company and love. And with Jupiter's change of emphasis after the 24th, you're ready to change your outlook on men in general, whether it's for a raunchy adventure with one you *know* you can trust or will never let you down. Or simply establish a new friendship with someone who could turn out to be your soulmate one day. Deep in your heart, you know that you have to make a choice about an ex who seems still intent on getting you back. Were his feelings for you as genuine as you'd like them to have been, or were you playing a role just to keep him? By the end of the month, you know you can't go on dwelling on what might have been. So make it clear you have your own boundaries and your own individuality, and you won't return to a relationship where you had to pretend to be something you're not.

Best days for romance: 18th, 20th
Best days to seduce: 12th, 16th
Best stay at home day: 26th

December

Love pleasures continue, the intrigue goes on, but work issues begin to take precedence when you'd rather be out and about socializing early in the month. But, by the 11th, you begin to relax and take time out to enjoy the company of those who can help you in the corridors of power. Now, please, don't take this the wrong way, but you must admit you are a bit of a power-tripper. And I know it's only because you feel acutely vulnerable inside and you have to compensate for that sense of powerlessness. This December, if you're single, you use your wiles and seductive ways to get you into a position on the professional ladder. Of course, if he's worth seducing for his looks and sex appeal as well, you'll have a double whammy of success, but do remember why you have to take control. Awareness doesn't mean you have to stop doing so and become a dull wallflower, rather it means you can seduce knowingly and with emotional honesty of what your true motivation or intentions are.

If you're attached, there's a brief testing time on the 7th before you can get down to seriously good times. You come to terms with why he doesn't seem to know whether he's coming or going. And you realize it's because you're not truly communicating what you think or feel. (Scorpios are very reluctant to give the game away.) Outbursts or tiffs will inevitably arise on the 12th, so use your gentle and serene ability to avoid causing a mindless conflict of interests. You need to feel secure in your relationship before you give too much away, so take a break away from the hustle and bustle of the normal festive angst, and with your man at your side take time to reflect on where you both go from here. If you still fear to make a deeper commitment, perhaps it's because you fear rejection at a later stage? Don't forget, as big-time Uranus is still waking you up to a whole new vision of relating – and will be doing so for the next few years – don't make any long-term plans. Just love the one you're with, enjoy the commitment you have in the here and now – and, possibly, the future. It's in the very moment of thinking about the future that you will begin to see it. Clear, uncomplicated and the magical expression of your desires coming true.

Best days for romance: 2nd, 14th
Best days to seduce: 5th, 20th
Best stay at home day: 30th

Sagittarius

The Archer

November 23 – December 20

Love Check

Why you're fabulous

- You inspire friends and lovers by being an eternal optimist.
- You are utterly romantic and always enticing.

Why you're impossible

- You rarely relax, and restlessly search for new experiences.
- You can deliver verbal punches without thinking whether they'll hurt.

Your love secrets

- For you, sex is a celebration of life.
- You need personal freedom more than anything in the world and are happiest single.
- Domesticity is the last thing on your mind. Sex is the first!

Your sexual style

Direct, passionate and highly provocative.

Who falls for you

Action men, adventurous rogues, intellectuals who adore your get-up-and-go attitude to life. Practical possessive types who want to tame you.

Who you fall for

Independent hustlers, men who've travelled, experienced no-nonsense tycoons, celebrities and rich kids.

You identify with

A fast-paced and action-packed career, a love of life. The unknown or anything which challenges your mind – particularly men.

Your greatest temptation

Making wild promises you know you won't keep.

Your greatest strength

A hilarious approach to life and love.

Passion Profile for 2006

Cupid's got nothing on you this year! You're aiming love arrows everywhere you go – and hitting dead on target. With feisty Mars in your love corner from February through to April, men just can't resist you. Your sexual needs are met, encounters turn to intriguing affairs, and a feeling that you can ride the waves of sensual bliss keeps a permanent smile on your face. With Venus taking over the sexual hunt in June, take the road towards a new challenging lover and what you truly want will follow. Make it a year to stand up for your freedom-loving personality, and don't let anyone try to force you into making compromises. There will be friends who squirm a little with envy as you indulge in romantic scenarios throughout the autumn, but your heart is set on one goal, and that is to be loved for who you truly are. With your ruler, Jupiter surging into your own sign at the end of November, your greatest fantasies can come true. The end of the year is set to be most transformative where relationships are concerned. And what about you? Well, you are as desirable and larger-than-life as any sexual diva.

Best bets for Mr Right: Leo for show-stopping fun, Aries for wild days and steamy nights, Gemini for tantalizing conversation.

2006 Month by Month

January

The arrows are aiming all over the place early in January. When confronted by close partners or lovers, you feel that life has suddenly begun to throw some very complicated obstacles in your path. Do you own up to your feelings about someone, or do you guard your secret behind that hilarity and zest for adventure? With Saturn backtracking through fiery Leo, it seems that partners or new boyfriends just won't bend to your rules and you are forced to make hasty rearrangements with regard to certain dates or plans around the 6th. Then, to cap it all, Mars and Jupiter's tension on the 14th triggers off a run of theatrical performances between you and him. Does he understand the reason behind your behaviour? Whether he does or not, release all that energetic enthusiasm into some sexy strategies and please both yourself and him. It's far more satisfying to express yourself through physical indulgence than mental power games.

If you are single, the powerful planetary activity this month also brings a run of mood swings. One day, you wonder, 'what's the point of relationships anyway?', the next you're flirting with every available man, whether your colleagues or your best friend's boyfriend. Deep down you want romantic fun, and around the 22nd you can be assured of some tantalizing encounters or a surprise call from that admirer who's been dying to take you out.

Adventure is your watchword, whether single or attached, so get out and create new romantic scenarios, but just don't make promises or commitments on impulse. It might all sound good on paper, but at the end of the month you might regret what you eagerly offered to do earlier on. Biting your lip is one thing, but don't bite the bullet too quickly too soon. There are far more antics and amusements to come.

Best days for romance: 11th, 23rd
Best days to seduce: 4th, 13th
Best stay at home day: 31st

February

After the ups and downs of last month, February is set to put you in the limelight of friends and lovers. With a seductive ability to organize yourself and your man, it's hardly surprising you wonder why the time just flies past. Freedom is still on your mind, and keeping your head clear and focused is a safer bet than rushing headlong into the kind of trap which will make you feel like a caged tiger rather than a free bird. With Mercury reminding you that your domestic situation needs attention from the 9th, you prepare your love nest, invite friends and lovers to help you redecorate the place, or simply entertain in your benevolent style. However, the Full Moon on the 13th triggers a feeling that you need to get away from it all, and you're ready to pack your rucksack and head off to some exciting destination alone. Complications if attached, complimentary admirers if single. And Valentine's Day brings an unusual missive in your inbox. Can it be that blast from the past you never really forgot who is trying to angle his way back into your life? Tread carefully, he's attached to someone else now.

Then, thank your lucky stars, or rather Mars winging his way into your love corner, you're blessed with the kind of attention that only a celebrity would have. Conquests pile up in you're single, and if attached, just take care with your lover's heart after the 17th, when jealous eyes could be watching your every move. Innocently, of course, you are flirting here, there and everywhere, and, on the 23rd, you cause a silly but highly frenetic misunderstanding. By the 25th, the twinkle in your eye and his have returned, and there is nothing to stop you indulging in the sexiest fun and mutual passion.

But, remember, living your life as if it were a game of chance, throwing dice and seeing what happens next, and if luck really is on your side, is one thing. But refusing to see the truth because it might just not be as enticing as the vision you have for a perfect love affair, can make you break off a relationship too easily. What is it about commitment that scares you? Is it perhaps that without your freedom to play, flirt and bring joy to others, you'd feel like an old hen trying to incubate the same old eggs?

Best days for romance: 17th, 29th
Best days to seduce: 1st, 14th
Best stay at home day: 22nd

March

Caution is not exactly something that you could claim to be one of your finest qualities, but with the planetary line-up this month, you might find yourself caught up in all kinds of scenarios you'd rather avoid. Like saying one thing and meaning another to a very distinguished rogue around the 4th, when Jupiter, your ruler makes a U-turn in your chart, and as much as you'd like to keep shtoom or keep a secret, you just can't help tactlessly spilling the beans. Then you start thinking, maybe I should take a more careful approach about getting involved (or tangled up in the sheets) with someone who isn't worth my time and effort. But with Venus moving into sparkling Aquarius, friends, lovers and strangers in town still provide you with delightful encounters and you begin to sort out the rough from the smooth. There will be smart, intriguing admirers around and they'll be slick, two-faced, bad boys, so discrimination, again not your strongest point, is all important.

By the middle of the month, you're fired up by someone's dreamy presence in the workplace, and your lust factor is on a high. If you're attached, you demand more time for fun and games with your man, and if single, you simply enjoy all the attention. The Full Moon on the 14th reminds you that you'd rather be out in the big wide world than stuck at home scrubbing the floor. And grand ideas about taking off again into the sunset trigger late nights with your partner flicking through travel and property magazines wondering – just wondering – if it's worth jacking it all in for a different landscape and better lifestyle. But dream houses or dream places inevitably become your own back garden again, and the new and the different becomes the known, dull and staid. (Rather like relationships, you think darkly.) And if you're single, hot-headed dreamers hold you fascinated and your lust for life is rekindled. And with a wonderful link between Venus, Mars and Neptune on the 25th, someone reveals their true feelings, and you begin to realize you can make those dreams come true and still have the challenging lifestyle you crave. The solar eclipse on the 29th confirms your romantic assumptions are right, your intuition regarding this Mr Right Now is spot on, and a very tantalizing relationship is about to lead you off down the road to adventure. Even if you are single, you'll be in your element with the urge to create sexy tracks towards one gorgeous hunk upfront in your mind.

Best days for romance: 3rd, 15th
Best days to seduce: 20th, 25th
Best stay at home day: 1st

April

You're nobody's April fool on the 1st, but you might feel you're missing something in one relationship and then propel yourself very quickly into another without thinking of the consequences. And, if you're single, you do have a restless need to find new blood in town. As much as your appear to be carefree and capricious about love, independence to you doesn't mean loneliness. But how to have your cake and eat it? With an idealistic Full Moon in Libra on the 13th, followed up by Mercury's eye-opening influence in Aries on the 16th, you realize that if you fall for someone who has the same need for space and freedom as you, then maybe it would work. You begin to sparkle, socialize in all the right places, and happen to be at the right place at the right time for professional opportunities, and then, lo and behold, here comes a fellow spirit. If he's an Aquarius, Sagittarius or Gemini, open your arms and embrace him as a like-minded soul. Any other sign, apart for an Aries (who, although very single-minded, does like to think he is the only one who can do his own thing), avoid like the plague. You don't need cookbook romance with a Cancer, nor dreamy poetical stuff with a Pisces, what you need right now is pure spontaneous relating peppered with pure spontaneous sex. If you're attached (and your partner is not one of the goodies listed above), don't panic. But do remember that if you feel like roaming around the world, your social circle or just down the local pub, he's got to understand you aren't cheating on him, merely entertaining yourself.

Around the 20th, you are the bees knees when it comes to partying, socializing and being the life and soul. A rather dull but good-looking charmer is worth getting to know on the 21st – at least as a friend – and he could be useful to you later this year in your professional world. Don't let an important date pass you by on the 25th. If you are single, this heralds a new romantic liaison, if attached you're making realistic but exciting decisions together – and ones which will give you welcome anticipation for the summer ahead of fun.

Best days for romance: 16th, 20th
Best days to seduce: 13th, 21st
Best stay at home day: 4th

May

Early on, you wonder if anyone will ever understand your emotional needs, and maybe it's time to admit that you have feelings as much as anyone else. Your lover, partner or a new love interest can't quite make you out. Have you lost that recent passion and zest for life? So prove them wrong on the 7th, when Mars and Jupiter's dynamic link reminds you that deep down you may be an extremist but you're never going to give up on your quest for perfect relating. It's those people out there who are subdued, they're the ones putting off dates, changing plans, being noncommittal or in two minds about the future. You, on the other hand, are passion personified and raring to get on with love and life. When it comes to relationships, you need to take a few risks and gambles along the way, or you wouldn't be you!

With Mercury surging into your romantic corner on the 19th, followed by the Sun on the 21st, you're feeling on top of the world. Strangers notice your smile, admire your hilarious approach to life, and, if you're single, a challenging romantic situation is just the tonic you need to bring out the best in you. A spot of retail therapy, a new hairstyle or a radical change of make-up, and you're scoring dateable points wherever you go. With a delightful New Moon on the 27th in airy Gemini, beg, steal or borrow that man. Or simply curl up in the arms of the one you love on this early summer evening. Though you are not fond of emotional scenes, you at least begin to see how to deal with one sensitive issue. Without energy being sapped, you understand that he has a will of his own too, and you reach the end of the month accepting that your rush forward into the unknown may not be compatible with his more practical approach to what's round the next corner. But you are proving you have vision, self-belief and common sense, but most of all the intuition to realize you are a star who is shining brightly on the romantic stage – and you're never going to get off.

Best days for romance: 19th, 27th
Best days to seduce: 21st, 30th
Best stay at home day: 7th

June

An unusual encounter on the 5th puts you in the mood to set off on a secret rendezvous a few days later, when on the 11th the Full Moon in your own sign bathes your love life in a very tantalizing light. Do you involve yourself in a clandestine affair, or do you walk away from a delectable offer? If you're single, your erotic aura attracts an equally charismatic reaction from a lover or new admirer. And, on the 19th, you feel that love has taken a different route from the one you had planned. Crossroads, remember, are challenges not restrictions and they add impetus to the dynamic way in which you seduce. But which road to go down? Sometimes you wonder if you make a choice you will regret it later on. But don't forget, like any road, you can turn off at another junction and find another far more satisfying. You are not foolish enough to believe that the perfect relationship exists, but you are feeling rather idealistic in the first few weeks of the month – and quixotic enough to feel dissatisfied with one aspect of your love life. Whether it's a lack of personal space that's bothering you, or a difference in sexual needs, a part of you is wondering whether you shouldn't re-think your living arrangements and reassess one particular relationship.

Working too hard at love around the 21st takes the pleasure of romance away and plans that may have been thought out carefully will suddenly have to be changed or rethought. Sometimes men just can't deal with your ability to adapt at the last minute, and Venus moving into your love corner on the 24th helps you manoeuvre a path through an emotional minefield and come up smelling of roses. Such a positive outcome puts you in the mood for celebration. Passions run high and fun is on the cards. You have catered to someone else's needs for too long and now it is time to live for yourself. The adrenaline's positively bubbling through your veins — enjoy it to the full, you've earned it.

Best days for romance: 11th, 14th
Best days to seduce: 2nd, 8th
Best stay at home day: 26th

July

With your ruler, Jupiter moving forward again through erotic Scorpio, you feel high-spirited and enthusiastic about love. Venus's quirky link with Uranus on the 4th sparks off a string of exciting encounters, dates and decisions. If you are single, is one glamorous rogue really too good to be true, or is he truthfully good for you? By the 10th, it seems as if one lover is talking absolute nonsense, and due to the Moon's deceptive link with Neptune, you just can't trust anything anyone says. And that includes yourself, so take care you don't get too enthusiastic about making joint plans which you won't be able to fulfil at a later date.

A spot of brainstorming at a social bash inspires you with noble ideas on the 14th. But a flashing smile from Mr Someone-to-die-for gives you a few wicked thoughts too. You'll know what to do next, just make sure it's legal and utterly delightful. Around the 19th, you wake up to that kind of 'wow' feeling. All you want and need from love is well within your grasp. Catch your breath, choose your moment and be courageous. Venus is giving you the panache and persuasion to get away with anything.

With a fiery New Moon in Leo on the 25th in the sexually driven area of your chart, you take a leap in the dark. After all, life's for enjoying, and this is one chance to defy those friends who see everything as an uphill struggle. Flirt, laugh and make eye contact. It's the look in his eyes that says it all. Remember, the heat is on, so either set off on holiday, or simply indulge in all the delights of summer romance.

If your lover or partner is being awkward around the 26th, or playing hard to get, then don't assume it's your fault. Sometimes you have to let go of the feeling that you're responsible for every mood he's in or gesture he makes. All this getting nowhere fast will at least give you time to think clearly about your own needs. Rather than jumping to conclusions, take it as a learning curve for you both.

Best days for romance: 5th, 18th
Best days to seduce: 3rd, 17th
Best stay at home day: 9th

August

It's summer time, and the living is easy – or is it? Friends are talking romantic holidays, or sinful beach parties, and although you are torn between what feels good and what feels right, discussing the finer details of a relationship which you think you've outgrown helps you realize that it's not you who is at fault, but the combined dynamic of your personalities. Any lover demanding more of you than you are willing to give inevitably frustrates you and by the Full Moon on the 9th the mist disperses, showing him in a less rose-tinted and more realistic light. Yes, he's human and like all humans he has faults, but trying to pull a veil over his imperfections is like sweeping dirt under the carpet. Both the dirt, and the flaws appear again when you least expect them. When Mars opposes Uranus on the 13th, whether single or attached, you feel strangely isolated, and you would benefit from listening to the advice of a close friend who not only makes you feel good about yourself, but also forces you to ask the right questions. Never has it been a more constructive time to make objective decisions about what needs discarding and what needs to be nurtured in your love life.

Forget the softly-softly approach – only commitment, black-and-white responses and plane-loads of fervency will give you the incentive to stick with one man. If he's too weak to honour your needs, make it clear that you might just be heading off into the sunset on someone else's arm. Frankly, when threatened with the loss of something he thinks is rightfully his (ie, you), you'll soon be the one calling the shots. And isn't it nice to be in that kind of demand? With a romantic link between Venus and Neptune on the 27th, the twinkle in your eye has returned, and your volatile spirit and sexy smile gains you the kind of attention you truly deserve.

Best days for romance: 12th, 25th
Best days to seduce: 1st, 19th
Best stay at home day: 27th

September

Not only are close friends and social whirls playing a special role in your life this month, but they are also enabling you to see that one admirer or lover needs careful handling. Hot-headed and impulsive though you are, it's often the dreamy, elusive men who keep you on your toes. And one such dreamer is either already in your life or after the recent high heat of summer, you now realize it's time to be hunted, rather than be the huntress.

With a host of planets moving through your most idealistic corner of your chart, seduction will play a big part in proving that you are in control of the flirtation stakes. But how to do it without being obvious? Passively you sit and wait, tap fingers, wait for phone calls, mails and texts. Everyone else is out and about, dates abound and yet you are convinced this is the right way to reel him in. But with Mars moving into Libra on the 8th, followed by Mercury on the 12th, you begin to be more rational about it all, and realize that not all romantic attractions lead up the aisle, more like down the garden path. In fact, once the dreamy stranger does begin to show interest around the solar eclipse on the 22nd, you turn down his offers instead of turning up the heat. Another beautiful face in the crowd stirs you into radical action on the

25th, when Venus's sinful influence on Pluto in your own sign triggers off a feeling that you've met this man somewhere before, and last time you missed out. Take advantage of your high profile, charisma and charm, and by the end of the month you will know you're on the right track.

If attached, you begin to take a more philosophical perspective about relating. If you can enjoy your professional interests, if you can still have your space and your chance to flirt with life and not be condemned for having a smile on your face 24/7, then why not accept that this relationship works as well as it is going to? For now anyway. You know there is something in the wind, a change of status, personal power, and a bevy of admirers who are just waiting to fall at your feet. By the end of the month, all is fair in love, but if you're in the mood to battle for someone's attention and he's not your Mr Right Now, then take care.

Best days for romance: 12th, 30th
Best days to seduce: 8th, 10th
Best stay at home day: 26th

October

The realization that your partner might not be able to live up to your high expectations is getting to you. It's a niggle and when you're feeling irritated you let the whole world know about it. This includes your gaggle of friends who can't imagine what you have to complain about. After all, isn't he the most gorgeous hunk this side of the ocean? But you're simply restless for fun and for sexier, scintillating adventures. It's not that you don't care, and you love to be loved, but maybe, just maybe this is one man who can't fulfil the things you really want in life. Whether it's a partner who can make love at the crack of dawn, leap out of bed and drive off into the sunset on a whim, and still have the energy to surf all day at the beach, or a dynamic entrepreneur who knows all the right people, it's time to think about your true needs.

Yes, of course you love to charge into forbidden territory without a thought for the consequences, but early on this month you might find that your 'trespass, who dares' philosophy triggers off a veritable test of your emotional mettle. With a fiery Full Moon in Aries on the 7th, frying pans may fly rather than rest easily on the shelf, and leaping into a sexier fire makes you realize just how much you can really get away with. And to cap it all, the intricacies of a clandestine affair based solely on sexual desire are far more complex than you would like.

If you're single, that restless urge to cut ties or look for new blood reaches boiling point on the 25th. But as much as you glorify independence and the quest for personal freedom, loneliness is another matter. Carefree, spontaneous and impulsive? I know those qualities are very precious to you. But gradually you are beginning to understand that you also need a man who honours your vitality but can also be your equal. As much as you adore charging around like a rampant huntress, the love you have for yourself will be doubled when you respect (which is what real love must include) your partner too. So make any double-act as exciting and visually spectacular as courting tigers, when romance returns with a bang at the end of the month.

Best days for romance: 7th, 22nd
Best days to seduce: 23rd, 30th
Best stay at home day: 4th

November

You are finally realizing that where one close relationship is concerned, you have no choice but to ask for more space and time to do your own thing. Cards have been put on the table, and you have experienced moments when surrendering to duty seemed an easier option. But now those true desires need to be expressed. Don't fear the truth. After all, if he doesn't understand you are a woman with a mission, then maybe he's missing the real you. So make the most of Venus's move into your own sign on the 17th to stir a little spice into your love life. It's not that you're bored, nor indeed wondering where to go from here, because you usually know exactly where you are heading. But you do need some mental stimulation just to lift you onto another level of communication. Trust in your ability to turn any dull or static scenario into an operatic performance. And make it clear that adventure, challenge and excitement are what love is all about for you personally.

If you're single, by the 12th you are entertained by a dream-boat who knows that you are a woman of action and passion – but just make sure you're not deceiving yourself about how you feel. With Neptune's illusory influence, infatuation is fine if you're just after a short-term fling. But what you see might not be what you get, so take care, never stop expressing your playful spirit and enjoy the attention.

It pays to sit tight and not get impatient around the Full Moon of the 20th, particularly where one intimate relationship is concerned. With your ruler Jupiter hovering on the cusp of Scorpio aligned to the Sun on the 21st, there's a real sense of change in the air. However much you want things to be resolved, there has to be a bit of give and take. And probably the giving will have to be more from you than anyone else. After the 24th, your ruler Jupiter finally alights in your own sign. You feel buoyant, alive, revitalized, raring to go. And at the end of the month you can have it all, whether socializing with a host of strangers, unusual meetings or simply indulging in wicked flirtations at the workplace. Of course, it takes guts to ask for what you really want. But at last you know that love is in your hands, not in the lap of the gods. So take responsibility for your own happiness, and lead the dance.

Best days for romance: 17th, 24th
Best days to seduce: 25th, 29th
Best stay at home day: 9th

December

You're feeling all lost at sea again on the 1st, but with a Full Moon in your love corner on the 5th, and Mars moving into your own sign on the 6th, you come alive and realize now is the time to restore your courageous, pioneering romantic character to its full glory. With Mercury joining the Sun in your sign on the 8th, the planets are truly shining a light on your ability to make some serious promises for your future. Your ruler Jupiter is still boosting your desire to make life perfect, and while the rest of us make do, you are forging ahead to secure your ideal partner – if you haven't snapped him up already.

But around the 15th, domestic demands and festive pressures stop you from following up a spot of romantic spontaneity. Around the New Moon on the 20th you are feeling feistier than ever and you don't feel like backing down when a lover decides he knows what's best for you both over the Christmas period. But temper your tendency to think you are the only one who has the answer. Sometimes, even you have to compromise, and if he really isn't the man for you, then season of goodwill or not, you will have no other choice but to discuss uncertainties about your romantic plans with friends and family who know you best.

Impatient as you are for perfect romance, remember the cosmos is just giving you time to really think about what you truly want. Is this love affair or relationship just a rush towards the same old ending. Duties, guilt, pangs of boredom and the same old routine? Or is it more that you need love to unfurl in such a way that there is always another route to go down, always something to explore both sexually and mentally? Always a dream to chase and a rainbow to discover? Whether single or attached, attractive strangers appear in your life around the 25th, when Mars gives you a craving for a seductive game you just can't resist. Take those romantic risks, but never doubt your ability to give the best of yourself to the right person. A New Year lover is waiting for a new, revitalised you.

Best days for romance: 6th, 8th
Best days to seduce: 5th, 20th
Best stay at home day: 25th

Your Love
Horoscope
2006

Capricorn

The Goat

December 21 – January 19

Your Love
Horoscope
2006

Love Check

Why you're fabulous
 You never stop believing in yourself.

 Men can't resist your sensual aura.

Why you're impossible
 You can become too controlling in a relationship.

 Holding back your feelings means no one really knows where they stand.

Your love secrets
 Erotic conversations beat partying any day.

 You want the best, and will often wait forever for the right lover.

 Money and love do go together.

Your sexual style

♑ Cool to begin with, passionate beneath the sheets.

Who falls for you

♑ Sensitive, needy types who want to be organized. Self-starters who like the idea of someone as ambitious as they are. Experienced lovers and traditional meat-and-potatoes men.

Who you fall for

♑ The poet, the stranger, hustlers and noncon-formists. Or you go to the other extreme and hunt for a man with something classy or classically smooth about him.

You identify with

♑ Bosses, workaholics and people who are honest about their past. Control, realism and a dry sense of humour.

Your greatest temptation

♑ Having sex in the office.

Your greatest strength

♑ Being self-reliant and never depending on anyone.

Passion Profile for 2006

Amazing, graceful, serene and composed. Who is this? Well, it's simply you this year as you climb into your hammock of self-sufficiency and self-worth. Even though life is proving to be more of a challenge than usual, and love testing you to say the least, in a strange way it's all actually making you more determined to take control of your life. So make it your own and don't let anyone tell you otherwise.

Determination and integrity are your allies through until March, so spend more time on self-dedication and less on worrying about what someone thinks about you. During the summer you glow with charisma, and radiate good feelings all round. Indulge in your sensuality and don't feel guilty about your hedonistic streak. You can be simultaneously mystical and down-to-earth, and all it takes is the right companion. And he's out there waiting for you if you're single. By the autumn, you stir the ingredients of love carefully and the magic begins to take effect.

Best bets for Mr Right this year: Taurus for stunning sex, Scorpio to support your ambitions, Virgo to light your fire.

2006 Month by Month

January

The way you handle your relationships is a bit like your cash flow this month. Friends are dependent on you for advice and you're not sure whether you should be more generous with your time. Likewise, you're saving money, and you feel guilty when you spend it. If you give too much away of yourself, you worry that you are missing out on your own needs. But what about intimate relationships? You know that the most important thing is to be loved and to give love and this month you can be assured of plenty of opportunity for new romance if single, or a deeper closer bond if attached.

A high-spirited friendship intensifies after the 4th, and you'll be ready to let him see the real you by the 13th. Just take care you don't give too much away, since with Venus reversing through your sign until February, keeping secrets won't be easy. But with a Full Moon in Cancer on the 14th, you'll also be at your most stunning. So accept every invite that comes your way and attend every party or event (if it's your own birthday party, make sure you invite all those gorgeous male colleagues). An exciting new encounter gives you a feeling that at last you're waking up with a smile on your face. So take the chance and prove that you're not just pleasing others, you're pleasing yourself too.

With Mercury blazing through your own sign until the 22nd, you'll be at your most witty and wise, so choose your words with care in all conversations regarding your future aims and you'll be sure to get what you want. Romantic offers will come to you in the most magical of ways. You experience exotic encounters in local haunts, and a run of dates with a new admirer in your professional circle puts a wicked smile on your face. This is a month for renewed conviction of your own self-worth.

Best days for romance: 3rd, 11th
Best days to seduce: 19th, 23rd
Best stay at home day: 4th

February

With Venus moving forward again on the 3rd in your own sign, you're urged to strut your stuff and show the world you mean business *and* pleasure. Naturally enough, you are aware of someone's magnetic presence, but although it would be easy for you to merely rationalize the circumstances, this time you're not sure how to take the attraction. It certainly seems to be a two-way thing, and what's wrong with that? Perhaps it's worth remembering to respect your own powerful desires too. Whether single or attached, Venus brings you fresh self-confidence and a wave of easygoing encounters with flirtatious characters.

Deep down you know that a sense of humour is invaluable, and you're beginning to free yourself from the pain of the past and leave it behind with a wry grin on your face. I think that you're in an excellent position now to ask for what you truly want from one admirer or lover, and with an electrifying link between Mercury and Uranus on the 14th, your real sexual needs can be met. Then, on the 17th, you suddenly feel you are back to square one. With Mars's move into the discriminating part of your chart, the feelings you believe to be true and right are being scrutinized by your own inner judge and jury. It's like you're in court facing yourself. Are you guilty of self-deception or are you innocent? And with a run of confusing links to the Moon around the 24th, you begin to wonder if it's worth making the effort to be the sparkling, soft-hearted person someone loved you for. Why is it romance dies, you wonder? And even though you accept the reality of relating, remember that you are still a secret romantic beneath the down-to-earth hard-working soul that everyone assumes you to be. Don't give up on the dream, it's yours to play with right now.

Best days for romance: 16th, 21st
Best days to seduce: 3rd, 17th
Best stay at home day: 10th

March

You feel confident enough to speak up about your more unusual ideas for creating a purposeful partnership on the 5th. But be prepared for someone special to attempt to seduce you into changing your mind, or to get out and free yourself from emotional pressures. With Mercury stalling in your chart until the 25th, you have the time and the objectivity to work out what exactly are your romantic plans for the future. A little exotic holiday in the spring sun might not go amiss, so get on the internet, find the best deal and then surprise a lover or new amour with your initiative. Single, or attached, you need to chill out and get away from the rat race. This month you are full to brimming with brilliant ways to achieve your personal success and make your love life as wicked as you want it to be.

Wicked, did I just say wicked? Yes, I'm afraid I did. The kind of wickedness I'm talking about isn't sinful, and neither is it about vanity or egotism. It is giving way to your true desires. And, perhaps, finally you are coming to terms with the fact that you are an individual in your own right. Don't stop being you just because someone you love hasn't caught onto the fact your autonomy is sacred right now. By the end of the month, Venus and Mars will have blessed you with confidence to put yourself wholly, madly and deeply into the relationship of a lifetime. If he's already part of your life, then don't resist. If you have to break down a few barriers, then maybe it will also free you up to be honest enough to face the truth. And that's one which will take you on a romantic journey towards deeper understanding.

Best days for romance: 2nd, 16th
Best days to seduce: 5th, 24th
Best stay at home day: 17th

April

With Mars moving into your love corner on the 14th, you can and will make your love life the inspirational, yet resourceful experience you truly desire. But don't hold your breath on the 5th (especially if you're single), when a chance remark and a brief flirtation puts a wry smile on your face and you wonder if this could be the start of a brief fling. Saturn's change of direction gives you a feeling someone in power is more than a fine example of trust and loyalty. In fact, he's got more to gain from knowing you than you think, so don't give away any secrets, nor give away your heart too soon. Even you can be tempted by something which you know will never lead to a perfect arrangement.

If you're single, offers of dates start well around the 10th, but niggling feelings of insecurity about rejection return to haunt you. Once bitten, twice shy is a fair enough response, but if you don't take a risk or face your personal doubts and fears, then you're simply not going to meet Mr Right. Around the 20th, the Sun's move into Taurus makes you more philosophical about love and life in general, your aspirations seem more viable, and romance takes over. One male friend confesses he has similar worries about relationships himself, and together you realize this could develop into a long-term rapport, and one that's worth working at.

If you're attached, don't sabotage a good thing around the 26th. Of course you both need space and time alone, and just because he's not 'communicating like he used to do', doesn't mean he's straying. It's simply a bout of misunderstanding rather than incompatibility that makes you both react in a negative way. By the end of the month you will be wondering what all the fuss was about anyway.

Best days for romance: 20th, 28th
Best days to seduce: 1st, 13th
Best stay at home day: 11th

May

Thanks to Mars's dynamic influence in your chart, you just want to crusade on behalf of everyone else. And while you are one of life's success stories, it's likely that if you are single you'll fall for the underdog in your professional world. Mars drives you to introduce him to useful contacts, but make sure that your trust isn't abused when the Full Moon in Scorpio on the 13th sets off intrigues, mischief and deception in the workplace. With Mercury moving into your creative and romantic zone on the 5th, you discover the power you have within you and how you can actually make things happen just the way you want them to when you're feeling instructive and intuitive. You'll be able to communicate to someone special that you want to spend time with them alone. Take the opportunity to also let them know your sexual needs and show that you're irrepressible right now.

The celestial line-up drags sex kicking and screaming into the equation by the 29th, and whether you are still with that wonder man of a few months ago or involved in a delightful spicy relationship with someone new, Venus's move into your romantic corner on the 29th demands that you drop a few of those emotional boundaries to let love in. Honour the fact that it's the only way it can enter, lower the drawbridge and discover how outrageously naughty you can be when aroused by this current man, even if love is not destined to last forever. Live for the moment.

With the planets giving you the voice and confidence to speak your mind, and to ask for what truly turns you on, both physically and emotionally, your man just won't be able to resist you. There's a deeper truth developing between you, so don't fall into the blame game (you know – 'it's *his* fault I'm un-happy', 'it's *my* fault he's lost his job), or start acting out the vic-tim/saviour plot just because you both fear being yourselves.

Best days for romance: 8th, 29th
Best days to seduce: 3rd, 26th
Best stay at home day: 5th

June

A blast from the past surprises you around the 3rd. Yes, he is still attractive, but do you want to dig up old emotions? The problem is that if you feel vulnerable, angry, threatened or tingly in his presence, then you need to resolve why you react that way. Venus's tense link with Saturn reminds you how much you miss certain things about him, but this time don't let him leave without being honest about your feelings.

Relationships never end, and even if two people are no longer together, there is still a mysterious and timeless energy which flows between us. Somehow, you can never break the bond, no matter how long it is before you see that person again, even if they seem to be different. Once back in the spell, the entity of the relationship continues in its own way, and probably was already there before you even met. This might sound weird, but I think it's really important to see that a relationship is not just about your feelings or his feelings, it's actually the creation of an energy or force in its own right. The synchronicity of meeting may be the initial flame, but oddly enough, the sparks and the dormant embers were already there, waiting for the catalyst – the pair of you.

Now that your relationships are going through a period of transformation, this is a sure sign that your confidence is back on track. You have learnt that detaching yourself from intensely emotional situations is not the solution, and that you are missing out on many of the wonderful things love can bring. The New Moon on the 25th ends a period of idealistic notions and sets you towards creating a gentler, more realistic phase in your love life. Plain sailing needs a breeze, just like getting to know someone properly takes time and energy. As the Sun moves on through your love corner, you'll be thinking positively, taking love seriously and pulling out the stops to achieve your heart's desire.

Best days for romance: 3rd, 15th
Best days to seduce: 14th, 25th
Best stay at home day: 9th

July

Casting off the constraints of unstable relationships and moving towards a more satisfying love life becomes tangible around the 4th, as Mercury's U-turn in your chart forces you to look closer at your previous bonds. Whether single or attached, the way you react to current or potential mates is about to change. You are discovering a determination to rid yourself of old habits, pointless behaviour and unsatisfactory partners around the Full Moon in your sign on the 11th. It is time to welcome a fascinating period of self-knowledge and growth. Be prepared to search deeper into the underlying motivations for your attraction to certain people. It will ease emotional tensions and open you a whole new awareness of your true needs.

Tantalizing developments with one special hunk are on the horizon, if you don't allow outdated feelings of insecurity to make you question his intentions. By the 19th, Venus's surge into your relationship corner brings a meeting of minds and bodies and you wonder if you've found your soulmate at last. He's attentive, he's handsome and he's interested in you, but don't imagine he's faultless. Drop unrealistic obsessions with perfection and learn to love him for his minor inadequacies. After all, a totally faultless man would be pretty dull. (You don't want a robot, you want a love god, don't you?) Live for the present, rather than worrying about what will be and what his prospects are. Enjoy the influence of the sexy New Moon in Leo on the 25th, which allows you to be totally comfortable with your body and yourself. And that's the very self which will create the sparks of love you've desired all along.

Best days for romance: 4th, 19th
Best days to seduce: 11th, 27th
Best stay at home day: 21st

August

With Mercury and Venus bounding into the sexiest part of your chart on the 11th and 12th respectively, your mind is working overtime and you are being drawn into a romantic situation which is beyond your control. For that matter, it could also be beyond your rational understanding. Don't spin those mental wheels too hard or fast, as it won't bring you any closer to happiness. Instead, use this energy to meet new people and engage in a variety of social activities. With the help of Venus, you'll discover you have the voice to verbalize your needs, dreams and fantasies. Emotionally and sexually, this could be the breakthrough you are looking for.

After the 19th, just take care you don't get carried away in the thrill of it all. Hold on to your current belief that there has to be more than just pleasure for the sake of pleasure in a relationship, and make the most of an incredible opportunity to gain insight into your deepest emotional needs. Find a way to accept what is happening, rather than fighting it, and with the adventurous New Moon in Virgo on the 23rd, use your imagination to enrich your real world. There's an electrifying buzz within you right now that isn't going to be gratified by the usual means. But around the 26th, you rediscover emotional equilibrium, and like a calm after the storm you desire everything to be perfect for the one you love. With Venus's enriching link to your ruler Saturn on the 27th, all will be forgiven and a night of heightened passion makes those temporary moments of emotional uncertainty worthwhile. It takes a little upheaval in life to help us relish the gifts we already possess, like that of unconditional adoration. Not everyone's so fortunate as you, so enjoy.

Best days for romance: 17th, 31st
Best days to seduce: 7th, 23rd
Best stay at home day: 29th

September

Remember, whatever experiences come your way are simply there to help you develop your full potential as a poised Capricorn who inevitably becomes an authority on love's difficult ways. Take the chance to make your relationships more how you want them to be, and even if you think you sound needy, it is far better to be honest than to sweep feelings under the carpet and expect them to go away. They won't.

Sensuous nights of mutual passion replace evenings of feeling that you are merely the best cleaner in town after the

6th, as Venus moves into your adventurous zone. And the lunar eclipse on the 7th in escapist Pisces makes your current lover totally up for a romantic adventure. You, on the other hand, start worrying about the money, who's going to feed the cat, dare you delegate your important work deadlines to anyone? For once, just drop the anxiety and enjoy the unpredictable. After all, some fabulous changes in your love life are due you right now, and this is one of those months to make them happen your way. Dump your doubts and fears and be liberated while the doors to emotional happiness are wide open for you and your man.

If you are single, there is always a feeling that if you let slip the knowledge that you have deep insecurities and a lot more self-doubt than anyone imagines, you'll be left stranded or abandoned at the starting post of any new romance. Any offers of dates are scary mid-month, simply because you are unsure if you can maintain your poise and self-confidence while you go through one of your insecure moments. But by the 26th an older, wiser male colleague gives you some much needed advice and praise over lunch. Your professional image is polished again, and with it your seduction tactics are finely honed. You're back on track for romantic success.

Best days for romance: 13th, 28th
Best days to seduce: 1st, 15th
Best stay at home day: 30th

October

Someone you have been getting close to is only just discovering what a true romantic you are. And you go from the sublime to the ridiculous and things couldn't be better where romance is concerned. He'll adore your intimate text messages, sensual e-mails and sexy postcards sent on a whim because you're in love and you want to tell the world. But most of all you want to make your partner feel more loved than he ever has before. The planets make it feel so good, that you know it is right. And with a positive approach, you think seriously about changing your way of life. This is your chance to devote more time to loved ones, rather than be overloaded with material matters and domestic responsibilities.

Saturn in your intimacy corner encourages you to spend more time making yourself beautiful for your man, sprucing, preening and pampering yourself, so that his desire for you is a mix of sensual memories which he takes with him wherever he goes. It is not always easy for you to let anyone know the private side of yourself, but however much of a loner you are, remember that no man or woman is an island. To be truly happy you need to enjoy life's smallest pleasures with someone you love. On the 25th, Venus's influence helps you to share one of the most important pleasures, your love of good timing. If you can express words of love, wisdom and laughter with your partner at the right moment, you know that you are onto a winning formula. Don't close up. Be sure to open up both physically and verbally, let him know how deeply you feel, and the intimacy you create will shock you in its levels of passionate intensity.

If you are single, enthusiasm for adventure or a brilliant new work scheme gives you oodles of opportunities to meet new friends this month. Their positive reaction inspires you to forge ahead and make firm plans. By opening yourself up to fresh experiences you attract a string of new admirers and tempting offers. Take up the man who is most in tune with your mindset and enjoy a run of sensuous nights after the 25th. Remember, you are strong, bright and irresistible, you know where you are going and self-doubt has no place in your life. Dump it and shine.

Best days for romance: 2nd, 18th
Best days to seduce: 11th, 26th
Best stay at home day: 10th

November

You go through degrees of feeling like you're being pushed and pulled between current reality and a deep-seated desire for a different way of life. This month as Mercury moves backwards until the 18th, these contradictions are stronger than ever, making you wonder if what you have is what you want and what you want is what you need. To cap it all, Mars is demanding you make a serious commitment before the 16th, and it feels like you are no longer in control of your destiny. Momentary lapses of loneliness around the 11th back up your need for a partner who understands you. And you might have to consider that even if it means forsaking a little independence, the rewards will be far greater than the cost. With a fabulous Full Moon in down-to-earth Taurus on the 5th giving you the motivation to get the best out of life and make your home nigh-on perfect, it's a great month for enterprising change. Once you accept what kind of lifestyle you truly want, your place will soon be silk-sheeted and ready for seduction.

As Venus moves into impulsive Sagittarius on the 17th, your love life is full of surprises and you are the one pulling the rabbits from the hat. Whether you suddenly indulge your partner's fantasies, or allow him to leave his toothbrush in your mug, it is a serious step for you and the beginning of a breakdown of all those difficult barriers. As Jupiter moves into Sagittarius on the 24th, your closest relationships will never be the same again. This is the most sensitive part of your chart, where you begin not only to understand what love really means for you, but also show someone special what you mean to them. And all that means one other thing – love will start to be exactly what you want it to be, not just in your head, but in the whole, fabulously physical, three-dimensional real world.

Best days for romance: 14th, 27th
Best days to seduce: 5th, 11th
Best stay at home day: 20th

December

This is your time of year. You know the winter solstice brings you back full circle to your birthday time, and the chance to start afresh if need be. It's not the calendar year ending that is important, merely the Sun's move into your sign on the 22nd, which reflects the changing light, the rebirth of nature's cycles and the beginning of your solar year. Make the most of this wonderful influence in your own sign to shimmer, seduce, indulge and pump up the passion rather than plumping up cushions for your festive friends. Think of yourself this festive season – with Venus moving into your own sign on the 11th, you really have no choice but to enjoy the company of male admirers if you're single, or live it up a little in the social whirl if attached.

Yet with Saturn your ruler turning backwards in your chart again on the 6th, you realize that it is time to be sensible, honest and pragmatic about your love life. If you want to make any long-term commitment, it is probably better to put it off until the New Year when Saturn moves forward again, but if you want to remind him that you are a force to be reckoned with, the power behind his throne, or simply the reliable lover or partner who will always be there for him, this is the month to do so.

This month you feel a sense of awakening, as if someone says a key word which triggers a whole change of attitude to yourself and your future. Watch out, though, that you don't make any hasty decisions around the 18th, concerning your most personal of feelings. That very special person seems to be acting negatively towards your future ideals, but it is simply because he is confused about your feelings towards him.

By the end of the year, you have sorted it out between you, and on New Year's Eve the sense of a deeper and long-lasting bond seems not too very far away. If single, you cruise into the New Year, knowing at last your independent spirit is being noticed by someone who respects your self-sufficient lifestyle as much as you respect his. A love merger is on its way.

Best days for romance: 11th, 22nd
Best days to seduce: 23rd, 31st
Best stay at home day: 30th

Your Love
Horoscope
2006

Aquarius
The Water-bearer

January 20 – February 18

Love Check

Why you're fabulous

 When you dedicate yourself to a cause, you'll never give up the campaign.

 You believe in independence and don't resent your man his freedom.

 Because you're a sexual maverick men drool after you.

Why you're impossible

 You ask for things you want in a very roundabout way.

 You often make irritatingly radical statements just to wind him up.

Your love secrets

 Beneath that cool intellect is a very romantic soul.

 You can feel jealous, even though you always deny it.

 You ask for sex in the most outrageously public places, just to shock him and everyone else.

Your sexual style

🔯 Cool, experimental and different for the sake of
being different.

Who falls for you

🔯 Conventional business tycoons, rugged
backpacking types who want you to go on safari
with them. Conformists who see everything in
life as a personal battle or victory.

Who you fall for

🔯 Rogue mavericks, men who think about the
universe more than themselves. Freedom-lovers
with witty brains, and glamorous, successful
entrepreneurs.

You identify with

🔯 Freedom, cosmopolitan friends, men who aren't
interested in commitment, humanitarian types
who save whales, but surf waves in their free time.

Your greatest temptation

🔯 Telling him you have all the answers when he
hasn't any questions.

Your greatest strength

🔯 Knowing that universal love does make the
world go round.

Passion Profile for 2006

Vivacity is one of your more magnetic qualities, and this year everyone wants a share in it. Particularly those platonic male friends who have an interest in your happiness. But one of them isn't quite as innocent as they seem on the surface, and unless you are up for a secret liaison, or a risky date, you might have to make it clear where your true loyalties lie. By the spring, Mars boosts your sexual energy levels, so if there is more to be had from your man, or from a new face in the crowd, this is your chance to take it. Be wonderfully generous with your other talents too, but keep a little back for one special person this summer. Saturn continues to gives you further glimpses of what's really behind one dreamy liaison throughout the autumn. But are you discovering that you might be hoping for something that can never exist? At the end of the year, you realize where your limitations lie, and get on with a real relationship rather than craving an impossible dream.

Best bets for Mr Right this year: Aries for thrills and spills, Libra for a great social life, Sagittarius for giving you the freedom to be you.

2006 Month by Month

January

For a long time you've been waiting for ideas to unfurl and romantic feelings to grow, and it's all getting very exciting. So do exactly what it is that pleases you from day one of this sparkling New Year. Yes, you can make those ambitious plans succeed, and you can cultivate relationships to work for you. In fact, you have all the necessary tools to hand. And, more importantly, the talent to craft yourself a marvellous future.

Being tied down to dates and pinned down to promises is something you would rather avoid, even with close friends or partners. And motivated by sheer obstinacy, you prefer not to let others know what you are up to but, of course, this can cause a great deal of suspicion and jealousy. It is times like these when your apparent outgoing and friendly nature can actually be your worst enemy.

During the first half of the month you are unreliable but everyone's best friend; if attached, your man can't quite work out why you prefer the company of your male colleagues over and above him. If single, you make the odd promise of a date then cool off just before with excuses about how 'tied up' you are right now. But with the Sun moving into your own sign on the 20th, followed by Mercury on the 22nd, the end of the month sees you in a far more positive mood about romance, and you begin to enjoy the unpredictable flow of energy that you express so naturally.

If single, be gregarious and charming at a work meeting around the 17th, and a sexy associate's mistake gives you an opportunity to pitch your best ideas. An unexpected, light-hearted chat a few days later in the office kitchen or corridor turns into something more bewitching, and your romantic prospects are looking great. But with sober Saturn still lumbering backwards through your relationship zone, it feels that just as you're about to take one step forward, you take two very large steps back instead. Don't worry, you're just going through a period of adjustment and preparation for the amazing sexual and romantic activity that is to come.

Best days for romance: 22nd, 29th
Best days to seduce: 3rd, 20th
Best day to stay at home: 1st

February

You are in the mood to dress glamorously and act outrageously, and you're so busy accepting party invitations that you have trouble giving those closest to you your undivided attention. Everything is exacerbated around the 6th, when stroppy Saturn's influence gives you those 'I should be spending more time with my nearest and dearest' guilt trips. However, don't let domesticity stop you from enjoying the social whirl around Valentine's Day; you've worked hard and deserve to play a little, but share out your time across all your relationships. If you're attached, spend quality evenings with your lover, rather than just bumping into each other on the way home. Doing things together, like making holiday plans, decorating the kitchen (while still gazing into each other's eyes) is the best path to sexy happiness, and you need that too.

Around the 11th, someone from your past you'd prefer kept secret ripples life's perfect waters by pitching up. Is it because he makes you question where your heart really lies that you are nervous? The excitement of a clandestine meeting gives you a high and you wonder if domestic bliss is all it's cracked up to be. But remember, eventually everything becomes routine. Your need for equilibrium is one thing, and you do love the occasional rollercoaster ride, but you'd hate a permanent rollercoaster lifestyle because it would simply prove to be just as routine as everything else.

By the 13th, the Full Moon in your opposite sign increases your need for security and the hearth rug beckons. You know what you want and by the New Moon in mystical Pisces on the 28th your man is sharing your romantic vision and he wants it too. What could be better than two people sharing the same dream – perhaps two people sharing it across a romantic dinner in your favourite haunt?

Best days for romance: 17th, 28th
Best days to seduce: 6th, 19th
Best stay at home day: 11th

March

Usually, at this time of year, you are determined to make a few more resolutions about finding perfect harmony. But, frustratingly, with Mercury backtracking through your chart until the 25th, it's hard to get the kind of easy response you're hoping for. Between me and you, if you really want to create balance, if you really want someone to blend, merge and honour your needs, you'll just have to accept that harmony isn't about perfection. It is about knowing that we all have flaws, irritating habits and Achilles heels. This month, remember that love is about acceptance and tolerance of those niggling faults that we often hide in the early stages of romance, and that then loom large later on.

With a sensuous link between the Sun and Uranus, your ruler, on the 1st, you'll either be swayed by beauty or seduced by an enigmatic stranger. A face in the crowd, a glorious voice on the phone – whatever the attraction – it could lead you into tricky waters. And whether single or attached, it is the lure of romance itself that is the actual temptation, rather than the real person behind the facade.

Around the 15th, the links between unpredictable Uranus and the Moon trigger off either a wild affair, a change of heart or an electrifying night of sexual bliss with your lover. And it's in those moments of surprise events that you'll find the most pleasure. Watch out you don't try to tip the scales in your favour on the 25th, when Venus and Mars jostle for power to trigger off complicated conversations. It will only leave you with a feeling that you don't know where you stand. By the 29th, you and your man are more objective, detached and civilized. It is time to sort out who's doing what to who, and what games you are really playing. With a powerful solar eclipse on the 29th in uptight Aries, there's a growing realization that the more you talk about the practicalities involved concerning each other's long-term goals, the more likely you can get down to the business of commitment and true love.

Best days for romance: 5th, 7th
Best days to seduce: 21st, 22nd
Best stay at home day: 17th

April

Why do other people think you are nervous and restless? Is it because they don't realize how difficult it is to be you? After all, you have both a genius at communication, progressive ideas and vision, and yet have a profound understanding of human nature. With Mars surging through your love corner, you can break the rules, be groundbreaking and breathless in your creative ideas, and also play the love game any way that suits you. In fact, you've had too much work and no play recently, and it's time to reinforce and balance all your energy levels (and that includes sexual ones too). The restless romantic in you needs expression, and it's time to get yourself into sexier action. Okay, you know you hate sitting around tapping your fingers or playing solitaire – you'd rather be out and about – so plan a jaunt to the countryside with your lover around the 5th, or play strip poker. Saturn moves forward again in your relationship corner and you feel like taking life less seriously. If you are single, a run of dates, flurries of intriguing encounters and a host of anticipatory admirers are likely to bring your world to life again.

With Venus sidling up to your ruler Uranus on the 18th, you feel positive about your romantic escapades, whether single or attached. After all, you're now going to be the centre of attention and grace someone with your electrifying presence, aren't you? So cast all doubts aside and enjoy a whirl of sexy flirtatious activity for the rest of the month.

Best days for romance: 13th, 25th
Best days to seduce: 4th, 10th
Best stay at home day: 28th

May

Reassure your man you're still there for him around the 8th. The powerful link between Venus and Saturn is making you very self-absorbed. And he might just start imagining that you're only interested in gazing at your own reflection in the mirror rather than into his eyes. Of course, he probably won't make a fuss because he's sensible enough to know it could cause a silly wrangle, but better to avoid provoking him. Novelty is everything around the 10th, so go on a romantic picnic. And Mercury's move into playful Gemini on the 19th brings out your fun-loving side, ready for a romantic but wicked sexual rapport.

Jupiter's long-term effects on your ruler Uranus are still giving you pause for thought. Are you just putting off making a commitment because it is easier than taking responsibility for your actions? Of course, letting your man make all the choices is very noble, but if you take the path of least resistance, you might just end up in mental knots. Some things are certainly better left unsaid around the 20th, but by remaining secretive you might be accused of all kinds of things which aren't true. This is your chance to make every effort to be honest and less evasive. Although it might feel like you are baring too much of your soul, in fact it could provide you with a delightful response of the kind you need to move on and invest in your emotional needs.

If you're single, around the 24th someone's interest seems very restrained, but don't think it's because they're not on your wavelength. In fact, they're probably far more enthusiastic beneath the surface than they make out. Could it be that your ambivalence is actually more challenging than they would like? For once, assert your needs, charm him with your grace, beauty and languid sensuality, and you never know – this could be one man who could unleash you from those self-imposed chains of self-doubt.

Best days for romance: 8th, 26th
Best days to seduce: 10th, 17th
Best stay at home day: 5th

June

Love, of course, does make the world go round, and you know that as an Aquarian you are everybody's friend, particularly when they love to have you around. The less neglected you are the more able you are to share yourself, even though, for all your charming cranky humour, sometimes you seem distant. Your wit and wild pranks and gags make you the centre of your social circle. You often lead close partners into situations and outrageous fun before they even know it. This month looks set to be one of those manic, fun-packed months. Romance is in the air thanks to Mars swooping into your relationship corner on the 3rd, although it could trigger off sexier, confrontational relating if you're already attached. You are ready to get out and about, and, with the Sun in romantic but cheeky Gemini until the 21st, there's a definite feel of summer fun, and new love could creep up on you before you know it.

Taking your time to form intimate relationships can be a hazard, because you miss out on the chemistry flowing and the adrenaline pumping. It's great to want friendship first, deeper sexual love second, but this month you've just got to go out there and play the seductive game. The more original or different the object of your desire, the more he'll sustain your interest. And one comes out of the blue on the 18th, if you're single – older, wiser, intellectually bright, but living a very different lifestyle from the one you do.

If attached, the 18th marks a turning point. With Mars and Saturn's push-pull collusion, you really can't be sure of anything. Feelings are distorted, you want to commit to something, but you fear you'll lose your freedom. You long to remain unpredictable and contrary, yet a voice in your head keeps saying, 'there's no room for anarchy in intimate relationships', and the other bit of you rebels and says 'yes there is, that's what makes love so complicated, endlessly mysterious and downright provocative.' These feelings and thoughts continue right through until the end of the month, so don't make any decisions just yet. Go with the flow, and the power of love will go with you.

Best days for romance: 11th, 24th
Best days to seduce: 1st, 18th
Best stay at home day: 29th

July

You're still feeling the exciting effects of Mars in your rela-tionship zone till the 22nd, reaping romantic rewards and awakening a sudden attraction. It's like looking in a mirror as encounters with others enable you to see the bits of yourself you might not normally notice. Even if trust and communication have been a problem in the past, with

Mercury's influence you are now discovering new ways of being open and honest about what you want from your current partner or a prospective lover. For once, don't be afraid of wearing your heart on your sleeve, or at least of baring a little more of your soul than you have in the past. The Sun is urging you to try harder and being the brilliant strategist you are, you know exactly how to play your cards to capture or enflame the heart of that special someone.

From the 5th, the dazzling combination of Mars and Neptune has that handsome hunk gazing into your eyes and hanging on your every word. But love is never totally glitch-free, and around the 14th a few heavy-handed comments could create waves in your millpond romance. You can try to fight the incoming waves or you can roll with them. Either way, a few unexpected ripples are nature's way of stirring things up to make you appreciate the calm. Handily, they also create a great excuse for blissful moments of making-up. After the 22nd, the scintillating summer Sun highlights your love corner, and you can charm the birds from the trees. Events are unfolding in ways that can totally transform your life. So if there is anything you want, ask now. The New Moon on the 25th in fiery Leo will bring your heart's desire. So, if you're single, watch out for someone who spends time listening to your every word because they want to understand your way of thinking.

Best days for romance: 14th, 26th
Best days to seduce: 2nd, 7th
Best stay at home day: 20th

August

Single, or attached, you are in the mood to enjoy some amusing escapades or romantic encounters. With Mercury and Venus moving into fiery Leo on the 11th and 12th respectively, you are at your most flirtatious and willing to go out and shock a few of your favourite men into dating, hating or loving you. The Full Moon in your own sign on the 9th reminds you also that this is one month where you're going to have to make a choice between independence and a loving bond. By the way, the latter doesn't necessarily generate *dependency*. (Yes, I know you hate that word!) You'll also feel like making firm decisions about your personal needs and confirming your feelings to a lover or friend. A wonderful sense of being special and adored will put you into one of your most extrovert moods, so make sure you are out and about and expressing your altruistic nature. Fill up your diary, book those exotic holidays, go for those long lunches with colleagues, and feel truly in harmony with the summer sun.

With powerful links between Venus, Neptune and Saturn at the end of the month, if you are attached you are suddenly unsure if you are a romantic escapist or seriously up for a long-term commitment. He may be prevaricating or quaking in his boots, but either way you have to communicate what you truly want in the here and now. Perhaps just more honesty, perhaps more space, a new lap-top or a houseboat to live on – who knows? But focus on what is right for you and you alone. If he can understand that you are a slightly eccentric, fun-loving, unpredictable and original woman who is loved because she is exactly that, then it's time he stopped trying to change you into something else. If you are doing the Aquarian noble thing of believing all is fair in love and therefore his needs are just as important, so therefore you can't tip the balance or it's not *equal*, then think again.

If you are single, a chance encounter around the 27th turns into something more tangible – a real live person, flesh and bones, with eyes that twinkle like the stars – and he's determined to show you that he's not just interested in physical pleasure, he's also one of the most humorous intelligent rogues around. So get out the seduction claws fast. Or a sneaky colleague might get hers into him first.

Best days for romance: 12th, 27th
Best days to seduce: 21st, 25th
Best stay at home day: 3rd

September

Cherish the words of an old pal around the 6th, and remember that even if you live in different worlds now, there is still something mysterious which keeps you in touch. There's no point in trying to rationalize what that 'unknown factor' might be, it's just another reality. Understand that friendship this month is based on your ability to keep people amused because you hate to see them bored or suffering from love or work problems. If you are not out and about chatting, making new contacts and joining in the last of the summer spirit, then this is your chance to get cracking. Be joyful for yourself – as you will be for everyone else.

If you want to know who is doing what to whom and why, or whether you're missing out on some kind of fun, then you have to be a bit of a prankster, seductress and wit all rolled into one. Well, this month no one can stop you from indulging in all kinds of social antics and amusing entertainment. You're on the ball, ready to bluff, amuse and persuade a lover or new dreamboat that love is truly in the air.

Mars moves into indecisive Libra on the 8th, and triggers off a few days of confusion. You have to look within, without and all around you to see where you are really heading. If attached, are you truly living the kind of lifestyle you want, or have you made too many concessions? Do you compromise for the sake of argument, and then seethe beneath the duvet wishing him far away? If single, did you really want to split up with an ex because he played too many games, or was it simply that you wanted more than he could give you? Flamboyant, fabulous and feisty though you are, don't deny the deeper motivations and undercurrents of your feelings. With quizzical Mercury moving into your adventurous corner on the 12th, you become focused, and aware of the fact it's time to put your foot down. Gently, of course. And if you have a really gut instinct about changing your lifestyle, then go with it. Motivated and dynamic, just take care on the 19th, when a loved one wants more of your time than you can afford to give. Don't fall into the trap of boosting their ego at the expense of your own.

Best days for romance: 8th, 12th
Best days to seduce: 5th, 30th
Best stay at home day: 25th

October

Love becomes an even deeper passion this month, as Venus proves that absence makes the loins, as well as the heart, grow fonder. Only a fool would think that the romance fever can last forever, but it's good while you have it and it's reminding you what matters most in life – LOVE – a four-letter word which makes it all seem worthwhile. While romantic dreams merge into reality and you're feeling all floaty and rose-tinted around the 16th, you still can't avoid the drag of Saturn: keeping your feet firmly on the ground and your mind on business. One minute your head is filled with thoughts of your last smoochy hours together and the next you're on the phone to your work contacts. This is a month where you'll have to practise your feminine, airy multi-tasking skills to a greater degree than ever before. But, luckily, it's what you do best, and with Mercury at the highest point of your chart until the 28th, you're eminently capable of whispering sweet nothings into one phone and negotiating a property deal on the other.

Family dilemmas throw a temporary spanner in the works around the 16th and you could find yourself taking your frustration out on those you love most of all. Don't be afraid to say you're sorry. So much can be gained from such a small word, and so much lost without it. It costs very little, and that kind of unconditional love will show a strength even greater than pride. The rewards of mutual understanding are so much better than you imagined possible.

At the end of the month, Neptune's change of direction in your own sign releases all those pent-up grudges and resentments, and the soft words of a lover or new amour put you into a time-warp of love's mysterious ways. There's a sparkle in your eye, a glimmer of something unfathomable in his. The magic you are looking for is about to be cast by your mutual conjuring trick.

Best days for romance: 22nd, 23rd
Best days to seduce: 3rd, 18th
Best stay at home day: 11th

November

The love planet, Venus glides on through your professional zone until the 17th, and it's there, down the corridors of power, in the lunch-time meetings, or by the coffee machine that you'll meet the kind of man who puts the T back into temptation. With a host of planets moving into idealistic Sagittarius this month, your more anarchistic views on love and life are put to the test – and most of all your liking for rebels, dissidents and non-conformists. Around the 10th, you have to choose between a tried and trusted friendship, and the lure of an eccentric stranger whose alternative lifestyle seems appealing. He may not be socially or professionally accepted by the status quo, he may be outrageous, foolish and enviable, but you know that whether he's just another friend, or a lover, you must get to know him better. A partnership is not always your only aim in life, and love is often simply part of friendship. This month, with the number of social contacts increasing by the day, you can't do any better than to enjoy a far-reaching and mind expanding relationship with this very special somebody.

If attached, your fascination for a new goal, vision or marketing ploy is taking up a lot of your time. In fact, the professional world seems to be far more enticing than the romantic one. Your partner or friend shrugs his shoulders, buries his nose in the computer and pretends that all's right with the world. But if you look closer, take a few minutes to see what's happening between you, then you might glimpse a widening gap of mutual interest. Take some time out together around the 20th to be together, talk of your motivations, desires and goals, express your thoughts, tell each other about your day, otherwise either of you could be in danger of falling in love with someone new. With Uranus moving forward again in Pisces on the 20th, this is your chance to make amends or break loose.

Best days for romance: 5th, 19th
Best days to seduce: 10th, 24th
Best stay at home day: 4th

December

The constant demands and requests for your attention haven't got much chance of being fulfilled, with so many people wanting a piece of you after the 5th. But with Mercury's influence, your ability to deal with them is impressive, and Mars's presence boosts your popularity rating even more. Much as you hate to deny anyone the pleasure of your wisdom, this is a period when a clear head and the eyes of a hawk are called for, so learn to manage your time carefully. If you really can't, at least learn to leave a party before everyone else has gone home. That way, you'll be level-headed enough to deal astutely with the puzzle that Venus's link with Jupiter throws at you on the 20th.

If you're single, you know it's time to grab your favourite friend – male or female – and set off to foreign climes. Book that impromptu package deal or exotic jaunt for mid-month, or simply the lusting eyes of beautiful men will be turned in your direction wherever you go. Whether single, or attached, sparkle that fabulous smile around you, and always look like the naturally feminine woman that you are. Irresistible romantic adventures beckon after the 25th. And with the growing realization that knitting circles and web-site forums aren't exactly generating the kind of interaction you really crave, you consider joining in with a more creative group of people. Oh – just make sure the ratio of male to female is at least ten to one. With Mars surging on through adventurous Sagittarius you have a stunning opportunity for an experiential awareness of love's deeper magic. Don't hesitate, leap in.

Flirtatious friends and tantalizing strangers bring you closer to a sense of what love really means for you over the festive period, and you are determined to socialize and enjoy the company of every admirer. Now, there might be resistance from your partner if you are attached, but you are more likely to induce in him a feeling that if he can't beat you, then he'll join you. By New Year's Eve, you'll be playing the kind of mind games that bring out the best in you both. In a way, it is a kind of healthy competition to see who can out-flirt the other into the new year. Why not? At least you know he is as confident about your love for him as you are about his.

Best days for romance: 21st, 26th
Best days to seduce: 6th, 19th
Best stay at home day: 30th

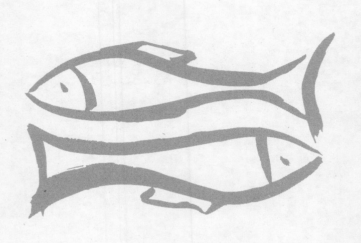

Your Love
Horoscope
2006

Pisces

The Fish

February 19 – March 20

Love Check

Why you're fabulous

 Sensitive and imaginative, you are the goddess of romance.

 You always care about your true friends.

 You rarely argue and are always the peacemaker.

Why you're impossible

 Rather than face reality, you prefer to live in a dream world.

 You often play the blame game to defend your vulnerable side.

Your love secrets

 You need someone to understand your changeable nature.

 You're often confused about your role in a relationship.

 A sensitive compassionate lover makes you feel truly adored.

262

Your sexual style
Hypnotic, dreamy and always seductive.

Who falls for you
Visionary dreamers and addictive personality types who want you to save them. Refined, rational intellectuals, who are hooked by your romantic personality.

Who you fall for
Physically beautiful men, perfectionists, priests, gurus and musicians, loners who want to be rescued and mystery men who won't tell you anything about their life.

You identify with
Mystics, actors and martyrs. Healing, theatre, films and the imagination.

Your greatest temptation
Drifting off in a dream world rather than facing the reality of phoning him.

Your greatest strength
Coming to the rescue when he's got problems.

Passion Profile for 2006

Define yourself this year. Highlight your virtues, circle your weaknesses, but be sure you know what it is that turns you on, off or indifferent in romance and sex. Draw an outline of who you are and where you are going rather than drift with any old tide. It's time to indulge in your true needs, rather than become prey to those who are love's parasites. There are those who do not understand the magic of love's mysterious way, yet you do. So early in the year show one special person that you have definition, that you are distinct, not a thumbnail sketch, but a three-dimensional living work of art – both warm, mutable and giving, but also self-contained and self-motivated. With an army of planets moving through your sign in the spring, followed by feisty Mars in your romantic zone from April through to June, you will be loved, and there is no one to stop you from loving someone back. All it takes is to see the difference between falling into a slap-happy co-dependent affair, and one enriched with individual respect, tolerance and harmony. The affinity you feel towards someone continues into the summer, as passion becomes as addictive as chocolate. There may be bittersweet days around the eclipse of the Moon in early September, but with Venus and Mars linking up late October in erotic Scorpio, you're on the road to a deeper connection with someone. The only litter on the wayside is all that emotional baggage you've carried for far too long.

Best bets for Mr Right this year: Leo for romance and large wallets, Cancer for understanding your elusive nature, Scorpio for enticing power-play.

2006 Month by Month

January

Your compassion is heartfelt, but early in January your magnanimity is being usurped by those who rely on you too much, so it's time to get out and about. The romantic Full Moon on the 14th in caring Cancer wakes up your emotional resources, so, if you are single, don't hesitate to scoop up a lucrative offer which comes your way. A change to your personal outlook on life will bring a change within, but don't let it alter your fundamental nature. With Jupiter pressing on through erotic Scorpio all month, you begin to work out how to cut free from a relationship which is too demanding. But, on the 18th, don't drop your guard and lose your self-respect in a moment of sudden desire for someone you know you can't ever be with in the long term.

You are not normally aggressive or pushy about the things you want in love, but, if you are attached, you are about to be rewarded. The evocative link between Venus and Mars on the 22nd brings romantic offerings, a flurry of sexual amusements and a sense of light relief. Whatever has been inflicted on you in the past is no longer valid, and you find your emotions gathering strength at last for a renewed sense of mutual happiness. If you are single, you take on a new lease of life, and you launch into a sizzling run of new admirers. With your idealism on a high, this month you deserve all the love and attention you can get. It feels that you are gradually finding out that however much you try to be something you're not, it's actually your own unique individuality that is attracting the right kind of attention. In truth, you are preparing yourself for the big changes that are coming your way this year. Remember what I said about defining yourself? This is the first step on the pathway. A clear-cut you, rather than a misty image of what you long to be.

Best days for romance: 13th, 25th
Best days to seduce: 1st, 19th
Best stay at home day: 24th

February

With Mercury entering your sign on the 9th and supplying the energy to fuel you into action, you are determined that one special person will sit back and take note of your presence. By the 10th, you're on a quest to make your mark. And whether you are up for a slow seduction, or ready to e-mail or text a sexy response, you're going to make an unforgettable impact. With a cheeky link between Mercury and Uranus in your own sign on Valentine's Day, get ready for the kind of magical evening you love best. In fact, you're making a deeper impression on someone than you imagine, and around the 18th when the Sun also surges into your sign, whispering explicit turn-ons will be music in his ears as well as your own! Just take care you don't commit yourself to plans, dates and travel without really thinking through your own duties and responsibilities. Work is demanding, and family equally so, yet you're raring to get away from the rat race and indulge in the most exotic escapism. But Mercury's mischievous influence scrambles the lines of communication on the 23rd, and you wonder if you were simply dreaming of what could be when commitments and work demands put you back in the land of reality with a bump. Yet the dreamy quality of the life you yearn for returns to haunt you and leads to extrovert thrills on the 25th. With a heavy weight of duty off your shoulders, your moods change to light-hearted fun and a dazzling social life – with or without that handsome rogue.

Revealing too much of yourself feels like overexposure at the end of the month, and you resort to extreme 'give nothing away' behaviour around the 29th, when Mercury's tension with Pluto puts the cat among the pigeons. If you're single, the fun begins, the wheel is turning and you are jumping on the bandwagon of love's wicked ways. If attached, you realize that your special person is human too. Don't play too many unreliable games, face the truth about what you have and take each day as it comes – just don't give too much of yourself. Your individuality is at stake right now. With Uranus bringing a much needed boost to your mental energy levels at the end of the month, you can see more clearly how you want to be loved, rather than how you are led astray by other people's personal desires.

Best days for romance: 14th, 23rd
Best days to seduce: 17th, 28th
Best stay at home day: 1st

March

Mercury's backtracking through your own sign until the 25th makes you feel less inclined to socialize. You want to drift away into some fantasy world, or escape for a while into a good book. Because you swing from mood to mood so easily this month, partners or lovers might find it hard to keep up with you, or difficult to understand your innermost needs. This misunderstanding is most likely to happen around the 9th, and again on the 12th. There may be the odd upset, battle of wills or simply a pillow fight ending in a sexual embrace. But with a Full Moon in your relationship corner on the 14th, you begin to make your needs understood, and you're at your most sensitive. So make sure that whatever it is you want to say or do is really coming from your heart and not just what you think someone wants to hear.

By the 20th, you begin to come out of that escapist world. So, if you're single, make the most of your seductive skills to woo the perfect partner. He's out and about in your social scene, and on the 25th, when Mercury moves forward again in your own sign, you begin to feel those wonderful tingly feelings every time you are close to him. Wait for those text messages; they're coming your way by the 27th.

But whether single or attached, you are feeling charismatic and spring is almost in the air – if not in your step. Just take care on the 29th. The powerful solar eclipse in fiery Aries creates delusions about what you really want. One minute you know deep down you need commitment and emotional security, the next you just want to be free-ranging and brazen. Your mood creates a sizzling tension between you and your new friend, lover or partner. Make use of this eclipse energy to make an important decision which will create both an important closure and a new beginning. It's not simply about dumping one man for another, but more about the way you can now create the magic you yearn for with someone. Drop the old methods that don't work and welcome the chance to adapt while maintaining your individuality.

Best days for romance: 5th, 19th
Best days to seduce: 7th, 26th
Best stay at home day: 11th

April

This is a month filled with seduction, fun and, most of all, a whole new romantic inspiration between you and a lover. With Venus finally alighting in your own sign on the 6th, you are the goddess of love personified. But take care on the 7th – you also have a sudden craving to communicate all kinds of fascinating and juicy gossip, and friends and their romantic problems take up most of your time when you could be out there enjoying yourself in the arms of a desirable admirer. Look around you, drop the strategy-planning for every pal, and think of number one.

With Mars also boosting your self-esteem after the 14th, whatever romantic success you are hoping for, remember when you are at your most enigmatic you can also be acutely shrewd. Take advantage of an affectionate male friend on the 18th, when Venus colludes with experimental Uranus. He could seem as if he is just being ultra-flirtatious, but he could be an important contact for your long-term ambitions too. Don't give anything away, be at your most insightful and instinctive, and keep an eye on his moves. This is one you don't want to get away. Either he'll help you to achieve more in your work, or he could have a lust factor to die for. Remember, all that emotional baggage is a thing of the past. You've dropped it. And if you feel like taking a weekend jaunt with a new man or current amour after the 20th, take advantage of the wonderful cosmic line-up in your chart. Mars is making every encounter a sexy one, and with a wonderful link between Venus and Jupiter on the 20th, blow the dust off your suitcase and arrange a fabulous trip while you're in wanderlust and lusting mood. It will do wonders for your vitality and most importantly your emotional and spiritual well-being.

Around the New Moon in Taurus on the 27th, you either bump into an ex, or you start thinking that maybe you made a mistake in splitting up. An ex could be confused himself, so stay unruffled and calm. What matters this month is your inner peace, not other people's chaos. You know you still care about him, but the kind of relationship you had was static and uncreative. Now you can look back, not in anger, nor regret but with memories of the good bits, while you simply drop the bad.

Best days for romance: 4th, 18th
Best days to seduce: 14th, 27th
Best stay at home day: 16th

May

With Mercury moving into your friendship zone on the 5th, you bump into a colleague or barfly who seems to understand you. Maybe they could become just a good male friend, the kind who listens to you when you've got troubles and who you can advise when he's got his own? That kind of love is just as important in your life as the deeper, emotional and passionate kind which you often find difficult to handle. Oh, at the Full Moon on the 13th in sexy Scorpio, don't forget to dress to kill when a social extravaganza puts you in a wicked mood. Whether single or attached, the only tears before bedtime will be those of ecstatic bliss.

But the long-term effects of Jupiter's link to Uranus in your own sign puts the spanner in the sexy works. Your professional world has become more important to you, and a moment of idealistic ambition clouds the importance of your relationship. You might want to go out to lunch, flirt or take the chance for a promotional break with a tycoon or VIP in a key position. But make sure you keep your mobile switched on – there's a chance your dreamboat might just call you to say that love is more precious than a vault full of diamonds.

With Mars still coursing through the romantic area of your chart, the communication channels are well and truly open between you and a lover or partner. And it works both ways. He's more open, you both chat away the evenings, knowing that at last there is something unbreakable between you. That deeper connection you've been waiting for is now being made. But even if this lover isn't ready to bond forever, at least you know in your heart that you are loved for who you are, not for pretending to be something you are not.

Life is really pulling you in more directions than you've ever been pulled before. And the choices you've made so far this year have been hard and have tested your determination to do the best for yourself, and have the best lover in town. Somehow change isn't so bad when you instigate it yourself. So remember, your heart is changeable, your mind sometimes scattered and restless, but like any butterfly when you land on the right nectar you know it's the one for you. Even if only for now.

Best days for romance: 13th, 29th
Best days to seduce: 5th, 17th
Best stay at home day: 20th

June

Because your whims and moods are all over the place this month, you might not even notice that someone special is feeling down and rejected. Sometimes men just can't deal with the feelings that run through them, so don't take it personally if you get accused of anything from the 'cause of his headache', to the reason he's lost his car keys. If you're single, tact will get you out of a tricky double-dating challenge on the 5th, flirtatious manipulation will simply get you into relationship trouble.

The revelation of a male friend's secret doesn't come as a shock on the 13th. But tempting as it is, try not to share it with twenty of your closest pals. One of them might be involved in more ways than one. You're dining in style, accompanied by a host of inventive male pals, and besotted by new places to play. It's in your nature to expand your network wherever you go, so don't feel that you're giving up on your girly group at the expense of the male one. Roam between the different camps and enjoy being liberated. Don't resist those temptations if you're single, party till you drop and flirt with every stranger you dance with. If you're not expressing that joy around you, you simply won't be prepared for the amazing change of romantic fortune that is coming your way. Wait for it – it's blazing like a forest fire out of control, and it's coming in your direction!

But around the 19th, you feel caught between the devil and the deep blue sea. Why do you think you've got to justify your intentions anyway? The only validation needed is that you are free to plot, plan and live your life the way you want. The pleasure will be all yours as long as you don't fall into the trap of thinking you won't be loved if you do your own thing. You might not get approval for your actions, but who needs false smiles, when you could win true love? Friends may raise their hands in horror, wonder if you're a two-timer, a femme fatale, or simply have just gone bonkers, but the dizzy days and magical nights that you're experiencing are worth every moment. Attached, or single, you are simply in the mood to dance with your lover by night, get on with your vocational needs by day. Don't throw away the chances you have right now for a really tantalizing summer ahead.

Best days for romance: 11th, 12th
Best days to seduce: 3rd, 19th
Best stay at home day: 12th

July

The ghosts of past insecurities return to haunt you until the 16th, bringing you closer to a lover than you have allowed yourself to be in a long time. It's this feeling of proximity which brings the encouragement you need to take things further and as Venus lines up with Uranus on the 6th, boundaries are lowered and you find yourself on the verge of an emotional diving board – 'boiing ... should I? ... boiing ... shouldn't I? ...' The areas in which you have experienced disappointment are those you most fear, so it's hardly surprising that you sometimes wonder if you were dished up a short supply of the love gene. You love so deeply and consequently have been hurt so badly (you'll be surprised to hear, on fewer occasions than most), that the minute someone tries to get intimate, up goes that thorny barrier to avoid experiencing pain again.

On the 19th, Venus's move into intuitive Cancer reflects that you have to open yourself up to every opportunity, whether financial, work-related or emotional, otherwise you will find yourself living in a restricted, loveless world. The time has finally come to accept those fears and deep feelings lurking within, whether you do so privately or by talking them through with someone you trust. The last year or so has been a high-seas, life-changing personal journey – thoroughly rewarding, but tough too. But imagine how dull life would have been on a straight, narrow path and think how much you've grown. On the 29th you get excited about initiating the beginning of a passion-filled romance, or changing the rules in a relationship. Your fated existence is now in your past. Look at what and who you have loved, to discover what you truly want, and you are already halfway to achieving it.

Best days for romance: 5th, 19th
Best days to seduce: 1st, 31st
Best stay at home day: 15th

August

A lonely Pisces isn't a happy one. You know you need some-one who can provide both the fuel to light your sensual fire, as well as the security and commitment for mutual ambition. Working at relationships takes two. And it won't be long before you know which partner makes up that contented coupledom. Single or attached, the planets are now working in your favour, and towards the end of the month pursuing relationship priorities will become a major factor in your life. Ambitions and responsibilities are one thing, but you are all woman too, so don't give up on your physical and emotional needs for the sake of what others think of you.

Around the 13th, thanks to Mars electrifying tension with Uranus, you will want to break new ground in your social world. It's almost as if someone radically different is making you aware that it's time to get cracking and make important plans for the future. Even if it's merely helping them prepare for a party, or a fun-packed adventure holiday, get to know this person. They could be the route forward to unleashing the most dynamic and active part of yourself.

What about that sixth sense of yours that you worry about so much? Sometimes it's finely tuned, others you just can't work out what it's trying to tell you. The romantic New Moon in your opposite sign of Virgo on the 23rd, will give you all the clues and signals you need to realize that you are up for adventure, passion and sexual happiness. And if the one you love is truly the one who loves you, then the rest of the month will flow by like a beautiful dream. The empowering, charismatic influence of Venus and your ruler Neptune on the 27th, is a day to iron out your problems rather than the shirts, make a commitment or prove that you've got absolutely nothing to lose. And by the end of the month, the sensual rewards will be as welcome as the practical ones.

Best days for romance: 2nd, 9th
Best days to seduce: 10th, 17th
Best stay at home day: 25th

September

With Venus moving into your love corner on the 6th, you really are in the mood to dally a little longer in romantic escapism. And if you're single, well, there's a spicy stranger who's fascinated by your enigmatic smile and hypnotic aura; he makes a brief entrance on the 16th, followed by a more vivid action plan on the 22nd. Make the first few days of the month a time to seduce, dazzle and play the mating game. Now, that doesn't stop you from doing so for the rest of the month, but with a string of planets surging through the idealistic part of your chart, you might just get carried away in all the excitement. Then intense days follow, lights are dimmed and that feeling of something worth changing your whole life for beckons. But what if it's all an illusion? Don't believe everything you hear (not that you normally would) because the partial eclipse of the Moon in your own sign on the 7th makes everything and everyone acutely attractive this month. And this effects your energy level right through to the solar eclipse in Virgo on the 22nd. Your instincts aren't reliable around the 18th, so work hard and lie low, and use your head and not your heart to make any key decisions. This eclipse could also trigger off a desire for someone who's already attached. Obsessive thinking keeps you craving their company, fine if you're single, but dangerous if attached. By the end of the month the love fever is over, and you at least realize that passion isn't just about a moment's infatuation or an indiscreet fling, it's also about a real commitment to your soul's harmony.

You're a sensitive, sensual woman and need to be treated as such. Whether you've been single or just under-sexed for too long, your body is waking up to the fact that it's time for romance. It's about time you put yourself first and around the 26th say no to family demands. A sudden surge of renewed vitality gets you noticed and adored by a rogue who makes you go all weak at the knees when you gaze into his eyes. Don't panic, he'll be literally falling at your feet.

Best days for romance: 6th, 22nd
Best days to seduce: 7th, 19th
Best stay at home day: 14th

October

Finding yourself amongst new friends who don't know anything about you encourages you to let slip a few secrets this month, but the best secret is that you know there's more love out there than you imagined. Mercury flying into your adventurous corner on the 2nd brings an end to a superficial way of relating to your pals and helps to open doors to social opportunities. At the same time, Venus inspires you to throw the sort of party that brings together the right people, and create the perfect atmosphere. You are charm personified. So use it, abuse it, but most of all get out there and subtly glow in the limelight.

Casting off the constraints of unstable relationships and moving towards a more satisfying love life becomes tangible around the 4th, as Jupiter forces you to look closer at your previous bonds. Whether single or attached, the way you react to current or potential mates is about to change. You are discovering a determination to rid yourself of old habits, pointless behaviour and unsatisfactory partners around the

23rd when both the Sun and Mars move into transformative Scorpio. It's time to welcome a fascinating period of self-knowledge and growth. Be prepared to search deeper into the underlying motivations for your attraction to certain people. It will ease emotional tensions and open you a whole new awareness of your true needs.

If you're single, tantalizing developments with one special rogue are on the horizon, if you don't allow outdated feelings of insecurity to make you question his intentions. By the 26th, you wonder if at last you've found your soulmate. He's attentive, he's handsome and he's interested in you, but don't imagine he's faultless. Live for the present, rather than worrying about what will be and what his prospects are. Enjoy the influence of Venus after the 24th, which allows you to be totally comfortable with your body and yourself. And that's the very self which will create the sparks of love you've desired all along.

Best days for romance: 1st, 23rd
Best days to seduce: 24th, 25th
Best stay at home day: 31st

November

Being elusive is one thing, but don't forget you are human too. If you're single, one handsome rogue in the workplace is thinking aloud, and they seem to be divulging some interesting information about how they fancy you. You may have been vaguely suspicious of them in the past but listen with an open mind. It could lead to the kind of liaison you're seeking.

Uranus's move forward in your own sign on the 20th will make your lover take note of your sensual power, sit up and probably kiss you to pieces. You can't resist that kind of attention, but if he's a Scorpio or a Capricorn, take note; he's got plans for you even though he's keeping it all hush-hush and they are the kind you will like. Meanwhile, a blast from your beautiful past could show up when least expected around the 28th. But then, isn't a little wicked wistfulness what makes you so magical? Current admirers will be texting you 24/7 if you're single, and if you're attached, revel in the attention, rather than those fantasies about 'what might have been'. Then suddenly it is back to reality. The admirers are having to work rather than play, and you're nodding wisely to bosses and family about in-house politics. (When you'd rather be dreaming of Mr Right.)

With Jupiter moving into your career corner on the 24th, you begin to wonder if you want to give up all you have for a new and better lifestyle. But at what price? Does it mean an end to a close relationship, cutting ties and truly loving someone, or do you give up those grand schemes and imaginative plans for success for someone else's happiness? These kind of questions will be on your mind for some months to come. So right now, promise that you won't give up on yourself. That sacrificial streak of yours is all too ready to relinquish your long-term dreams for the sake of being loved. But if you love yourself first and foremost, the rest will follow.

Best days for romance: 7th, 20th
Best days to seduce: 13th, 29th
Best stay at home day: 3rd

December

With Mars and Jupiter in raunchy Sagittarius you're in the mood to party and won't let anyone stop you from enjoying yourself to the full. Saturn is making you think through a major re-invention of your image and you are far more confident about your love and working life than you've been in a long time. Your bold ambition and fresh outlook is hyper-attractive and you'll be surprised at the attention you suddenly experience from a handsome colleague. Don't let a past emotional disappointment stop you from getting in-volved if you're single, and if you're attached, open up to your partner and let him know what you're really feeling and how to please you. Deep-seated fears must be cast aside for you to go one step beyond. The Full Moon on the 5th makes this much easier than you imagine and you may even find yourself showing off in a public display of hugs, kisses and hand-holding at a major social whirl. As Mercury moves on into cool Capricorn on the 27th, you'll find that you no longer need to work at a relationship, but that it falls into place naturally.

Enjoy love for love's sake, make a list of your desires and surrender it to life. Don't force issues and you'll be surprised at how much better things work out than when you insist on taking control. The cosmos has designs for you, much grander than any you could begin to conceive – all you have to do is give them a chance to happen.

Don't sell yourself short around the 29th and your talents won't go unmissed, whether you change the way you work, the way you think or the way you act and react, friends and lovers will be astonished at how focused you are. This doesn't mean that you'll walk roughshod over them – you'd never do that – but you do finally know what you want. But by New Year's Eve your romantic ambitions are clear and you're no longer dealing with the past. You are wrapped in the arms of someone you've desired for a very long time, and he's the present you've been dreaming of since the beginning of 2006.

Best days for romance: 5th, 26th
Best days to seduce: 10th, 31st
Best stay at home day: 4th

Your Love
Horoscope
2006

Love
Compatibilities

Who's most likely to be Mr Right or simply Mr Right Now? This section of the book tells you all you need to know to seduce any man of the zodiac, how to handle him month by month for 2006 and who you're compatible with. Knowing who's compatible and who you might find hard work will give you insight into your own emotional, romantic or sexual needs too. Some zodiac signs want romance or a 'no-strings attached' relationship. Others want marriage or a highly workable professional partnership. This brief compatibility guide will give you some clues to whom you might find a challenge, a pushover, a one-night wonder – or simply the man of your dreams.

Sign-to-sign compatibility

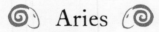 Aries

Aries woman/Aries man

Immediately a powerful rapport, but who's the boss? Both of you are impulsive and vain, so there could be a few arguments about who gets the bathroom first. You both leap hell-bent into relationships, but neither of you bears any resentment towards the other if you part.

Aries woman/Taurus man

You enjoy a mutual fascination for your very differences. You admire his cooking skills, he's glad you prefer to be boss in bed. Luckily this means you can have sex all night and a gourmet dinner every evening. Together you'll have sex anywhere from a sauna to a bunk bed, but watch out he doesn't fall asleep just when you're ready for more.

Aries woman/Gemini man

You both experience physical bliss in this relationship and he's quickly aroused if you play out some of your sexual fantasies. You love his quick wit and restless spirit, but he's not so fond of being dominated. Incredibly stimulating for both of you, as long as you both give each other space.

Aries woman/Cancer man

Initially you're convinced he's ambitious and self-centred. This is only a cover-up – he doesn't want you to see his gentle side. Excellent for a short-term affair, but you may tire of his indirect way of dealing with life when you'd rather just get on with it.

Aries woman/Leo man

Expect to get on like a house on fire, to begin with anyway. You both need to dazzle and shine, but Leos tend to be ultra proud and your flirtatious sparkle may make him jealous. Good for a glamorous partnership, but not strong on intellectual rapport.

Aries woman/Virgo man

Together you are the most virtuoso performers imaginable. You enjoy a perfect sex life, but you have to be ready to match his performance and take his criticism. Both of you have little in common mentally or emotionally, but physically sparks can fly.

Aries woman/Libra man

This is often a combustible relationship, but always sexy and challenging. Your fiery approach to sex is both compelling yet threatening to his more aesthetic ideals about love – he needs beautiful surroundings and subtle provocation. Always fascinating and seldom forgettable.

Aries woman/Scorpio man

This man can be too intense and deep for your more dynamic and extrovert style. You'll enjoy an exhilarating sex life, but there's a danger he wants total commitment. Giving up your independence is unlikely, so be prepared for a long haul of emotional battles.

Aries woman/Sagittarius man

Could prove to be the biggest romantic thrill. Sex is just one big adventure once you've fallen into his arms, but heroes have a knack of disappearing at a moment's notice. Good for laughs and physical romps, but be prepared to cross canyons to find him.

Aries woman/Capricorn man

He may be more conventional than you about how your sexual relationship develops. You love taking risks and having fun, and initially he finds this totally mind-blowing.

But he prefers the kind of risks that lead to business success rather than simply to bed.

Aries woman/Aquarius man

There's an interesting rapport here, with both of you needing oodles of freedom. He adores your impulsive nature but often prefers to observe life rather than get involved in it. Good for long conversations into the night. The only problem is you're hot and he's sometimes just too cool.

Aries woman/Pisces man

You both have totally different social needs. He wants to be everyone's friend, you don't. He's dreamy, elusive and often unpredictable, and you're flattered by his sensitivity to your sexual needs. He either falls hopelessly in love with you or runs a mile when he sees how volatile you are.

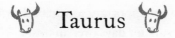 Taurus

Taurus woman/Aries man

An instant magnetism pulls you together. He is impatient, dashing and vain. You have to keep your cool and adore him for his sexy smile and good humour. Don't try to force him to make any commitments and he'll stick around longer than you'd imagine.

Taurus woman / Taurus man

You're likely to be spending most of your time on the horizontal. Both of you love sensual pleasure and both of you enjoy indulgence. There's lots of silent tenacity and mutual defiance out of the bedroom, but a wonderful earthy rapport as long as you both remember to communicate.

Taurus woman / Gemini man

You adore his ability to play any role you desire, both in and out of bed. But don't ever get possessive about him or he may disappear faster than he appeared. Good for romantic fun and erotic sex, but he's totally unreliable and utterly flirtatious with your friends.

Taurus woman / Cancer man

You both require tenderness and both need time to allow your sexual secrets to unfold. Your fantasy world intrigues him and his might take a lifetime to explore. Warmth and companionship are important to you both; your only test is when you both sulk for days over an upset.

Taurus woman / Leo man

There's oodles of sexy magic between you, but you have little in common emotionally. Both of you communicate in very different ways and are liable to stubborn moods. It's an incredibly strong relationship if you respect each other. He needs loyalty and to be treated like a king; you love sensually indulging him.

Taurus woman/Virgo man

Your earthy sensuality lifts him off to a different plane when he realizes you're the most perfect woman he's ever met. You might find him too clinical about sex and he might eventually decide you're too self-indulgent. Good for a long-term stability, but lacking in passion.

Taurus woman/Libra man

As long as you give him plenty of space to socialize he sticks around. But remember he lives in his head and doesn't like to be brought down to earth too often. Both of you like winding the other up in public, but in private you just like to laze around in each other's arms.

Taurus woman/Scorpio man

This is one of the most erotic combinations of the zodiac – you're sensual and steamy, he's torrid and sexually demanding. He's drawn to your earthy needs and you to his extremes of passion. A transformative relationship that can be total love or total hate.

Taurus woman/Sagittarius man

You could have problems. He's a rover and doesn't really want to be committed. If you're prepared for him to wander and return to your side when he feels like it, then you'll be rewarded with a fabulous lover and friend. Not easy for long-term commitment.

Taurus woman/Capricorn man

Once you establish a rapport with this man there's usually a strong bond between you. Sexually, you're more sensual than he is – you need tactile warmth, he usually prefers to be plotting business coups. Maybe it's time to teach him some new tricks? Good for long-term commitment.

Taurus woman/Aquarius man

Both of you are fascinated by your very different personalities. Aquarians love to be alone or with a million pals and need more freedom than anyone else. Good for a fun-loving affair, as long as you can tolerate his ex-lovers being his friends.

Taurus woman/Pisces man

You can get lost in his imaginative world and are fascinated by his sensitive nature and intuitive talents. He's far stronger than he appears on the surface and you're emotionally deeper than he realizes. Together you can establish a long-lasting instinctual rapport.

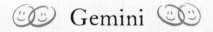

Gemini

Gemini woman/Aries man

Initially his crazy ideas bewitch you and you fall for his impulsive need for spur-of-the-moment sex. There's a great physical rapport here, but he's too egotistic at times. It's a passionate but exhausting relationship. Intellectually he can't match you, so you may tire of him long before he tires of you.

Gemini woman/Taurus man

You are instantly attracted to his very feral masculinity. His body intrigues you and his sexual performance thrills you. However, he does love routine in his life and you prefer anything but that. Excellent if you want stability and constancy, not so good for variety and fun.

Gemini Woman/Gemini man

You're like a couple of identical twins. Intellectually stimulating and always buzzing, both of you are adventurous and on the lookout for new ideas. Good for mutual understanding, but you're both easily led astray by a beautiful face, so chances of instability high.

Gemini woman/Cancer man

This captivating rogue makes you feel cherished, for a while anyway. However, he's home-loving and possessive and you're extrovert, flirtatious and need space. Physically compelling, but difficult to sustain.

Gemini woman/Leo man

He's generous, warm and sincere and you adore his dramatic and fiery nature. However, you could find it hard to keep playing the role of the ultra-glamorous celebrity. Great for sex, sex and more sex, but he can get too arrogant about his performance.

Gemini woman/Virgo man

You both feel an instant attraction or an instant repulsion. Intellectually he could assume you're not as clever as him and he's liable to criticize your every move. Could be fun for a crazy fling, but usually lacking in long-term mutual passion.

Gemini woman/Libra man

His idealistic, romantic nature bewitches you. Out and about you probably discuss the world, play mental games and enjoy romantic adventures. Good intellectual rapport, but he likes everything to be ultra perfect, so remember to wear beautiful lingerie and clean the bath.

Gemini woman/Scorpio man

Very different natures at work here, so often an erotic connection. Can be a complete love-hate drama. Sexually wild and often unpredictable, passionate and volatile. If you like leaping in at the deep end, then this is the man for you.

Gemini woman/Sagittarius man

You've met your match. Not only is he your opposite sign which means there's an extraordinarily powerful attraction between you, but also he's the most exciting lover. Passionate and heroic, he leaps into your life bringing adventure in his wake, but he can disappear equally as fast.

Gemini woman/Capricorn man

You're put on the spot and feel like you're being cross-examined. Not only do you feel restricted by his conventional attitude to life, but you also get impatient with his calculated plans. Physically worth pursuing purely out of Gemini curiosity, but unlikely to be a long-term affair.

Gemini woman/Aquarius man

Your mind fascinates him and he spends hours analysing every inch of you. You quickly establish a genuine and permanent intellectual rapport. Can be an unpredictable but long-lasting relationship. Secret: he may prefer more sexual freedom than he's willing to admit.

Gemini woman/Pisces man

Here's a man who can adapt to your own changeable and restless nature. He drifts with your needs and indulges in your fantasies if you ask him. He's just as happy to talk through the night as he is to be utterly sensual.

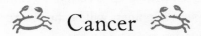

Cancer

Cancer woman/Aries man

He's drawn to your cool sensuality and you adore his fiery sexuality. His passion is naked; yours is clandestine and secret. Words like commitment and security send him running. Great for a fling and a wild passionate affair, but he's not interested in your feelings – he's only interested in himself.

Cancer woman/Taurus man

Both of you have a need for closeness, although his is more physical and yours more emotional. Together you can create a serene lifestyle because neither of you wants to score points over the other. Excellent for sexual pleasure and long-term happiness.

Cancer woman/Gemini man

He loves to talk about his sexiest fantasies, while you prefer to keep your sexual thoughts to yourself. His nature is geared towards variety and intellectual stimulation, while yours is towards feelings. Could be okay for a casual affair, but not easy if you want commitment.

Cancer woman/Cancer man

Both of you are equally evasive, especially about your private fears and desires. And both of you fear rejection more than anything else, so opening up to each other could take a long time. But physical happiness will be the most profound and magical of experiences if you do.

Cancer woman/Leo man

Flamboyant and impulsive, the Leo man's egotistic needs are very demanding. But you adore his protective attitude and he loves to be loved. If you can reveal your true warmth, he is utterly devoted. The only downside is his stubbornness and your evasiveness.

Cancer woman/Virgo man

Meticulous beyond belief, he believes that what you see is what you get, while you have mood swings and need to experience the mysteries in life. Both of you feel deeply but rarely open up to each other.

Cancer woman/Libra man

You respond eagerly to his idealistic vision of love and he adores your sensitive, sensual nature. But as you begin to slowly open up and reveal your feelings and changing moods, his airy, abstract approach to life may not rest comfortably with your emotional world.

Cancer woman/Scorpio man

Apparently the master of sexual pleasure, he's the most irresistible man you've ever met. But he won't be able to stop himself from wanting to own you. Good for an erotic, deeply emotional relationship, but take care, this man can destroy that which he loves.

Cancer woman/Sagittarius man

Because you have such different ways of looking at the world, a powerful magnetic attraction pulls you together. He adores your secretive side and you love his sparkling optimism. A creative relationship but short-lived. He wants freedom and a nomadic lifestyle; you need commitment and a nest.

Cancer woman/Capricorn man

You need to feel in control of your emotions and he needs to feel in control of his life. So you both play sexy games of one-upmanship to defend your vulnerable side. Your mysterious femininity keeps him hooked. An ambitious relationship, deeply satisfying and often long-lasting.

Cancer woman/Aquarius man

Different energies here – he needs detachment, you need closeness. He may make you feel sexually liberated, but once he's uncovered your secrets and told you about everything under the sun, he won't hang around for long.

Cancer woman/Pisces man

You both have an intuitive understanding of each other's feelings. He knows how to please you and you know what goes on behind his role-playing. A very private relationship, but one where you have to make the decisions if you're ever going to get out of the house or on to the next party.

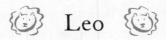 Leo

Leo woman/Aries man

He is impulsive and vain; you are always proud and uncompromising. Your fiery enthusiasm can burn itself out and there's always a danger of you both tiring of each other's competitive attitude to love. Great for fun flings, but long-term happiness can be difficult.

Leo woman/Taurus man

This man is a sensual artist, but he doesn't aspire to flamboyant behaviour. Great for physical fulfilment as long as he doesn't get a little frustrated by your desire for glamorous living and always acting the part of queen bee.

Leo woman/Gemini man

The big problem here is that he lives in his head and you live through your heart. When he's with you he's an entertaining prankster, but also a bit of a gangster. You want loyalty and probably this is the last man on earth to give it, especially when he'd rather be flirting with your friends.

Leo woman/Cancer man

He's moody and often silent; you're passionate, vibrant and glitzy. He's inspired by your fiery nature and need for complete honesty and loyalty. A love affair of passion – your only problem being his need to retreat when you'd rather be socializing every night.

Leo woman/Leo man

The passion you generate together could become a battleground of wills. You both have a natural desire to out-pleasure each other. Fiery and rampant, neither of you has time to consider making commitments. Highly compatible, if you can both remember to honour those hidden emotions.

Leo woman/Virgo man

Workable but not necessarily long-lasting. It is a very creative relationship as you respect each other's different approach to life. But he could resent your constant need for glamorous socializing, while you might get fed up with having to be the cleaner.

Leo woman/Libra man

Both of you love to get out and about, look good and enjoy a glittering social scene, but his indecisiveness may eventually irritate you. Wonderful for sexual fun and to feel truly adored, but difficult to pin him down or make any long-term plans.

Leo woman/Scorpio man

This relationship is a battleground for two powers intent on their own emotional and physical fulfilment. You are showy, teasing and dynamic; he is smouldering, intensely serious and often difficult to satisfy. Don't flirt with anyone else and he could be yours for as long as you choose.

Leo woman/Sagittarius man

Dynamic and impulsive romance, but don't expect him to make commitments. This man prefers his freedom and he isn't terribly loyal when variety is at stake. Great for physical fun, but he's a roamer not a fixture and fitting.

Leo woman/Capricorn man

The rapport between you is exciting, dramatic and erotic, and this often makes for a steamy sensual relationship. He loves your outrageous sexual style; you adore his potent, earthy libido. A passionate and challenging relationship – your only problem is you both need to dominate in and out of the bedroom.

Leo woman/Aquarius man

He believes in non-exclusive relationships and you believe in utter exclusivity. You are proud and demanding; he's detached about his feelings and believes in universal love. An attraction of opposites which can succeed, but he's likely to stray if you get possessive.

Leo woman/Pisces man

A strangely rich and satisfying relationship in the beginning, where fantasy mixes with drama. He loves to be dominated but may find it hard to keep up with your passionate demands. Great for escape, romance and intrigue, difficult for long-term companionship.

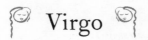

Virgo

Virgo woman/Aries man

He's arousing and enticing, while you enchant him with your cool and classy charisma. Definitely an attraction of very different types, and it could be seriously romantic if you can accept his very extrovert needs and he can understand your need for privacy.

Virgo woman/Taurus man

This is one of the most potent and often long lasting of zodiac relationships. He is practical, earthy and has similar sexual needs. He's a sensualist and you're a perfectionist, but together you can make a superb workable relationship.

Virgo woman/Gemini man

You adore his mischievous phone calls and witty one-liners. Both of you are mentally seductive. He warms quickly to your earthy sensuality but may prefer a more uncommitted relationship than you. Great for a laugh, difficult for long-term bliss.

Virgo woman/Cancer man

Immediately you feel comfortable in his very needy arms. You love being wanted, but his moods and unpredictability could be too disorganized for your methodical approach to life. An enriching rapport, but only long lasting if you let him close enough to your heart.

Virgo woman/Leo man

You easily relate to his high standards of beauty, sexual attraction and polished performance. But don't ever suggest he needs to make improvements – he believes he's already perfect. A warm sexy relationship if you've both got the patience.

Virgo woman/Virgo man

Here's a man who understands your basic earthy approach to life. But he probably won't awaken your passionate wild side.

Great for trust, friendship and a working partnership, but ultimately not a dynamic relationship.

Virgo woman/Libra man

Physical and mental harmony for both of you. He's idealistic though and wants only the most complete romantic experience every time. Both of you are gentle lovers and need refinement, but he's the real perfectionist, so make sure you never slip up.

Virgo woman/Scorpio man

You feel like you've been thrown in the deep end. This man's magnetic sexuality is very intense. You're compelled into a deeply transformative relationship but may not be able to accept his need for domination. Great for a fling but remember he has a sting in his tail.

Virgo woman/Sagittarius man

He's a great sexual adventurer and usually loves to roam free, but he adores your feminine mystique and your cool earthy approach to life. Both of you are adaptable, so a relationship could prove highly exciting if you can tolerate his unreliability.

Virgo woman/Capricorn man

Together you enjoy a wonderful sexual rapport that relies also on a bond of companionship. Likely to be a seriously long-lasting involvement – he gives you that sense of stability and you keep him enchanted with your easygoing but materialistic approach to life.

Virgo woman/Aquarius man

A highly original and quite unusual relationship. He's fascinated by your sensible streak, you by his detached view of love and life. However, this is a relationship based on intellectual rapport rather than a deeply potent one. Great if you want a truly loving friendship.

Virgo woman/Pisces man

A wonderful sexual rapport – you take pleasure in his very intuitive romantic style, while he adores your earthy sensuality. Both of you can adapt to the other and you enjoy a deeply connected sexual and emotional relationship. Often long lasting.

♎ Libra ♎

Libra woman/Aries man

You've met your natural opposite and like any polarity this could be a knockout relationship. You're romantic and idealistic and this man usually fulfils most of your dreams. He loves to be in charge; you adore having decisions made for you.

Libra woman/Taurus man

His practical approach may not gel with your image of an ideal heroic lover and your need to be mentally amused could be frustrated by his desire for the facts. But together you can make a pretty good double act because you both love the beautiful things of life.

Libra woman/Gemini man

You're at home with his sexy and hilarious mind. He's not too emotionally intense and you're both adaptable enough to keep the relationship light and free-spirited. Great for fun and romantic sex, as long as you keep him amused.

Libra woman/Cancer man

An unusual blend of sexual spice and mystical attraction, both of you are enchanted by each other's different way of perceiving the world. Excellent long-term rapport, but you might just find his moodiness hard to handle.

Libra woman/Leo man

Both of you enjoy pleasure for the sake of pleasure, as long as it's mingled with compassion and love. He adores glamour; you love playing the part. Good sexual companionship and usually long lasting and sparkling.

Libra woman/Virgo man

Together you physically and emotionally understand one another and your quest for an ideal could end with him. Your only problem is that he can accuse you of all kinds of faults and flaws when in fact he's actually not that perfect himself.

Libra woman/Libra man

There's an instant rapport between you, simply because you

are so similar. You both have an aura of romantic tenderness and adore all kinds of sexy fantasies, thoughts and games. A harmonious affinity, but only if one of you makes all the decisions.

Libra woman/Scorpio man

You fall into a very deep and intense sexual relationship, bewitching each other with your very differences. It's intensely passionate, but you might feel at times you want more space and a decent social life, while he wants to draw the curtains and be alone with you.

Libra woman/Sagittarius man

As long as you can keep up with his roaming lifestyle this is a fun relationship. He needs independence but also loves to be loved for who he is, so give him loads of space and he'll be back for more. Sexually exciting, with few emotional storms.

Libra woman/Capricorn man

He has a very different approach to sex and life from you. He thrives on straightforward, earthy, no-nonsense relationships – you prefer the romantic. Excellent as a discreet fling, but long-term there could be power struggles about money and property.

Libra woman/Aquarius man

You enjoy a fantastic physical rapport based on mental games. However, he's more fascinated by your mind than your body and his independent lifestyle may conflict with your need for a constant companion. Wonderful for a fun-loving, easy-going relationship.

Libra woman/Pisces man

Escape into a land of romantic fantasy. You enjoy an instant sexual rapport and often it's a successful relationship. He is looking for the ultimate experience and you're looking for the perfect one. But imagination may not be enough to keep you together when good old reality kicks in.

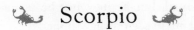

Scorpio

Scorpio woman/Aries man

Assured of physical action, you have dynamic fun wherever you go. He's challenging and impulsive but has a very different nature from your own. Your possessiveness could push him to the limits and his need for independence could leave you lonely.

Scorpio woman/Taurus man

Taurus is your natural opposite in the zodiac and this means the tension between you will be like a magnet – this is a love or hate relationship in the extreme. You hold an erotic fascination for each other which is often long-lived but can be exhausting, possessive and emotionally challenging.

Scorpio woman/Gemini man

You want to plummet into the depths of his amusing, ambiguous personality. He needs constant variety and is fascinated by your secret side. However, he avoids emotional intensity, whereas you prefer exclusive closeness. Great for mental games, difficult for long-term rapport.

Scorpio woman/Cancer man

Fascinated by one another's very private nature, you both crave complete physical and emotional closeness, and together are assured of dedicated companionship. Good relationship potential, but he may not be as passionate and as wild as you might secretly have hoped for.

Scorpio woman/Leo man

Although for a while you're happy to play his games, your need for a serious physical involvement could alarm him. Both of you are demanding and enjoy challenging the other, but his line-up of glamorous friends and exes may make you jealous.

Scorpio woman/Virgo man

Needing an earthy and ordered love life, he's discriminating and laid-back. You, on the other hand, have a more passionate, chaotic approach to relationships and could feel emotionally unfulfilled. Especially as he prefers to keep a big distance from his own feelings.

Scorpio woman/Libra man

He craves the perfect relationship and loves being subjected to your intense mystical power. You both enjoy his fantasy world and have a great sexual rapport, but you both have very different needs and desires. You want all or nothing; he wants to be free and easy.

Scorpio woman/Scorpio Man

There's an instant affinity between you, both sexually and emotionally, but you could both end up playing too many power games. Exciting and intense, but often too stormy too soon, unless you truly enjoy the danger element of who can outwit the other first. Sexy and wicked.

Scorpio woman/Sagittarius man

You're attracted to his opportunist nature, but his fiery spirit doesn't involve feelings. He needs to be free to come and go as he pleases, whereas you need to know exactly where and what he's doing. Sexually exciting and great for a fling, but could be a very steamy, torrid affair.

Scorpio woman/Capricorn man

Both of you are aroused by power and there could be some fascinating conflicts surrounding your mutual need to be in control. He learns from your intense passion for life and you from his pragmatic one.

Scorpio woman/Aquarius man

This is a highly magnetic and erotic relationship. But you want total involvement, he doesn't. The main problem is that his freedom means more to him than you do. Great for an unconventional relationship if you can defuse your jealous streak.

Scorpio woman/Pisces man

You enjoy a sensual rapport, but this relationship is highly challenging. He's a social animal and prefers to roam his social circle telling everyone about you. You're discrete and don't want your intimate life broadcast around town. Good for sexual affinity, but lifestyle needs are very different.

↗ Sagittarius ↙

Sagittarius woman/Aries man

This is a sexually exciting and passionate relationship, but when the flames die down, what's left? Probably the desire to go your own way. A fun-loving, challenging relationship, but difficult long term as you both have very strong views about living independently.

Sagittarius woman/Taurus man

Strangely, can be extremely satisfying, as he's down-to-earth and very sexy with it. As long as he doesn't get too possessive, a long-term rapport can develop, simply because you need to feel there's always someone reliable around.

Sagittarius woman/Gemini man

You're natural opposites in the zodiac, so there's bound to be fireworks. You enjoy a magnetic sexual attraction, where your sex life is usually fast-paced and furious. Long-term this can work, as long as you accept that he looks at the bigger picture of life, while you want to work on the details.

Sagittarius woman/Cancer man

Hmm. He's home-loving, but you're not exactly fond of leaning over a hot stove more than you can help. But he comes up trumps if he agrees to be the domestic saint while you get on with your hi-flying career. Sexually inspiring, but don't forget he's looking for a mother figure.

Sagittarius woman/Leo man

Daring, risky and often drawn together through your social scene, you both enjoy glamorous parties and flirting with everyone. Great for your image, but often doomed to separation, as you're both likely to get led astray by a gorgeous face.

Sagittarius woman/Virgo man

He can be enchanting enough to keep you guessing and has the sense of humour to put up with all your jokes. But he needs punctual dates and the same old friends. You prefer the unknown, the surprising and being late. Great for a sexy fling, difficult for long-term togetherness.

Sagittarius woman/Libra man

You're an utterly romantic duo when you first get together. And you feel as if you've finally met the man of your dreams. But take care when he starts saying 'we' at every possible moment, while you'd rather be saying 'I'. Great for sex and romance. Only long-term if you're willing to make compromises.

Sagittarius woman/Scorpio man

A very steamy relationship. He's compelling, sexually potent and irresistible, but he likes to be in control of the relationship, so watch out because he's jealous and provocative himself. 'Power play' likely, but physically breathtaking.

Sagittarius woman/Sagittarius man

You're drawn to each other because you see the best of yourself in each other's eyes. Can be a very long-term duet, but take care as you're both capable of being led astray after the initial fire has died down. Neither of you can have your cake and eat it, as you're both very jealous underneath that bravado.

Sagittarius woman/Capricorn man

Physically competitive, you're driven to out-seduce this man. But he's after conventional love and wants his woman – yes, remember those words, 'his woman' – to be the perfect business partner/caterer or career-seeker. You can handle the latter, but he won't be able to deal with your flirtatious side for long.

Sagittarius woman/Aquarius man

Excellent for a free and easy, 'no strings attached' relationship. You both need oodles of space and both avoid heavy-duty emotional scenes. A good friendship rather than a passionate torrid love affair, but isn't that actually quite refreshing?

Sagittarius woman/Pisces man

Sexy sparks abound. But he's even more elusive and unreliable than you are, so you keep missing each other on those last-minute impulsive dates. Great for romantic fun, difficult for anything which requires commitment or decision making.

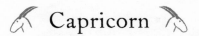

Capricorn

Capricorn woman/Aries man

A battle of wills, but a very physical magnetism between you. But he needs a woman to hang on his arm like a gold chain. Great for a professionally successful partnership with loads of sex thrown in. Not high on romance or peace and quiet.

Capricorn woman/Taurus man

Materially, physically and mentally you're in tune, but, and there is a but, you could end up in more fights than you imagine simply because you can both get fanatical about your beliefs. Great sexual rapport – just take care who's in control of the credit card.

Capricorn woman/Gemini man

Steamingly sexy to begin with, but he's a man who needs constant change in his life or boredom immediately sets in. Then he's off flirting the night away while you're doing the ironing. Not easy long term, but could be a laugh a minute while he's enthusiastic and kept amused.

Capricorn woman/Cancer man

You're opposites of the zodiac so you're drawn to each other like moths to each other's flames. This is a very sexy, extremely serious relationship and often it's successful in the long term. It's better if you're both ambitious to reach the top of your profession.

Capricorn woman/Leo man

A glamorous liaison built on a mutual desire for wealth or ambition. But he's very vain, so make sure you always treat him as if he were the only man on earth. Your only problem is that you can get tired of his self-righteous streak.

Capricorn woman/Virgo man

Stability is important for both of you, and as you're both Earth element signs, you have an affinity for the same pleasures in life. A sensually-fulfilling relationship, as long as he accepts your need to be in control and you can deal with his mercurial teasing side.

Capricorn woman/Libra man

Initially you're attracted by your very differences. He's romantic and idealistic, you're down-to-earth and want security. Long term he might still hanker for the perfect woman, even though you know you're exactly that.

Capricorn woman/Scorpio man

This relationship is challenging and often highly successful. You're both driven by power and both prefer a very private relationship. But you're more of a social animal than he is and he could become resentful of your ambitious achievements if he's not one up on you. Sexually great, emotionally exhausting.

Capricorn woman/Sagittarius man

If you can put up with his need for freedom then he might hang around longer than you'd imagine. But he does admire success and anyone who name-drops. Status turns him on, so make sure you're aiming for celebrity acclaim, otherwise he'll be off on another scent once the initial passion's worn off.

Capricorn woman/Capricorn man

Sexy rapport, but although you both understand the other inside out, you always feel there's something missing. 'Power plays' and rivalry likely, so good for a challenging relationship. But it might be you who falls in love with a wild romantic or lone wolf while he's out making money for the sake of it.

Capricorn woman/Aquarius man

Strangely addictive. You both love the other because you're so different but will probably want each other to adapt to your own way of thinking. Can be a highly successful relationship if he accepts you need things done by the book and you accept he needs freedom to do whatever he likes.

Capricorn woman/Pisces man

His very changeable moods could mean you get a little hot under the collar. Not an easy rapport, as you want things to be black and white and he prefers a few grey areas. Especially when he disappears when you're supposed to be entertaining your business chums. Sexy, but usually short term.

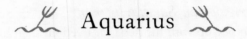

Aquarius

Aquarius woman/Aries man
Blazing with passion, he could be too physically direct for your more detached attitude to sex. But you adore shocking him with your sexual insights and flirting with his friends, and you send him erotic e-mails just to keep him on his toes. He's fiery and single-minded, you need independence. Watch out you don't burn each other out.

Aquarius woman/Taurus man
His physical passion is wild and untamed, but he does get incredibly fanatical about his possessions, which could include you. He may be too confining for your more detached, aloof lifestyle. An interesting experience, but rarely long term.

Aquarius woman/Gemini man
You alternate between finding him totally stimulating and totally frustrating. But a good long-term relationship, as he's fascinated by your mind and you love his ability to give you the freedom you crave. Watch out for his flirtatious streak though.

Aquarius woman/Cancer man

Could be a good sexual relationship if he's prepared to accept friendship is more important to you than 'coupledom'. But he's a 'one-woman man' so the problem arises when your male friends pitch up for coffee and he realizes you're not exclusively his. Very sexy attraction, but not often long term unless you want a 'man indoors'.

Aquarius woman/Leo man

He can offer you complete physical bliss, but he does require loyalty in return, which you may not be prepared to give to one man. He adores your independence and your wild, unconventional approach to sex. An exciting rapport as long as you accept his need for prestige.

Aquarius woman/Virgo man

Both of you avoid emotional involvement. You have stunningly different temperaments and therefore find each other very addictive, but you both might just forget to talk about your feelings and hurt one another unintentionally.

Aquarius woman/Libra man

This man's an idealist whose romantic sexuality could lead you deeply astray. A lively, fun-loving relationship with little emotional intensity, which suits you down to the ground. He needs romantic conversations and together you create a fascinating rapport.

Aquarius woman/Scorpio man

A powerful attraction of very different needs and desires. Both of you like to take control of the relationship. He wants to be the boss, but you just want to control those feelings. Magnetic and irresistible, you may find you have little choice but to fall into his arms.

Aquarius woman/Sagittarius man

This is one man who needs greater freedom and space than you. A highly successful physical relationship. You give each other enough time to do your own thing, without feeling suspicious or jealous. Good for an exciting liaison and an utterly honest attitude to life.

Aquarius woman/Capricorn man

You both have very different physical needs, as he needs a conventional lifestyle and you prefer anything but. Can be a lively, demanding and ambitious relationship, as long as he gives you your space and you give him the time of day in the first place.

Aquarius woman/Aquarius man

You share a natural affinity for the same physical and mental pleasures. Both of you approach relationships with a very open mind and experiment with taboo ideas. A great relationship – not deeply passionate but completely honest and mutually creative.

Aquarius woman/Pisces man

This man needs unconditional space, but he is still a romantic cleverly disguised as a pleasure-seeker. He's likely to become addicted to you, so watch out if you want complete freedom as he's so sensitive. Excellent for a romantic fling, but exhausting for anything long term.

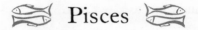 Pisces

Pisces woman/Aries man

Brimming with passion and audacity, he can't resist your lush sensuality and you easily surrender to his uninhibited sexual style. Difficult for a long-term relationship as you need to feel totally part of his pack, while he's a lone wolf.

Pisces woman/Taurus man

He won't understand the depths of your mysterious vulnerability but he treasures your sensitivity. You might persuade him to save a few whales, but he could be just too interested in making money to be charitable all the time.

Pisces woman/Gemini man

Both of you have ambivalent natures. At times he wants sexual fun filled with laughter, conversation and wine, and at others he disappears from your bed at dawn when he's on a mission. Enjoy those mind games, but you could get resentful when your fantasy world seems to be wasted on him.

Pisces woman/Cancer man

You're inspired by his sensual rhythms and varying moods of passion. There's a great sexual balance between you. He adores your femininity and your willingness to adapt to his unpredictable streak. The only problem is his need to be mothered – and yours to have a hero.

Pisces woman/Leo man

He's mesmerizing and you may feel like a princess, but he does need to know you'll be there for him on permanent stand by. You prefer to escape into your dream world, he'd rather he was the only fantasy you had. Superb sexual rapport, but real life is difficult.

Pisces woman/Virgo man

This relationship provides a great contrast between perfection and sensual beauty. Together you have tense and testing moments. The sexual arousal between you is profound and you can develop a haunting devotion to one another. The only problem is you want to escape reality and he likes to be part of it.

Pisces woman/Libra man

A very romantic kick-off, but his intellectual approach to life and love may begin to disturb you when you'd rather be drifting on the tide without a care in the world. A dreamy, almost unreal relationship, but sexually irresistible.

Pisces woman/Scorpio man

Excellent for a sexual fling, but you get defensive when he thinks he owns you. If he gives you enough space, then long-term prospects are good, but he'll have to accept your flirtatious streak. This is Mr Jealousy, don't forget.

Pisces woman/Sagittarius man

He's a bit of a sexual roamer, while you're interested in clandestine romance, so you might meet through a love triangle. He could prove to be the most exciting lover you've ever met. You enjoy a wonderful sexual rapport as long as you give each other space.

Pisces woman/Capricorn man

Preferring to keep his own feelings locked away, you may find his physical needs are just not enough to keep you deeply involved. You fall under his dominant spell, but not an easy long-term relationship.

Pisces woman/Aquarius man

His radical belief system may jar with your more ephemeral ideals and although physically it's all very arousing, there could be difficulties in the rhythm of your very different emotional make-up. Good for a short-term fling or affair.

Pisces woman/Pisces man

Because you are so similar you play the same games, changing the rules when one fears rejection from the other. Trapped in a mutual fantasy world, neither of you are interested in the reality. Totally erotic, but your dependency on one another may result in one of you acting the martyr through fear of abandonment.

Seducing your man – and managing him!

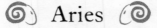 Aries

How to seduce an Aries man

If you're upfront, glamorous and direct the first time you meet, he'll be fired into similar action. It's a sort of challenge to him to prove he's a hero and god's gift to women. He's bewitched by the Extraordinary Woman. The one who doesn't start moaning about her past or how dull the party is. The extraordinary woman is one who is the life and soul, flirts with everyone, but has her eyes secretly fixed on him. Give a sexy smile and chat lines centred around him – 'What's your favourite sports car?' 'How exciting your work is!' Then drop in a few subtle carrots here and there that you know Harley Davidson's team of designers or that you go hang-gliding regularly. Soon he'll be wanting the kind of physical sport he enjoys most – the romantic chase and, of course, sex.

Be confident about yourself, but boost his ego with truck-loads of flattery, and then dash off from the party or pub when he's looking the other way. He thrives on the hunt, so be chased. Ignore his phone calls or texts for a few days, or keep your mobile turned off to really keep him guessing. When you do finally pick up the phone, provocative sparring with sexy innuendoes and a dash of wit will make him want to hunt you even more. Before he has time to suggest a time and place for a date, suggest the local skydiving club, or some-where you can dance. (He adores showing off, and the trick is never to look or even feel embarrassed by his antics; he can see right through any deception.) Make him feel very impor-tant – you know, 'Gosh, did you really do that? How exciting! Wow, are you going to do that, how amazing!' Frankly, he loves talking about himself, so be a good listener, but not a blank sheet of paper. Prove you're as independent as he is and, more than anything, not an easy catch.

Be as sexually exciting as he is when you get up close and personal, and remember you're his equal – not a sack of po-tatoes. He imagines you to be a sort of modern-day Joan of Arc who will never give up her own quest for anyone. Don't start trying to tell him what to do in his life, but be assertive about your own sexual needs. He won't ask what they are as he's usually more worried about his own. Sounds like a bit of an egotist? Well, if you get past the first few dates, keep up the fire-queen image he has of you, overpower him with your physical magic and maintain your independence, there's a man who will always be exciting, passionate and heroic by your side.

Managing your Aries man month by month

January

He's still in two minds about making a major life change. You do come into the equation, but like any algebra lesson, it isn't always obvious where it is leading to. Don't do any numbers on him. He's done his own sums, and if you want to be number one in his life, keep the flak down to zero.

February

You just can't pin him down to anything this month. If he's not hopping onto planes, trains or dashing between bars and clubs, he's leaping in and out of your bed. Try to tolerate his restless side. Jealously won't get you anywhere except left home-alone, while he's horsing around.

March

Well, you know he's a bit of a wild roamer, and if you're up for a fun social whirl this month you might be a tad concerned at his sudden desire to adventure forth alone. Give him loads of rope and he won't stray into other female territory. He only needs to crack on with his ambitious plans.

April

If he's reacting snappily around the 6th, he's more likely to be frustrated in his search for something to challenge him mentally, than seeing someone else. Help him find a creative outlet around the 11th, and Venus's gentle influence will bring out the romantic soul in your warrior man.

May

Expect the unexpected. After the 5th, if he's not drinking champagne out of your shoes, he'll be plying you with romantic texts. Mid-month, he's a step ahead of everyone in thoughts and actions and there's no way out. Frankly, when he's being this romantic, why would you want to leave?

June

This month you just don't know where you stand with him. One minute he has got amazing plans for mutual adventure, the next he is talking about his need for independence and personal space. If you can bear to go with his erratic flow, by the 30th he'll be far more inspired to share his dream than giving up on the one he already has. You.

July

The end of a project on the 2nd frees him up to spend more time together with you, but he seems to find it hard to stay in one place. His erratic behaviour makes you wonder if he is as committed as he says. With Venus's influence, there's no doubt that he is – he just needs encouragement to show it.

August

He's all finger and thumbs – well only when he's trying to undo your bra straps. His nervousness is simply due to him, the romantic fool that he is, beginning to experience feelings of the 'tender' kind. Don't let on you know, and keep him on his toes. His sex drive will reveal all.

September

With his ruler, Mars surging into his love corner, frankly he's going to be either kneeling down at your feet to make a commitment, or thrashing around in bed with you 24/7. Between you and me, I'd take all promises with a pinch of salt. As for the sex, go for it.

October

With a Full Moon in his own sign on the 7th, he has gone all moody on you. And a temperamental Aries isn't an easy beast to tame. Leave him to wallow in the pub with his pals. He's got big plans for changing his world to make it a better place. If you want to be part of it, keep cool and don't challenge him.

November

Adventurous travel plans take over from the social injustices – he's all leaps and bounds, and if you bought him a pogo stick, he'd probably hop to work on it. If he does go off on a trip without you, don't imagine the worst. If he takes you with him, imagine the best.

December

With Mars firing him into action everywhere but at home, you'll just have to keep up or get out. Yet that wanderlust look in his eye turns to lust for you by the end of the month, and if you show him you are the most loyal woman in the country, he'll take you out of yourself.

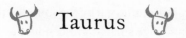

Taurus

How to seduce a Taurus man

Getting him fascinated isn't too difficult if you have exquisite taste, know the difference between quality and quantity, dress 'feminine sensual', or happen to have a large income. Yes, seriously, this earthy beauty-lover does place great value on material wealth, because money represents the key to his sense of security. Also, he wants to feel secure with you. Your sexual assets, your belief in him, your trust in him and, of course, enjoying and indulging in the simple pleasures of life are what seduces him.

When you first bump into him, he can take a while to be tempted into sexier gambits, simply because he likes to know what value you place on him. (The art of making him feel like a vat of gold is to titillate all his senses by subtly making it clear you adore his voice, his masculinity, his eyes, his skin, his work and his taste in cars. But you must talk quality words and give out quality body language.) Seducing him isn't too hard if you wear the most expensive perfumes around and don't dress like a tart. Remember, he's a sucker for femininity – with a big F! Empower him with a gentle touch to his arm now and again, kiss his cheek tenderly when you meet (no lipstick either, he prefers the natural look) and be divinely you.

Next, talk about music (even if neither of you is a classical music buff, he's impressed by the sound of the words) and drop in buff language such as 'crescendo', 'cello' or 'Carmen', and you'll get his sense receptors working overtime. And then if you talk about beautiful clothes, four-poster beds, how your favourite winter wear is cashmere, that your mother has wonderful antiques in her attic, works of art are worth investing in, and winter landscapes or summer skies are worth giving up the rat race for, he'll begin to realize you might be the ultimate temptress in his life. Emphasize your love of the simple pleasures of life, like eating, sex and nature, peppered with money matters. For example, how nice it would be to have a vault filled with gold bars, how you adore expensive jewellery, classic cars and antiques. How you adore going to restaurants, particularly ones where you can slurp country soups together before a roaring log fire, or gourmet banquets with an endless delight of different wines. Do avoid those little nouvelle cuisine-type meals which, for a man with a big appetite, will only leave him twitchy or walking out the door when the waiters hover round him like flies. Invite him to your favourite restaurant, or cook him something special on your own stove – he loves to be nurtured. But don't fall into the trap and think he's an easy catch. Once you've got him to the bedroom, he adores sex and, remember, quality is still more important than quantity. Always look good, wear beautiful underwear but never, never let him see you shaving your armpits or slopping around in rollers. This man is one of the most romantic yet sensual signs of the zodiac, and even though he can be downright stubborn, once he's yours, he's usually yours for life.

Managing your Taurus man
month by month

January

The Sun's glow brings emotional honesty to the fore and there is an in-love sensation between you and him all month. If you are feeling hemmed in after the 8th, just make it clear that you need your space. Boundaries are vital to you both, and if there's one thing your sexy Bull understands, it's a few fences.

February

He wants to be closer to you, but there's a fear that if he gives away too much too soon you won't love the real man inside. Don't tell him that you know men are just as vulnerable as women, because he'll just deny it. Instead, stroke his ego, back his ambitious plans and, hey presto, he'll be moving nearer than you ever thought possible.

March

His persistent hammering will eventually drive that nail into the hole. Whether that nail is related to work or relationship, there is no avoiding his determined efforts. And if what he wants is you, he'll woo you until you submit. Enjoy it, it'll be an exhilarating and evocative experience.

April

He keeps financial fears so well hidden that you could mistake money worries for disinterest, and after the 14th, Mars's shilly-shallying influence holds up his plans. If you're anticipating a lifestyle upgrade, don't panic, it'll come at the end of the month.

May

With Mercury in his own sign, he's up for some serious conversations about his future. If he doesn't include you on the agenda, don't get in a flap. He's just testing to see if you are as cool, calm and diplomatic as he imagines you to be. Pass the grade, and you'll rise to the top of his must-have list.

June

Mars and Jupiter test his cool on the 19th. Can he perform professional wonders, or does he need a miracle woman by his side? Probably both, so make sure you are as serious about his future as he is. Your eyes will say it all, so mean it if you say you'll be there for him through thick and thin.

July

Lo and behold, he's thinking big business and talking sweet nothings all at once. Finally, he's getting his act together, and it pays to realize he's serious when it comes to his future. Stick by his side, drool over his financial wizardry, and enjoy the pace.

August

He's getting a bit picky about your wardrobe co-ordination – or lack of it as he sees it. And in the nicest possible way he's trying to take control of you. If you let him, this could be the commitment you have longed for – if you don't it could be the showdown he's anticipating.

September

Luckily, he's realized you have a right to wear what you want to wear, as long as it doesn't clash with his good taste. And with Venus in earthy Virgo, he's beginning to remember that romance is an essential part of his life too. In fact, he's craving naked fun rather than all that dress-sense.

October

This month he's up for all-night sex marathons or jogging round the block. Either way, Mars is giving him the kind of body awareness that means you can have your wicked way too. It's all steamy windows and breakfast in bed stuff. Make the most of his roaring libido.

November

You can carry on giving him all that attention. Cook up some grub, soothe his brow, flex his muscles and he will only have eyes for you. The Full Moon in his own sign on the 5th means he's making secret plans for the future, and the New Moon in the 20th means he'll reveal them – to only you.

December

For once he wants to get away from all that festive routine. Family do matter to him, but adventure and foreign shores are on his mind. He is reliably predictable about where he wants to go though – anywhere he can lap up the peace, harmony and beauty of a luxurious package. Make sure you are the one wrapped up ready for the New Year.

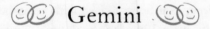 Gemini

How to seduce a Gemini man

Flirt, flirt, flirt and flirt again. And I don't mean just with him, but with all those other charming men around you. He's looking for an independent light-hearted woman to amuse him, who doesn't want to trap him, commit herself to a life of mortgages and responsibilities or be tied down herself. (Mind you, occasionally he likes being tied up in fun.) Attract his attention initially by being a witty, chatty, frivolous conversationalist, with a splattering of erotic innuendoes thrown in. (No clichés – you have to have a brilliant, clever, quick brain.) Then disappear to the heart of the throng, or just disappear to the bathroom, and don't come back. The more you play the hide and seek game, the more he'll be interested. Always be reasonable, and avoid being insecure or grumpy. For example, if he says something like, 'Hey, Emma is really cool and fun. She's so fanciable,' don't reply, 'Oh, I don't know, I think she's a bit of a tart actually.' He'll instantly rationalize your response as a jealous reaction. But if you say something like, 'Yes, I know, I can see why men fall for her, isn't she amazing?' that's impressive; It proves you are as objective and as observant as he is.

He's a game player, and will be ultimately turned on by what's coming from your mind rather than your feelings. And sex isn't a feely, sensual, sweaty body affair for this fickle and sometimes impossible to live with man. It's all about thinking sex too. He's not so bewitched by your looks, but he is seduced by the unpredictable woman who one day throws on an old pair of jeans, the next is in stilettos. He gets bored quicker than any other zodiac sign, and thrives on mind games, funny e-mails and sitting in bars observing human nature and how it ticks.

Be curious about him too. But be as popular as he is – or more. Joke, laugh with his pals, wind him up a little, then push off when he least expects you to. He's easily bored and wants to be amused in love. His innate curiosity will mean he'll follow any trail which is peppered with surprises. And if you can provide that kind of light-hearted and spirited treasure hunt, he'll turn up on your doorstep when least expected. If you tell him where you are, and then demand to know why he isn't there too, he'll probably be found chatting up Emma the following weekend. On the other hand, call him from your office and tell a little white lie to make him curious, for example, 'I've just popped over to Paris on business. We're having such a fantastic time!' and his twinkling eyes will be shining at you across the pillow a few days later while you chat enthusiastically about Sartre, Baudelaire and the Arc de Triomphe. Remember, research, research, research goes with the three Flirt factors – flirt, flirt and flirt again. Be scintillating in public places if it kills you. If you're stunning everyone else, and can talk your way out of any social corner or political debate down the pub, he'll be hooked. He's hard to pin down and notoriously unfaithful, but if you're as freedom-loving and people-loving as much as he is, you might just become his best lover and friend.

Managing your Gemini man
month by month

January

Jupiter's influence blows the winds of success in his favour and he's looking to you to celebrate with him. His personal achievement is important to him. But if he spends too much time at work around the 13th, he hasn't found another woman, just his true vocation. The good news is, you are part of it.

February

When he's in the mood to be down-right difficult for the sake if it, there's not much you can do about it. So let him get it out of his system. But around the 21st, you might wonder if you'll ever get a break. Luckily, by the end of the month, his cheek turns to tenderness, and his libido moves not only the earth, but the cosmos for you too.

March

Venus's influence puts him in a romantic mood before the 17th, but by the 28th he's craving something different. Seek out cultural things to do and places to see. Spicing up the everyday will give your relationship an inventive boost. He will be in awe that you can read his moods so well.

April

His pin-sharp perception of your thoughts makes it hard to keep anything secret, but he needs mystery in his life around the 19th. Play guessing games, get him to imagine your perfect evening – and act it out. It's also a great way of getting to do what you want for a change.

May

Of course, the physical chemistry is flowing between you, but he needs to know you have a brilliant mind and aren't going to turn into a clinging vine. This month, he's fascinated with his finances, so talk money and prove how self-reliant you are. Don't depend on him, and he'll be there for you.

June

He knows everything about human nature – apparently. But those fuzzy edges around emotions are still eluding him. This month, he's not too keen on discussing his feelings. So don't lose your cool when he'd rather plan his professional in-house rebellion than play romantic games.

July

Torn between inventing a new sex toy and just getting down to the nitty-gritty, he's got his mind on physical bliss. What better way to get through the dark nights than in his arms? Make sure he's not up all night at the drawing board though; he needs to be seduced.

August

His friends seem more important that romantic dates this month, and you really can't be sure what he's up to. Don't show any signs of jealousy or possessiveness or you'll be in big trouble. Calmly attend to your own social devices and he'll soon be back in your arms.

September

Oops! With a gang of planets in his romantic zone, he's either sweeping you off your feet every night, or swapping cheeky stories with new admirers in his workplace. If you want to keep him, make it clear you are turned on by hearing his seductive adventures. At least he won't lie to you.

October

Like any mercurial minded hero, indecision gets to him this
month, and he wants you to help him sort out his life-plan.
Does he go for that job, turn it down, or simply do something
radical such as leave the country. Make sure you don't make
his decisions for him, especially not based on what you want.

November

With Venus and Jupiter surging into his relationship corner,
you might think he'd want to settle down to a 'normal' relationship. But I'm afraid he's not quite ready for lawnmowers
and coffee percolators. He wants his space, so give it him and
he'll give you the kind of love that means he's hooked on you
anyway.

December

Mars bustles into fiery Sagittarius this month and he's restless for travel. If he goes off on an impulsive jaunt alone, don't
worry. He'll be back to whisk you away for another weekend
treat before the end of the month. Don't ask him where he's
been or who with. He's hot property and, wonderfully, he'll
still be all yours.

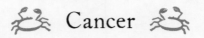

Cancer

How to seduce a Cancer man

One of the most complex signs of the zodiac, this sensual, but restless and insecure man needs a complicated seduction act too. First of all, don't talk about his mother unless he mentions her. The chances are she'll come up in his conversation at some point, even if it's just 'mum's the word'; or while you're engrossed in a conversation about life, he keeps referring to the 'maternal instinct' or how his mother always cooked wonderful mash. If he doesn't mention a 'mother experience', then take care because he might not be at all comfortable with seductive women. (They often represent the 'overpowering mother', and at this point you don't know what his relationship with his own mother is – he either adores her or hates the ground she walks on.)

More than any other man in the zodiac, apart from Pisces, this man innately empathizes with women and their sensitive side, but he doesn't particularly like the fact he does. He has feelings, but why? He has moods, but he doesn't get PMT. He needs to be loved, but finds it uncomfortable if he's smothered with too much affection. But – and there is a big but – if he's had serious issues with his mother, he might flip into King Cancer, the macho man to a fault, who can't deal with his moods, his feelings or his own very needy self. And then he's back to being unable to deal with seductive women, who he sees as an invasive threat to his vulnerable side.

So, how to get past the barriers he sets up for himself? And why would you want to in the first place, your best friend asks? Well, because underneath all that moody, defensive stuff, he's a sensitive, intuitive, sensual, imaginative and hilarious friend and lover. He's also pretty hot with money and is eternally loyal.

He's most attracted to self-reliant women. The ones who are secure in themselves, genuine, have integrity and aren't flippant flirts in a constant flap. Talk about the past – he's far more interested in what has been than what will be; not an arrogant appraisal of all your exes, but how things once were. Memories of films, school-kid stuff, the photos you have stuffed away in your cupboard, the music you listen to over and over again. He's also turned on by the self-sufficient air you have. That you can support yourself, have an excellent investment portfolio or are a whizz with finances. And, most importantly, that you are prepared to change your plans at the drop of a hat. Once he's realized that you can take him out of himself, his moodiness is forgotten when he's in your vivacious company and you make him laugh about life. Then you can also add unpredictable romantic carrots such as, 'I've never felt like this before', 'Let's have sex now', 'Let's grow tomatoes in your window box', 'I'm going to visit relatives this weekend.' First, it proves you care about him; second, that you are serious about being together, and third, you are clearly self-sufficient enough to give him time when he needs to be alone. If he feels like going out to dinner 'a deux', rather than the local curry house with a gang of friends, then be prepared to adapt accordingly. Then there's his sensual side. He likes to

339

be touched, he adores romance, candles, the lingering smell of your perfume on his shirtsleeve, and your phone number to gaze at while he's working in the office. Keep up the romantic, unpredictable, but reliable you, and he's a winner.

Managing your Cancer man month by month

January
He is beginning to seem far more feisty and less unreliable. With Uranus giving him surprising ideas about the future, attempt to understand him – or else. There's a light at the end of his tunnel, so make sure you're ready to go through it with him. Don't drag him into your own, just yet.

February
He's hardly put the phone down when you wonder if he's hiding something from you around the 1st. But by the 9th, Mercury gives him the courage to tell you what's up. Actually, it's just that he wasn't sure how to tell you about his exciting new plans for the future. And they do include you.

March
Adorable though he is, he's feeling restless for adventure and you just can't seem to keep him on his toes. Let him roam a little. He needs to chill out and lose himself in his dreams. By the 17th, he wakes up to the fact that he needs your motivated ideas to give him fresh direction.

April

Daydreamer that he is, he's used to creating castles in the air, but, for once, they are for real. Domesticity is something he thrives on, and by the 20th he's looking for a raunchy princess to share his domain. Make sure that you are dressed, or undressed, accordingly for that knock on your door.

May

Self-reproach sets in around the 5th, when he's wondering how loved he really is. Returning to the bosom of his family is one answer, but nuzzling into yours is much more fun. Help him find comfort in your arms and he'll keep coming back for more.

June

Yes, he's got amazing plans and he's sure that he can stick to them, but he begins to doubt himself again around the 10th. Boost his self-confidence and be as down to earth and motivated as you can. What he needs right now is genuine support and a woman who has the patience to nurture his needs. And that's you isn't it?

July

A look here and a word there are so easy to blow out of proportion, but around the 16th let your Crab express himself freely, or he'll flounder. Political correctness may be the norm, but debate is what he wants. Give it to him and he'll rise to your seductive bait.

August

Don't bother arguing with him around the 2nd, he's in contrary mode and will win any argument he starts – even if he's wrong. On the 11th, share his enthusiasm for physical passion, but make sure he's not playing devil's advocate with his affections.

September

He's guarding a secret and, try as you might, you can't get him to kiss and tell. An ex's arrival on the scene around the 10th might be bugging him, but it could just be a work matter he can't resolve. He loves escaping into the past, so prove that the present holds far more sensual pleasures.

October

Wicked whispers make for inspirational sex this month. And you know how he loves it when you talk dirty? Just make sure you give an equally passionate response to his plans for work changes. He knows what's best for him, so don't feel he's leaving you out in the cold.

November

Everyone wants to be his friend, and that means you've got a fair share of admirers as well. He gets particularly jealous about your mild flirtation with his best mate mid-month. He'll probably retreat, refuse to call you and pretend he doesn't care. But you know better.

December

The warmth between you creates sexy moves and fiery libido highs this month. It's all easy-going dates, blissful nights and a knowledge that you are the centre of his universe. But take care, if he gets it in his head you are a permanent fixture, you might find your personal goals are lost in the ether. Make sure he knows that you are number one in your life too.

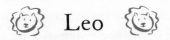 Leo

How to seduce a Leo man

Anything less than being the glamorous queen of his dreams won't do. This man is a sucker for fame, power, money, status and 'who you know'. Which is fine as long as the people you know are famous, rich, powerful, have social or professional status and aren't shelf-fillers. He needs a classy, stylish woman, who he can hang on his arm at social events, who shimmers coolly beside the pool and is smart enough to have spent her money wisely at a tanning parlour before she even thinks of getting to the beach. Yes, he is a bit of a snob, but he's also quite insecure about his own specialness. So the more special you are, and the more you tell him that he is, the more attracted he'll be to you and the more he'll be attracted to himself.

If you've already got your eye on him, then check out his favourite places and plan to be there. Dress to kill, be ultra-stunning and look like you've just been on stage. Super-model status isn't essential, but at least play up your vivacious pulling power, be daring and provocative. Smile like a film star, act like one, and he'll be twirling the black tie, the coins in his pocket or the champagne glass between his fingers in anticipation of what's to follow.

He needs a challenge to bring out his passionate streak, so make it clear that you're far more interested in your own success than anybody else's (apart from his). You probably won't even have a chance to take the initiative, but if you do, strike up a conversation about your favourite champagne and how you know the proprietor of various vineyards in France. Tell him about your friends in the city (one of course is a multi-millionaire) and that you once had a Ferrari. (All of these little white lies will do wonders for his libido, and if you can't bear the thought of telling fibs, then stay away.) Because even if you don't have this kind of status, he can imagine that HE does, and it will arouse him enough to desire you to fulfil his kingly role with him.

Once you've laid the bait for a date, keep up the super-woman image, take his mind off all your wealthy (and probably imaginary) friends with your richness of body, personal ambition and quest for power. Sexually he wants to be in charge, but is up for pillow fights and a woman who knows what she wants too. Make mad passionate love in the wildest, outrageous places. He's a bit of an exhibitionist, so don't panic if he's more interested in sex in public places than he is in your cosy love nest. But if you can rustle up a breakfast fit for a king the following morning, and still look like a squillionaire, he'll be back for more.

Remember, ultimately he has to be the centre of attention, the most special person in all the world. If you draw the crowds first, that's fine, but he'll want to take over the limelight. If he feels you're getting more attention than he is, the Little Lord Fauntleroy act takes over. 'Spoilt? Me? Never,' he laughs. 'I'm simply the best, and I deserve the best,' he'll remind you. Agree that perhaps he does, and seeing as he chose you, then that's exactly what's he's got. Stay dazzling, talk zealously about his future, while still being subtly creative with your own. Always tell him he's wonderful and his loyalty will be unshakeable. Just take care you don't resort to sloppy clothes, cheap deodorants and yawning in front of the TV when you could be sipping champagne. That means you'll shatter his dream of the perfect princess and, like the child he is, he'll be off on another quest for the queen of his dreams.

Managing your Leo man month by month

January

He's sprucing himself up, admiring his reflection and shining those twinkly eyes at you. And when he puts himself first and disappears without a 'by your leave', you wonder if he'll ever sing to a mutually desired tune. Probably not, but wouldn't life be dull and predictable if he did?

February

One minute he expects you to try moves from the Kama Sutra and then, around the 14th, he wants to jet off to Hawaii alone. Let him travel, he values his independence like a priceless jewel, but don't be his whipping boy. Remind him that the best Karma comes from mutual respect.

March

Well, what do you expect? With Venus in his opposite sign, he's passionate about everything, from your sexy lingerie to his stack of car magazines. Motivated and raunchy, he might need a little more leeway in his social life. Don't be jealous, he's just in the mood to strut his stuff.

April

Saturn moves forward in Leo on the 5th, and he's going to be on the hunt for a new crusade to inspire him. Don't worry if he talks about himself all month. Luckily, his passionate fury means he'll also be in the mood to sweep you off your feet over and over again.

May

Assert your own sexual needs this month. He is so worried about his own that he probably won't even think to ask about yours. The more you show that you're his equal, the less he'll assume that he can just do his own thing. He's buzzing with exciting plans for the future too, so keep up to date.

June

A few jealous moment around the 6th put you both in a grump, but subsequent attempts at making up are so deliciously rewarding that you're tempted to go another round. After the 10th, he's in charm mode which makes it impossible to find fault. Frankly, even though he's utterly devoted to you, don't even try.

July

Whispered sweet nothings around the 4th make you feel so adored. But by the 17th he's so consumed by a zillion new challenges he may forget to call. Enthuse, excite and wallow in the thrills of his potential hopes and dreams and you'll be the girl he wants to share them with.

August

As usual, he's got a fantastic vision for the future. But whether it includes you or not is a delicate issue this month. So don't push him for answers, don't question his motives or imagine he's up to something. He just needs space to sort out his life. Actually, the more you get on with yours, the more he'll be working out how to fit you into his game-plan.

September

It is often said that if you want something done, ask a busy person. Well, that could have been written about your man right now. He's enjoying a sense of control and the opportunity to lead and shine. Nothing will distract him;

except perhaps a bottle of bubbly and some very skimpy lingerie around the 16th.

October

Travelling is on both your minds, but he has to make a choice between a new destination, or sticking with one that he knows and loves. Opt for the different and be inspired by a whole new social crowd. He just adores an audience and a sea of fresh faces will make him feel like a star.

November

He's a born-again Valentino this month. All magic moments, romantic flurries and luxurious sex. You really can't want for more, or can you? Could it just be he still hasn't made it clear how he feels about you. This month, you won't need to ask, he'll be telling you across the pillow.

December

He' got a bee in his bonnet about something. What it is remains a mystery until after the festive bash. Then, in the dull light of the end of the year, he unleashes all his woes and troubles. Frankly, it's just because he needs someone to understand he's quite a softie underneath all that roaring libido and lion-taming act. Let him know you are the one who cares..

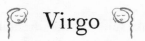 Virgo

How to seduce a Virgo man

Nine times out of ten, Virgo men are led astray by self-contained, efficient women who are poised, classy, intellectually bright and who stick to what he believes is the conventional formula for seduction. This means he feels as if he's in control, and can tick off the pros and cons about whether he wants to get further involved with you before it all gets messy and out of his hands – his worse fear.

So what are his version of the rules? As we know, you can't pigeon-hole romance, but if you want to get closer to him, then you have to accept that he believes in order, one step at a time, and the steps up to the altar or just his bed are unambiguous and conclusive absolutes. So, if you secretly know what they are and follow the steps in the chronological order below, then you can bewitch this sensitive, highly sensual and useful man right into your life.

What's going into your mouth, and what's coming out of it? If you want him to sit up and take serenely cool and fascinated notice, eat your mung-bean sprouts, tofu sandwich or vegetarian crudités with politesse. Avoid fast foods, calorie inducing fat and gallons of beer, all of which he usually detests and knows are bad for you. From his perspective, what goes down your throat is a clue to what goes on inside your head.

When you first have a conversation, which is usually when you've been formally introduced by a friend, colleague or other contact, make sure you have the ability to talk about 'Very Knowledgeable Things'. (The things coming out of your mouth are the biggest attraction factor to him on first acquaintance.) It's not just what you say, but the way you speak, the intonation of your voice, your use of vocabulary, the way you can laugh and smile without him seeing all your fillings. Don't forget, this man is obsessive about order and everything in its place – and that includes your teeth. So talk objectively about anything from the Roman invasion of Britain to how fascinating it is that not many people know the difference between entomology and etymology. (If you don't, intelligently check the words out now, because if HE doesn't know, then you're already one up on him. And he is a sucker for the Wise woman.)

Once he's confirmed in his head that you are 'Very Knowledgeable', you can attend to sexier pursuits. Lack of passion? Well, he's sensual, private and highly erotic when he chooses. But you can't force him, or even direct him into bed yet. First, he needs to be lulled into a feeling that he's actually in control of the situation. So don't ever get emotional on your first dates, don't ever get in a flap about the late train or the silly friend who forgot to give you a lift. Take it all with calm realism, a dose of clever humour and let him think he can be very useful to you. That doesn't mean you have to let him open doors for you (though he won't mind) or shake out your napkin at the table, but he is a gentleman.

Respect and Discuss. Of course you have feelings, and so does he. In fact, by now he's probably proved he's a whizz beneath the sheets and wants to make it a little more like a relationship than a jog round the park. Respect his ideas, his work and yours too. Prove you are a professional in your own way, and always agree to differ rather than rant and rave and have tantrums in his favourite restaurant – this would seriously upset his, dare I say it, Karma (he might use the word).

Finally, the sexiest thing about you apart from your trim body and sophisticated looks, is your mind. So the more intelligently you plan your seduction campaign, then the chances are you'll be rewarded with a complex, but honest, reliable and inexhaustible lover.

Managing your Virgo man month by month

January

With Mars in pig-headed Taurus, he's behaving like the determined earth-sign that he is. He wants what he wants and if you're part of that equation, one way or another he'll get you. There's no fooling him, his intuition is spot on and isn't that what you want anyway?

February

Blending his roles as model worker and energetic lover combines your need for fun with his lust for hard work. Around the 23rd, put on your high heels and demand that he satisfies your every whim. He is in the mood for domination and you can both enjoy the pleasure of his labours.

March

A Sun-driven surge of domestic bliss puts him in nesting mode and romantically he's infatuated with you. Be honest about your feelings, or you may find yourself swept away by the power of his enthusiasm. It's your call – he's so dizzy with desire you can write the rule book.

April

Okay, he's had a few disappointments recently, and he's now convinced his professional life is on the right track. But remember, he may be a realist but he's also fanatically security-conscious. Let him take control of anything he wants this month, whether it's the joy-stick or the kitchen. He'll thank you in the most sensually indulgent way.

May

It's hard to follow his train of thought around the 17th, when he's not sure what he wants and why. It's more likely to be a personal or financial problem that's bugging him than anything to do with you. Give him time to brood and he'll come running to seek love and approval in your arms.

June

If he seems preoccupied around the 14th, engage his mind, indulge his love of luxury and wrap yourself in things that are soft to the touch. Ensure that it's you who's acting out his fantasies, or he might act them out with someone from his past.

July

Quality time with you matters to him this month. So make sure you are ready for nestling up to him by night, and looking your most gorgeous by day. He's a little insecure about his finances (as usual), but if you suggest he does his sums on paper rather than in his head, you'll come up trumps.

August

You just can't stop him from doing his own thing. With potent Mars in his own sign, mountains will be moved, sex will be glorious, and he'll be up for pushing himself to the top of his profession. Stick by his side – it's worth being mere putty in his hands for the pleasures to come.

September

It's one of those 'must have it now' months for him. Although he's keen on financial security, he keeps spending his cash on all kinds of bargains and beautiful things. Keep your head, avoid the sales, and lure him into a night-time investment of the sexiest kind. You.

October

Time is money, he reminds you on the 13th, and you know he's waiting for a very important work decision. But he won't listen to your advice this month, simply because he doesn't want to admit you're right. Don't push him, he'll soon come round by assuming he thought of the idea first.

November

He can get awfully fanatical about his body, his keep fit routine and his diet. This month, he's obsessed with anything from your teeth to your hair colour. Let him rant and rave a bit, but don't change your look to please him. He's got to learn that you please yourself first, him second – sometimes.

December

Mistletoe is hung, parties are visited, friends are rowdy, and your man? He's decided that he wants 'out' from this year's glitz and fuss. In fact, if he doesn't invite you to spend time away in some exotic location, suggest it yourself. He's waiting to be told what to do, for once.

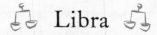

Libra

How to seduce a Libran man

Now, he might seem like an easy catch when you first meet him. Especially if you're beautiful, feminine and perfectly turned out. He's the social charmer, and falls quickly in love with anything from your eyes, hair, smile and breasts to your name if it resonates with his own ideal of perfection. (If you're called something unpronounceable or harsh sounding, it might be worth kitting yourself out with a pseudonym to be going on with.) The main problem is that Mr Libra is always going to be seduced by a pretty face. He's a natural flirt and a paradigm of seduction himself. He can charm monkeys out of trees and sell saunas in a rain forest. And he notices beauty wherever he goes. 'Wow, hasn't she got a beautiful face, it's perfect,' he whispers in your ear, just as you thought he was about to lick it. He's tempted by all women who look after their bodies and has visions of being the ultimate Romeo. (His perception of beauty is very classical. Gentle voice, feminine hairstyles, not too much make-up and a charisma that makes other men turn their heads when you walk in the room.) Easily infatuated by what he considers to be the Perfect Woman, the more you play the part, and the more you keep up the glamorous, female mystique as embodied by you, the goddess Aphrodite herself, the more he'll play along with the game.

When you first encounter him, his charm and his own appearance are cultivated, refined and aesthetically balanced. He knows how to be socially correct, he knows how to be the diplomat and the romantic, and he expects that of you too. Without much work you can turn him on with light-hearted banter, a winning smile, a sexy dress and a polished performance in public. On first meeting him, you quickly find out that you have to learn to be his equal – well almost. If he's drunk three glasses of wine, he's happier if you drank only two. Make sure you don't get drunk and become an embarrassment, because any kind of behaviour which isn't civilized shatters his ideal of the perfect woman and thus will crush all hopes of the perfect relationship. Then again, if you flirt with three men simultaneously, he'll be sure to be found flirting with four beautiful women. No wonder he's got a reputation for being a bit of a playboy. Why? Well, he wants to be wanted, he seeks approval to give him a sense of self-worth, he adores being flattered and proving that he can seduce anyone into loving him. He's a hopeless romantic, but hopeless romantics have a big problem. Once past the first few dates he often never really gets to commit himself in case there's someone more beautiful, more harmonious, more perfect round the corner.

To reel him and keep him well and truly hooked, elevate your feminine mystique to glamour princess status, and never let him get a glimpse of your spots, your unshaven bits and bobs, nor your face creams. Scrub your toenails and slap on the moisturizer when he's not around. Always stay cool, calm and collected about your feelings, show no jealousy when he chats about all the women who fancy him. Instead, turn it into a conspiracy between you – 'She wants to pull you, what fun! Do tell me what happens,' rather than a confrontation, 'You're with me aren't you? Don't you realize I have feelings too?' Well, frankly, no. Talking about feelings is fine, but expressing them is taboo.

Once you've finally got him into a bedroom, remember that ultimately he has to experience himself through relationship. And the more harmonious, dreamlike and perfect you are, the more he's likely to enjoy the experience of being himself.

Managing your Libran man
month by month

January

He's being so adorable you feel like bottling him. You can't
bear to be separated around the 7th. But what happens if you
bottle a butterfly? Don't suffocate him, give him the space he
needs and he'll fly home to you because he loves you and not
because he's trapped.

February

Sexy Mars sways through the seductive area of his chart, giving him the charm and sex appeal of Brad Pitt. After the 20th,
he may start seeking answers from a new kid on the block.
Give him the freedom to stray within your relationship and
he won't feel the need to.

March

Uranus is giving him innovative ideas, and you could offer to
prop up the bar with him, but he might get led astray by a
flirty friend. Pillow-talk is wiser. And even if you don't get
your wicked way, at least he'll rabbit on until he falls asleep
in your arms, rather than across the bar.

April

What is he up to? One minute he's gassing on about culture,
wine and the latest book he's read, the next he's moving his
furniture around. Be as sparkling and inventive as you can,

keep him amused and the changes he needs right now, will still include you.

May

Think 'humour' and 'light-hearted conversations' this month, and you'll be keeping each other amused from dawn to dusk. Be cool around the 25th, when he flirts with a female contact to get ahead of the competition. Tell him you think she's the perfect answer, and he'll think you are too.

June

If there's an obstacle to overcome or a fence to jump, he's prepared to leap it around the 5th. So, in the tradition of maidens of old, set him a task to complete. Give him a sexy quest and by the 25th he'll be whispering sweet nothings and demanding his promised reward. You.

July

Around the 2nd, he's so all-engulfing and passionate, and then on the 17th he's the iceman personified. Could it be that he's getting so emotionally attached that he's freaking himself out? Break down his fears by helping him to live for the moment, rather than panic about tomorrow.

August

He's worried about financial affairs, and just can't seem to settle into working routines. Remember, he needs time to go out and play, so suggest a weekend jaunt around the 17th, when he'll remember that you're just as fun-loving as he is. Liberate his inner child and he'll make you his favourite sex toy.

September
It seems as if he's three steps ahead of you around the 10th, when his craving for constant excitement needs to be fulfilled, so be sure not to be a damp squib. Share his enthusiasm and he'll think you are the greatest sex goddess since Aphrodite. Let him prove it too.

October
He can't resist winding you up around the 8th. And his mischievous streak causes uncomfortable moments at a social whirl. Is he really getting off with your best friend, or trying to make you jealous? The rogue in him is testing you, so show you've been to flirt school too.

November
His friends do include the female variety, and you have to accept it. But this month he seems to be spending a lot more time with them, and naturally you feel miffed. Chat up a few of his male friends on the 19th, and you'll soon have him hanging around you like a lost dog.

December
When he thinks romance, he acts it too. And this month you can be forgiven for imagining him to be the Prince Charming with the mostest. He's got it all, class, style, the right

clothes and body to match. The only thing that's missing is that he can't commit himself right now, so you'll just have to wait until next year.

Scorpio

How to seduce a Scorpio man

Smoulder with mystery at the business lunch or across the bar, look and act cool and 'hard to fathom' as if you've more hidden power than a nuclear reactor and you'll soon hook him. Now, he won't show that he's in any way fascinated at first. That's the clue. He's notoriously and innately skilled at pretending he's not remotely interested, because he needs to feel that he can control the seduction stakes later on. But the more aloof you are, the less you say and the less you show interest in him, the more he'll want to know you inside out. Once you do strike up a conversation, be awfully intense and passionate about your work, your ambitions and your interest in money-making enterprises. If you happen to know a lot about the stock market or 'futures', and you can discuss the masturbatory habits of Martians without flinching, then you're off to a rampant start. Never give away much about your personal life, don't rabbit on about superficial things such as your favourite TV programmes – and avoid gossip! Don't leave him your phone number, and don't call him. He'll find a way to encounter you again if he's seriously interested. Chances are, the more you play the 'now you see me, now you don't' game, the more he'll want to know you better. What he can't have, he wants, what he can have, he's likely to dispense with sooner rather than later.

Scorpio men live and love dangerously. That doesn't mean he's skydiving every weekend, although some Scorpios do take the danger thing to physical extremes. But he's born with the dark side of life more real to him than the light. He's shrewd, manipulative and very aware of the sexual intensity that flows beneath the surface of romance and relationship. That's why you've got to be a bit of femme fatale or a sexual vamp who's willing to dominate him in bed too. His own libido is all about tangled sheets and locked doors. So once you're both smouldering away in sexual oblivion, never reveal your bedroom secrets to anyone else. Not even your best friend. He'll instinctively know if you've told any tales, and he'll have left the neighbourhood before you can phone and apologize. It's all or nothing with this man, but you can never be sure how far down the relationship road he'll go. If you're up for a passionate fling or intense clandestine affair, then it's worth playing the game his way. And he can provide the most erotic, transformative and compelling of love experiences ever.

Managing your Scorpio man
month by month

January

If he starts getting all snuggly around the 10th, don't assume it's love; it might be a guilty conscience. Give him the benefit of the doubt, help him develop a plan which promises happiness for you both. Inspire him with your dreams and he'll start to believe they're his too.

February

Uranus makes his every move unpredictable. He'll use it to his advantage as there are some very slippery characters who he needs to keep one step ahead of until the 16th. He feels capable of taking the world on single-handedly – and that degree of strength is seriously seductive.

March

Everyone is mad as a March hare. But for some reason, your sensitive Scorpio is making it patently obvious he's the only one sober and correct. Jupiter's forcing him to be acutely self-protective this month. So spend more time wrapped in each other's arms than wrapped up in the pub spirit, or you could lose him.

April

Cook up a new recipe for relationship happiness. With the magic ingredients of support, emotional honesty and sexual spice, he'll feel secure enough to start planning your joint future. But make sure your culinary skills match your seductive ones. He needs a domestic diva too.

May

He's worried, secretly, that he's not pulling his professional weight around the 14th. And, of course, those niggling doubts and fears mean that he can't give you his full attention. By the 25th, he calms down, cooks up some sexy plans for the future, and he's all yours again.

June

At last he feels he can achieve his ambitions. All that self-doubt and moodiness disappears in the wind and he's beginning to wonder if you are the key to his brilliant future. If you want a share in it, then get seducing. He is so sexy when he's got that professional smile of success beaming across his face.

July

Leaving him to his own devices is an option you might regret, so stick by your Scorpion and he won't want to let you go. When he's tired of work around the 8th, surprise him with a secret trip. Whisk him off to the sea, let the waves relax him and his gratitude will be dizzyingly passionate.

August

You love his commitment and fearlessness, and he loves that you adore him for himself. Around the 10th, he wants a sounding board not a solution. Listen and nod at appropriate intervals. Don't demand immediate, all-consuming intimacy and by the 16th he'll be sharing his wildest dreams with you.

September
Harking back to his past might keep him nostalgically entertained, but it makes you wonder if he is feeling insecure about your relationship. It's time to come clean this month, and set the record straight. With the planets making him emotionally fragile, be gentle, but show you care and offer up your true feelings for him.

October
If there's something you want to ask him, or feelings you want to share, discuss intimate matters around the 3rd. While he is feeling uncharacteristically vulnerable, he'll open up. Set him a challenge, watch him succeed, and he'll be putty in your hands. Now you can mould him into the perfect man-about-you.

November
The New Moon in erotic Scorpio on the 20th, triggers off a run of steamy days and sensual nights. The package is just what you wanted. At last, he's getting the best of both worlds. And so are you. Just don't push him into making any promises – he won't be able to keep them.

December

All you wanted was a cosy festive season, but your man has other plans. In fact, curiously enough, he's up for every social bash and showing off his brilliant conversational pieces. But it is all work-related, so don't despair. He needs to make valuable contacts, so stick at his side and be the most valued of them all.

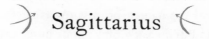

Sagittarius

How to seduce a Sagittarius man

Hilarious social skills are a way to attract him instantly. He adores a woman who's as freedom-loving as he is, who is funny, quick-witted and enjoys flirting with everyone. If you've got any desire to possess, trap or lure him into a life-time of routine, then don't even consider he's the one for you. What turns him on most is the spontaneity of any romance. And if you want to make it last, you've got to: a) keep up with his quest for adventure, his constant change of plans and his restless get up and go libido; and b) accept his need for personal freedom.

Be frank, outspoken and confident about yourself. Have wonderful visions for your own future (and never let on it might include him). Tell him you've travelled the world and are about to embark on another global trip (even if it isn't true, he exaggerates the truth himself, so it won't bother him that you haven't departed three weeks later), and that you never want to be tied down. Commitment, pressure and promises aren't what he's looking for, but fun, crazy romance and a little exotica are.

Dress simple, don't EVER rush off to the ladies to do your make-up (he hates all that preening and prefers the natural look), otherwise the chances are when you get back he'll already be chatting up someone else. Talk a little dirty too, and dance with his mates to prove you're as carefree and capricious as he is. But do ask for his phone number directly and then zoom off with a load of hilarious chums when he's about to buy you a drink.

If you get to the first date, which might never happen as he's just as likely to forget he made one as to remember exactly where, make it clear you're Miss Independence Unlimited, but you are also wild about his body and honest about your sexual needs. Don't forget, he's pretty irrepressible when it comes to sex, and the crazier and the more spontaneous the locations, the more fun you'll have. Socially, he's a bit of a snob, and it helps to know all the right places to be seen in. The food doesn't matter – he probably won't eat much anyway – but he does like to name-drop, and he does like to believe you could pull a few strings for him.

If you're truly able to put up with his horsing around, his late-night chats about how many women he's 'known', then you might even get to the 'let's travel' step. But never arrange to meet him in Paris for a dirty weekend. The chances are he'll make a fantastic promise, regret being put into a 'intimate situation', then fail to turn up at the airport with some amazing excuse about work or the car breaking down. He's a sucker for a woman who does her own thing. So far better to tell him you're off for a weekend alone, book your hotel and nine times out of ten he'll turn up when you least expect him. He's a wild rover, but if you're one as well it could be the most hilarious relationship ever.

Managing your Sagittarius man month by month

January
No one can stop him exuding that sexy, flirtatious, devil-may-care approach around the 5th, and, frankly, isn't that why you find him so attractive? Jealousy is a dangerous emotion, so don't try to play him at his own game, just enjoy knowing that in the long run he's chosen you.

February
The Full Moon in raunchy Leo brings an old flame onto the scene. This doesn't mean that you'll lose him, more likely that he'll decide at long last to bury those old dreams. Dig out your sexiest lingerie and remind him of present fantasies.

March
Suitably in his stride for every social event of the season, but with so much attention from the female ranks, you're beginning to wonder if he's merely draping you around him

like a designer watch to show off. Ensure he loves you for being you, not just because you make him look as if he's a millionaire.

April

Well, he's got that visionary look in his eye this month. You know: the future holds wonderful opportunities, and he must be the one who shines brighter than anyone else. That might mean you're not his pilot for once. But like any back-seat driver, you have more control than he imagines.

May

Self-assured and growling with pride, he's plotting how to overthrow the powers that be. Of course, that means he's thinking of himself first, and you second. But he's secretly proud of you too. Be his star, and you might even become the most celebrated couple in your social circle.

June

He's very aware of your social status this month. And the more you play up your glamorous image and talk about all those important people you know, the more he'll be a sucker for your charms. He secretly wants to impress all his friends, so get strutting and you will soon be in hot heaven.

July

The Sun's influence is stirring up those 'commit or run' sort of dilemmas, putting him in the mood to travel or find his 'spiritual side'. Don't try to force him to be someone he can't

– your understanding rather than your criticism will win his heart and bring him back down to earth.

August

He may seem as if he's in control but, around the 29th, there's an undercurrent of something deeper-seated than he's letting show. Stress is his secret enemy. Soothe his brow, massage his ego and be there if he needs to talk. You are the support he needs to achieve his goals.

September

Not one to sit around twiddling his thumbs, he is charging off at all tangents to make headway with professional plans. That means he might have less time to spare for love's wicked ways this month. Be prepared to be available when he needs you, and you'll still be his star.

October

He would sooner skip the country than tell the truth around the 13th, so don't hassle him to reveal what he's thinking. Give him time to prioritize his needs. Your understanding will be the back-up that he is sneakily relying on to do the right thing. After the 22nd, his plans unfold and your fears are as extinct as dinosaurs.

November

Chasing the odd windmill won't do him any harm. After all, when he's out and about he might bump into someone who can help him decide on his next star performance. I know he's very hard to keep up with, so best get on with your own life and he'll probably want to be part of it too.

DECEMBER
It's his time of the year, and with Mars surging through his sign, you just can't help but laugh at his antics, love his passion for life and adore his wit, humour and, of course, sexiness. He's oozing it, so don't try to possess him, just lap it all up and take each day as it comes.

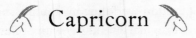 Capricorn

How to seduce a Capricorn man

Rather like the Rock of Gibraltar, you have to prove that you're solid, reliable and have a bit of interesting history. Family connections, money in an offshore bank or just good breeding are also things which turn on this power-conscious and ambitious man. You're more likely to bump into him in the office corridor, lift or company boardroom. He's power-hungry and into big business, although he's also a creature of habit and probably stops off at the local swish wine bar to down a little Chardonnay after work. Rather like Taurus, he's easily impressed by class and beauty. Cheap wine, cheap talk and cheap high-street fashion turn him off. He's seduced by expensive taste which isn't flash and a woman who knows the difference between claret and burgundy. But also make sure beneath that stylish and sophisticated facade you've got the sexiest underwear and the body to match.

Now the problem with Mr Capricorn is that he is awesomely serious about life and love. Maturity means a lot to him (it's a way of defending his vulnerable inner child which he is fanatical about never showing to the world), and any childish behaviour from you in public would turn him into a gibbering lunatic. He's very insecure about 'feeling' and his sensitive side, so he often over-compensates by being a bit of a control freak, both around the office (ruthlessly) and in bed (nicely). He's enchanted by flattery, he's seduced by being a VIP in your eyes, the fact that you know how to hold a conversation with anyone and that you're not scared of hard work. But he also needs to feel you'd give up all your worldly goods for him if the crunch came to it.

If he does make a date, be punctual. He's obsessed with time and, as he knows only too well, it waits for no woman. Discuss his latest enterprise over a candlelit dinner, and never chat to your girlfriends on the mobile while he's around. He demands utter indulgence, and if you're not pampering him between every mouthful, he'll feel his authority is being usurped. You'll probably notice he says, 'I think you *should* give up the job/speak to your bank manager/feed the birds/eat more spinach' rather than 'Why don't you?' or 'What is it you really want to do?'. This is where you'll have to go along with his judgemental side, swallow your pride and admit he's right if you want to take this ambitious (and potentially lucrative) relationship any further.

Only seduce him into bed with sensual gestures in private. He hates public affection and might not even kiss you in front of anyone else in fear of his reputation. Always be available on the phone, and if you have a busy social life, organize it so that he doesn't know you have one as important as he believes his to be. Once you've got past the first date – which he must decide where, when and how – he'll take control of the relationship. Where it's going, and how he is in command at all times. Keeping him hooked isn't hard if you don't rebel against his conventional expectations of love; keep up that cool yet supportive image and devote yourself to being the power behind his and, of course, your own throne.

Managing your Capricorn man month by month

January
If he seems pickier than usual, it is Venus in his own sign making him overly sensitive to the smallest things, and he has other things to occupy his thoughts. Don't take it personally – he's never been a flash-in-the-pan type – and by the 21st blissful equilibrium returns.

February
Friends want to pool resources but he is not sure if he wants

to be involved in a project he's not completely responsible for. Around the 11th, take him away for the weekend to prove that the freedom of irresponsibility is far more liberating than doing all the work himself.

March

He is sweating it out regarding one possible financial or professional gain. And the more you try to take his mind off it all, the more he'll resist. But, on the 11th, he realizes that your love is a serious business too. Choices have to be made, so make it clear what you really want.

April

He can be a bit of a grouch if he is not living out his true potential. And if he's sitting around minding his own business, it's your business to wake him up to the fact he needs to enjoy life, not avoid it. Enlighten him gracefully, show you are on his side, and you won't become the enemy.

May

He is more of a workaholic than ever this month. To draw his attention away from business towards sexier pleasures, make lots of lists and hang them on the fridge or mirror, or pop them in his diary. Among the efficient-looking 'don't forgets', include a splattering of references to a mutual body work-out.

June

Be very knowledgeable and intellectually vibrant this month. He is ready to make some big changes in his life and, if you want to be included, he will be swayed by your ability to work on a joint project. Even if it's only changing a light bulb, you'll soon be swinging from the chandelier together.

July

One minute he's gazing into your eyes and the next he's looking for the nearest escape route. Saturn's fiery influence is stirring up the rebel in him. So to capture his heart wait till the 19th, when he'll want to capture yours right back, and never let go.

August

Don't ever forget that his favourite pastime is putting his life in order. If you want to be part of it, file your receipts, look gorgeous and re-organize your underwear drawer. That done, it will put him in the mood to muss you up around the 8th, and you'll know he's worth the effort.

September

He's Mr Fix It this month. From the leaky pipe to the squeak in your bed. Remember, if he's interfering it means he is genuinely concerned about you. Let him get on with it, and be rewarded with his ability to turn your relationship into a balanced way of loving.

October

An ego boost and a back rub will work wonders on the 13th, when his confidence is low. Help him to aspire, dream and believe in himself. Fickle behaviour around the 17th is no reflection of his feelings for you, he's just giving too much of himself to too many people, as usual.

November

Now you see him, now you don't. He's a tad elusive this month, due to a worry that if he's not in the right place at the right time, he'll miss a very important deal or contract. Success is his middle name so, don't try to tie him down, and he'll soon be gently tying you up in the boudoir.

December

He's his own boss this month, thanks to the winter solstice, and Venus in his own sign. Charismatic, earthy, strong and as confident as a politician, he also knows it is time to work at love too. Don't let him down and he won't let you down either. He means business – especially when it's pleasure he's after.

Aquarius

How to seduce the Aquarius man

Make it very obvious that friendship is what you want first and foremost. Yes, you're fascinated by his body, and of course the physical chemistry is flowing between you, but he needs to know that you have the same kind of mind as his. Far more seduced by your brilliance than your fluttering eyelashes, he's easily tempted and lured into your life if you make it clear you're an unconventional thinker with no intention of depending on him. You must have progressive beliefs, staggering theories about mankind or be a serious crusader for the rights of anything which moves, whether it's a whale or a crab. What turns him on is abstracts and ideals. Philosophize rather than make judgemental statements. For example, if there's a rather sad person in a bar who can't get their act together, say 'It's extraordinary how mankind operates,' rather than 'Isn't he a pain.'

He'll find any overt sexual gestures almost threatening, so seduce him with your wit, humour, independent thrust on life and your social skills. Communication is top of his turn-on list, especially if you have brilliant ideas and plans for your own future and that of the world. He has a lot of friends, both men and women, and he'll expect you to have plenty too. So if in any way you show signs of being the possessive 'you're exclusively mine' type of seductress he'll run a mile.

Be prepared for his lengthy analysis of people, including you, and never get emotional or weepy. It's not that you have to be without feelings, but if you can talk about feelings in a rational sort of 'I own them, they don't own me' kind of way, he'll be open to any reasonable discussion without the heavy-duty sense of responsibility which terrifies him. Never talk about your exes with a pained look in your eye, or give away too much about yourself. He's a sucker for probing the depths of your psyche, and if you can keep a few surprises, the more he'll be turned on.

He's awfully unpredictable when it comes to dates and romance. And don't ever assume you know when he's feeling horny, because he'll always be one step ahead of you. Just when you think he's not interested is probably when he actually is. And then, just when you think he is, his mind is swayed by a far more abstract concept or idea. His is a complex sex drive, but if you want to swing from chandeliers or listen to Wagner and have sex in the bath, he'll be up for it. Just make sure you let him believe it was his crazy idea in the first place.

Managing your Aquarius man month by month

January
Mercury has him questioning his deepest desires and Uranus throws in a few unpredictable red herrings. As you'd expect, he wants recognition, remuneration and a jet-set lifestyle, but, before the 28th, he also needs to secure long-term happiness in his relationship. Get ready to get serious.

February
His domestic set-up is far from ideal and by the Full Moon on the 13th he is looking for somewhere which reflects his taste. He's moving up the ladder and needs a stylish place to entertain influential colleagues. His ability to network gracefully is enviable – help him carry it off.

March

Worn out by recent new responsibilities, he's quite fragile and needs hugs and kisses – even though he's acting all cool. But he's also a party animal and, around the 25th, a rival has her eyes on him with a vengeance. Give him a chance to prove it's you he truly wants – just don't let him out of your sight.

April

This month you wonder if he'll ever make it clear how he really feels. It's ok admitting he's 'very' romantic, but is that enough? Mars is going to make him provocative one minute, impossible the next. Stay as zen-like as you can, and he'll come round to your way of thinking – passionately.

May

Looks do matter to him, and that's that. Around the 13th, he gets into one of those slightly critical moods and you're in a flap. Do you change your wardrobe or make-up just for him, or remain defiant? Make your choice wisely. He needs a people-pleasing partner, and social grace above all.

June

He really can't make up his mind what he wants, and it's safer to just drift along with a beautiful smile and an easy-going approach to life. Be socially flirtatious and remember to slap on your moisturiser when he's not around. He wants a near-perfect goddess, so be divine in his eyes.

July

The sensitive creature that he is, he could over-react to any harsh comments made, especially around the 14th. His emotions are heightened, so feed his heart, boost his ego and, on the 21st, he'll be your very own genie – rub up close and your wish is his command.

August

He's torn between staying under the duvet with you, and dashing off to change the world with his business acumen. Send him to work with a smile, sex up his weekends and prove to him that life doesn't have to be a choice. He'll adore you for your logic.

September

Sometimes he seems more concerned about his own attraction factor than yours. But don't worry, this month he suddenly realizes that you're getting more than your fair share of admirers too. Keep him on his toes by smiling at the world, and flirting with life, and he'll be attentive to your every whim.

October

Mars gives him idealistic verve and if he's not saving the world, he'll be defending someone's right to chew gum. He's determined to make a stand, but steer him away from financial risks on the 25th. Over-investment could deplete his coffers – and, hey, that's your future.

November

When he's in one of his awkward moods, you just can't expect anything other than the unexpected. But this month he is full of tricks and ruses for sexy adventure. Don't hold your breath, though; it might all get defused at the last minute when a work brainwave comes over him.

December

Refuse to believe everything he tells you this month. Ok, so he's not always the most nostalgic or sensitive of rogues, but when he starts getting all soppy about an ex he bumps into, he's really just winding you up. Remember, he's with you now, and testing your nerve. Make sure it's made of steel.

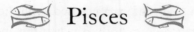

Pisces

How to seduce a Pisces man

It's not so difficult to lure him into your space, it's keeping him there that is. He's a social animal, adores to be adored, is a lover of women and is easily led astray. To reel him in requires a very simple hook. Be charming, stimulate his senses with romantic glances, gentle conversations, your feminine charisma and, above all, entertain him. That means not only do you have interesting things to say, but a fantastic bag full of escapades up your sleeve. (Like romantic locations you can take him to, fun kiddy things to do together.) You also need to be a little bit elusive, mysterious and sensually wicked. When you pop out to the loo, be sure to come back through a different door, just to make him wonder what you've been up to. If he looks like he's gasping for a drink (Pisces are notoriously good at finding their own entertainment through drink, drugs and rock 'n' roll), suggest you go to an art gallery, walk along the riverbank or go to that amazing gig he keeps talking about, but can't be bothered to get tickets. Organize his social life discretely, and he'll never have time to drown his boredom or sorrows in the pub. (Yes, he does have sorrows and often moans lengthily about painful relationships he's endured, and how he's a misunderstood genius.) Of course, if you're as gregarious as he is, can hold your own in any company and not be jealous when he gazes at a pretty face, then he'll realize you're a romantic player too.

But how to keep him hooked? The problem is he might just bump into another fascinating beauty in one of his more dreamlike moments down the pub or in the office. And the romantic that he is, he falls into raptures of physical desire and fantasies about how, after all, it might be someone else who could be his perfect soulmate. Falling in and out of love as if he was leaping in and out of the shower is one of the major issues you'll have to deal with. Not forgetting the floods of water on your bathroom floor every day. But to keep him, the art is literally to be his fantasy woman. He imagines you to be bathed in a kind of misty light. You have an aura of goddesses, divas and fairy-tale princesses about you. So live up to his imagination, opt for sensuality rather than assertive sexuality, splash out on champagne and candlelit dinners instead of takeaways, and never mention mundane things like mortgages and pensions. If he imagines you're rolling in money, he'll spend every penny you have, but if he imagines you're penniless he'll give you everything he owns. The Pisces man is searching for something profound, but he's not exactly sure what it is. Tell him it's you. Adapt and go with his flow, make every date or encounter dramatic, romantic and spiced with sensual temptation. Keep him guessing, and always play the elusive game, one step ahead of him, and he might stay longer than even *he* imagined.

Managing your Pisces man month by month

January

If he seems withdrawn this month, don't jump to any conclusions. Around the 8th, he decides to sacrifice his own desires for the sake of family responsibilities. His clan's blood is thicker than water, so help with his family problems and he might just invite you to join.

February

His devilishly good looks and winning ways gather admiration and bring a favourable end to a lucrative financial battle around the 14th. His ability to understand people is something to be lauded. But has he seen that torrent of passion running beneath your cool facade? Absolutely!

March

Never one to say what he really means, his ambiguous remarks on the 5th give you momentary doubt about your future together. Is he serious, or is he killing time? With radical Uranus making him very contrary, he's going to have to give you answers, or you'll be the one moving on.

April

Woe betide you if you don't discuss his future seriously. He's really confused this month, and even though he's moody with it, you know that deep down inside he needs your unsurpassable support. Be flexible, he could have the greatest idea since the man who invented tampons.

May

Remember how he wants to have the kind of sex that nobody's parents would approve of? Well, the electrifying link between Jupiter and Uranus this month adds a delicious angle to your bodily geometry. If you can out-filth him this month, the earth will move into a new orbit of sheer bliss.

June

Act as if you're very hard to fathom this month, and don't give away your secret desires. He's feeling sexually driven and Mars is giving him all kinds of passionate thoughts about taking things more seriously. Be consumingly hot by night, mysteriously cool by day and you'll win him.

July

He's worrying about keeping fit and obsessing at the gym after an overindulgence of summer punch. With Venus in his romantic zone, he'd much rather be spending time in your arms. Around the 11th show him how to keep fit with only one piece of equipment – you.

August

Around the 4th, don't get embarrassed if he shouts his love from the rooftops – or wants to make love on them. It's his way of showing the world how he feels about you. On the 25th, be ready to conquer the world with him, or he'll be off on his own adventure.

September

Money is on his mind, and that means he'll want to talk about it without being judged. Because he's so sensitive to what other people think of him, be as open-minded as you can. He needs a conspirator this month, and the more he can trust you, the more he'll begin to believe you are a permanent fixture in his life.

October

His determination is what attracted you in the first place, so when he heads off to make his fortune, don't get annoyed that you weren't consulted. Venus and Mars boost his libido on the 25th, so if you want to be involved in his plans, get him to agree to your demands before giving in to his wicked ways.

November

He's feeling incredibly adventurous and wants to roam away from home. In fact, he's so elusive this month, you are better off leaving him to his own devices. Eventually he'll feel lost without you, and soon be back by your side.

December

Reeling him in is one thing, keeping him hooked is another. And although you've no illusions about commitments and long-haul loving, you still wonder whether he might be becoming more of a permanent fixture than you thought. Don't try to trap him into making festive promises, right now he needs a woman who gives him his freedom, and he'll give you his all.

Your Love
Horoscope
2006

A Final Word

For further information about Sarah, visit her website:

http://www.sarahbartlett.com